▶▶▶▶▶INFORMATION: TECHNOLOGY FOR YOU

Stephen Doyle and Bob Sparkes

Hutchinson

London   Melbourne   Sydney   Auckland   Johannesburg

Hutchinson Education

An imprint of Century Hutchinson Ltd
62–65 Chandos Place, London WC2N 4NW

Century Hutchinson Australia Pty Ltd
PO Box 496, 16–22 Church Street, Hawthorn,
Victoria 3122, Australia

Century Hutchinson New Zealand Limited
PO Box 40-086, Glenfield, Auckland 10,
New Zealand

Century Hutchinson South Africa (Pty) Ltd
PO Box 337, Bergvlei, 2012 South Africa

First published 1988

© Stephen Doyle and Bob Sparkes 1988

Designed by Raynor Design

Printed and bound in Great Britain by Scotprint

British Library Cataloguing in Publication Data

Doyle, Stephen
Information technology for you.
1. Information technology.
I. Title
001.5   QA76
ISBN 0 09 172981 5

Acknowledgements

The publishers would like to thank the following for permission to reproduce copyright material:

Abbey National Building Society; Access; Ace Studios; Acorn Computers Limited; Ardea; BBC Hulton Picture Library; Bank of Scotland; Barnabys Picture Library; Clwyd Technics Limited; Digital Equipment Company; Eurotherm Limited; Mary Evans Picture Library; Sally & Richard Greenhill; Hitachi Electronic Components (UK) Limited; IBM United Kingdom Limited; ICL; Konica Ubix; National Westminster Bank plc; Nottingham Building Society; Picturepoint Limited; Psion Limited; Rediffusion Simulation; Research Machines Limited; Rocc Computers Limited; Ann Ronan Picture Library; Science Photo Library; Telefocus; Thorn EMI Business Communications; The Times Network System; Topham Picture Library; Trustees of the Science Museum (London); Wayne Kerr Datum; Willis Computer Supplies Limited.

Contents

1

Information technology and you

Figure 1.1 *Information technology is already here*

I am waiting at the ticket office of a famous London station. My ticket is being electronically printed with my destination and the cost. The digital clock says 16.54. The electronic display board shows that my train will leave from platform 9. An electronic voice announces that the train will be ten minutes late.

I pass by a PAYPHONE with an electronic memory to record how much time is left before the money runs out. If I don't have any cash, I can use the CREDITPHONE or the CARDPHONE instead.

With time to spare, I pop into a Casey Jones cafe. 'One coffee and doughnut, please.' The assistant presses the COFFEE and the DOUGHNUT keys on a keypad. The electronic display on the till says '65p'.

In front of me is RENDEZ-VIEW, a set of nine television screens each carrying different information. Some show news items; others are videos for electronic advertising. On a nearby photo-booth, an electronic text scrolls by with this message:

... YOUR PHOTO WITH SANTA... READY IN 10 MINUTES...ONLY £2.99...

Information technology is not something for the future – it is here, now (Figure 1.1).

What is information technology?

Figure 1.2 *Animal information*

Animals convey information by grunts and gestures. They tell one another about sources of food or approaching danger. The cat in the picture (Figure 1.2) is telling the dog, 'I warn you, don't try it!' Men and women use speech for similar purposes.

5

But even speech has one serious defect: words disappear as soon as they have been spoken. To leave information for a friend, early man marked signs and symbols in the sand. Eventually this became writing. Turning the spoken word into the written word was the first information technology (Figure 1.3).

Figure 1.3 *Some forms of data collection were very slow!*

In Europe, until the fifteenth century, books were handwritten. They were very expensive, so written information belonged only to rich people. With the invention of printing, books were less costly and the number increased rapidly (Figure 1.4). This allowed knowledge to grow at a faster and faster rate. The economic wealth of the western world is partly due to the invention of printing.

Figure 1.4 *The first printing press in Great Britain – the second information technology*

Today, computers can store vast amounts of information. They can also find or **access** that information quickly. The information that is wanted can be displayed on a screen and read by the user (Figure 1.5).

Figure 1.5 *Computers – the third information technology*

Communication

Another human need is to communicate over a distance. In early times this was done by lighting a beacon on top of a high mountain. At sea, sailors developed semaphore and flags for signalling between ships.

More recently these ancient communication technologies have given way to the telephone, radio and television. These allow the spoken word to be communicated rapidly over large distances and to huge audiences. Without technology, Jesus Christ spoke to a few thousand people from the side of a hill. Recently, the *Live Aid Concert* was heard by more people than existed in the whole world at the time of Jesus Christ (Figure 1.6).

Figure 1.6 *The 'Live Aid Concert'. Only a few thousand people heard the music directly. With television in their own sitting-rooms, millions of others heard the music before they did!*

Electronics

The link between communications and computers is electronics. Electronic chips are used to make powerful computers and worldwide communication links. Together, these make a powerful new tool, known as information technology or IT (Figure 1.7)

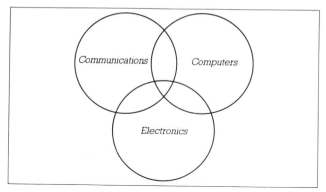

Figure 1.7 *Information technology – a powerful combination*

Information technology combines computer-based information with communications. Very soon, people with this technology will have access to more information than is presently in the biggest library in the world. Information technology will affect jobs, schools, leisure and the home. This book explains how and describes its consequences for you. To begin with, we shall look at just one possible result of IT.

The 'cashless society'

About 3000 years ago, money was invented. Before money, people used to barter or swap the goods they wanted to 'sell' (Figure 1.8). The miller would offer to grind the farmer's corn in return for keeping some of the flour. The ironsmith would exchange his spades for chickens (Figure 1.9). The number of chickens depended on how much the farmer wanted a spade and if, perhaps, another ironsmith in the next village would be prepared to take fewer chickens. The 'law of supply and demand' ruled everything.

Figure 1.8 *Barter and Carry!*

Figure 1.9 *Exchange rates!*

Problems came when a farmer had a large number of chickens to sell but there were no spades available. In such cases, metal tokens could be given to the farmer to represent the value of his chickens. Later, the farmer could exchange the metal tokens for the spades he wanted. This is how money began to be used (Figures 1.10 and 1.11). At first, the tokens were made from rare metals such as gold or silver. People would keep this money in safe places like banks to prevent it being stolen. Eventually, it became awkward to carry around bags of gold, so the banks issued **bank notes** instead (Figure 1.12).

Figure 1.10 *A money token at the time of Christ*

Figure 1.11 *Cash sales!*

Figure 1.12 *'The Governor & Company of the Bank of England promise to pay the bearer on demand Twenty Pounds'*

Originally, you could take one of these notes to the bank and exchange it for real gold or silver. But don't try this now! Many years ago the banks needed to issue more and more notes, but there wasn't enough gold and silver to equal the value of the bank notes issued. Hence the banks dropped the gold standard and now the bank notes themselves are exchanged for the goods that people buy and sell. Money, whether as metal coins or as paper notes, now only **represents** value. The paper and coins themselves have no worth at all.

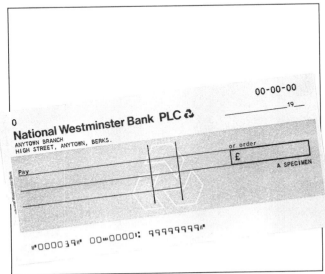

Figure 1.13 *'Paper' money of a different kind*

If you can be trusted, shopkeepers may be prepared to accept a **cheque** instead of money (Figure 1.13). To the bank, this is just another piece of paper. When the bank eventually gets the cheque, say for ten pounds, it will take ten pounds out of your account and add ten pounds to the shop's account. The cheque represents money in just the same way as the paper money issued by the banks.

When buying goods in shops, many people today do not hand over paper money or cheques, they use **credit cards** instead. A credit card is a plastic card, with the owner's name, signature and account number written on it (Figure 1.14). This card is better than paper money, which can be stolen and easily used by thieves. If a credit card is stolen, the thieves cannot use it except by forging the real owner's signature and thus committing a further crime.

Figure 1.14 *'Plastic' money*

When the owner want to buy something, the shop assistant fills in a form. This is then signed by the card owner and sent off to the credit card company. The company subtracts the amount from the card owner's account and adds it to the shop's account.

One big advantage of a credit card is that it can be used in many parts of the world. Queuing in a foreign bank to change pounds into pesetas, francs or lire is no longer necessary.

Figure 1.15 *'Electronic' money*

The credit card form that the shop assistant fills in, is only **information** about money; it is not money itself. As long as the credit card company knows the number of the card and the amount of money, that is all they need. This information can be passed directly to the credit card company along telephone wires; it does not need to be posted. Some shops have installed **electronic fund transfer** terminals **(EFT)** which do just this (Figure 1.15). This is better for the shop, because its bank account is immediately credited with the money.

More and more goods and services are now using credit cards. For example, British Telecom have problems with people breaking into public telephones to get at the money and they are now installing CREDITPHONES, which are operated by credit cards instead of money.

It might eventually be possible for everyone to use personal credit cards. If this happens, there may come a time when paper money and coins disappear completely. Here are two of the **possible** consequences of this.

No more robbery . . . if there isn't any money, it cannot be stolen! Bank raids will become a thing of the past. Also, there is no point in burglars breaking into homes to steal things, such as television sets. If there is no money, they will not be able to sell them later...
...*but much more fraud!* Some people may cheat by putting 'false money' into their credit card accounts. They may discover the secret codes needed to gain access to the bank's computer. If they can do this without being found out, they won't just steal a few pounds, it will be **millions**! We have no reason to

believe that people in the future will become more honest, but thieves will have to become much more clever.

This is just one possible result of using computers: to represent money, taking the place of notes. In a similar way, many other aspects of everyday life will be affected too. This is a reason for learning about IT. If we understand it, we will more easily cope with the change.

➢➢ Things to do _____

1 *Keep your eyes and ears open in a shop or supermarket. Make a list of all things that use electronics, computers or other aspects of information technology.*

2 *Electronic toys and household gadgets are very popular. Go through a mail order catalogue (such as Argos or Littlewoods). Find out which items are based upon electronics.*

3 *Imagine life in a 'cashless society'. What do you think it will be like? Describe a typical day in the life of a person who lives in the 'cashless society'.*

4 *Before you can get a credit card, the company will want to know if you can be trusted.*
   a *How do you think they will find out about your **credit worthiness?***
   b *Do you think it is fair that some people are unable to obtain credit cards?*
   c *How can you make sure that you are never refused a credit card?*

2

Data and information

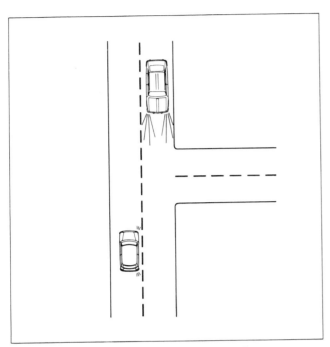

Figure 2.1 *What do the flashing lights mean?*

Figure 2.2 *Margaret Thatcher – Friend or Enemy?*

Data is not the same as **information**. Here is an example to demonstrate this. Figure 2.1 shows a motor car waiting to turn right. We know this because its right indicator is flashing. The meaning of the indicator is clear. It gives **information** about the intentions of the driver.

The picture also shows another car coming towards the first and flashing its headlamps. What does this mean? It might be the message, 'Watch out! Have you seen me?' or it might mean, 'You may pass in front of me!' It could also be a warning to another driver of a police radar trap ahead, or it might just be a friend saying 'Hello'. The meaning of the flashing headlamps is not clear. In all of these cases, the flashing lights are the **data**, and what they mean is **information**.

The same data can give different information to different people. Figure 2.2 is a picture of a well-known person. But is this person a friend or an enemy? The same picture conveys different information depending on what you already believe. Information technology, or IT, is not really about information at all, it is about data. It is humans who turn data into information.

Digital data

A person walking in the Scottish hills is advised to carry a torch. This can be used to send messages if the walker gets hurt. The torch-lamp has only two states – OFF or ON. Nevertheless, signals can be sent just by switching it on and off. In the same way, sailors send messages to one another at sea, using a lamp. Before information can be sent in this way, the sailors have to agree on what the on/off signals mean; they use a **code**.

Many years ago Samuel Morse found a way of signalling with ON and OFF signals. We call his method the Morse code (Figure 2.3). Each letter of the alphabet has a different code, for example,

ON/OFF is the letter E
ON/OFF/ON/OFF is the letter I
ON/OFF/ON/OFF/ON/OFF is the letter S

Representing **all** the letters like this needs too many ON/OFF codes, so Morse used both short and long ON signals. These are called 'dots' and 'dashes'. In this way, Morse was able to code all the letters (and punctuation, such as question marks and full stops) with no more than six ON/OFF codes for each. Figure 2.3 shows the Morse code for letters, the more common punctuation, and how to signal that an error has been made. There are also codes for the numbers 0 to 9.

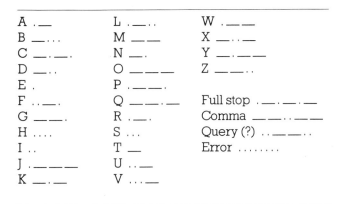

A .—	L .—..	W .——
B —...	M ——	X —..—
C —.—.	N —.	Y —.——
D —..	O ———	Z ——..
E .	P .——.	
F ..—.	Q ——.—	Full stop .—.—.—
G ——.	R .—.	Comma ——..——
H	S ...	Query (?) ..——..
I ..	T —	Error ....
J .———	U ..—	
K —.—	V ...—	

Figure 2.3 *The Morse code is used to turn ON/OFF signals into meaningful letters and words*

Computers also use on/off signals. They do this because it is easy to switch electronic circuits on or off. But the computers need a code to represent the different letters and digits in a message. In Morse code, the on/off signals are sent one after the other. We say that the data is sent in **serial** mode. Sending data in serial mode is slow, but with only one on/off switch there is no other way. Computers, however, need to work fast, so they send many on/off signals at the same time. We call this the **parallel** mode.

Two lamps side by side (in parallel mode) allow us to send four different messages. The indicators of a motor car do this. If the left indicator flashes, the car is sending the message, 'I am turning left'. If the right indicator flashes, the car is sending the message, 'I am turning right'. If both indicators flash, the car is saying 'Watch out! I have stopped'. If no indicators flash, then everything is normal. So two lamps give twice as much information as one lamp. This continues as the number of lamps increases.

Three lamps

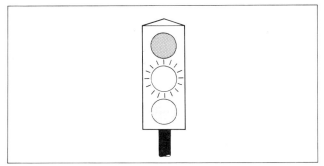

Figure 2.4 *Signalling with coded lamps*

A set of traffic lights (Figure 2.4) has three lamps. We usually think of them as red, amber and green, but this is not as important as their position. Even a driver who is totally colour-blind can tell if the top lamp, the middle lamp or the bottom lamp is on. Different combinations of lamps give different messages to the driver. Up to eight different messages are possible, although we only use four of these. Which four? And what does each message mean?

red only   red and amber   all three lamps on
amber only   red and green   all three lamps off
green only   amber and green

Four lamps

You already know of one particular way of coding numbers. In mathematics you probably learned the binary code. Figure 2.5 lists the first sixteen numbers of the binary code.

Binary	Decimal
0000	0
0001	1
0010	2
0011	3
0100	4
0101	5
0110	6
0111	7
1000	8
1001	9
1010	10
1011	11
1100	12
1101	13
1110	14
1111	15

Figure 2.5 *First sixteen numbers of the binary code*

Each digit in the binary code is either a 1 or a 0. This is the same as a lamp that can be **on** or **off**. One binary digit is called a **bit**. With four bits we can have sixteen different binary numbers. So four lamps, sending messages in parallel mode, could represent sixteen different messages.

A small microcomputer uses eight-bit binary numbers, which can represent 256 different messages. These numbers are written down in a special way. A binary number like 0111 is written with all eight bits, like this 0000 0111. We leave a gap between the first four bits and the last four bits to make it easier to read.

Bigger computers have even longer binary numbers, for example:

0000 1001 0101 0101 0001 1110 1011 1100

Numbers like this are very difficult to read, so we use a special code to make it easier. This counts to base 16, and is called the **hexadecimal** code (Figure 2.6).

Binary	Hexadecimal	Binary	Hexadecimal
0000	0	1010	A
0001	1	1011	B
0010	2	1100	C
0011	3	1101	D
0100	4	1110	E
0101	5	1111	F
0110	6		
0111	7		
1000	8		
1001	9		

Figure 2.6 *The hexadecimal code*

Now each set of four bits can be represented by a single symbol. For example, the binary number 0000 0101 1100 1111   becomes   05CF in hexadecimal.

A number like 1011 can be very confusing. Is it in binary, decimal or hexadecimal? To show hexadecimal numbers, it is usual to put a special symbol in front of them (and/or behind them). The following are three different ways of showing that a number is hexadecimal:

&A450   –   used with the BBC microcomputer and the Electron;
A450H or $A450   –   used with other microcomputers.

The 'binary number' stored in a computer is called a **byte.** In small microcomputers, each byte has eight bits. In bigger computers, a byte can be sixteen or even thirty-two bits. The size of each byte determines how many different codes it can hold (Figure 2.7). Each extra bit doubles the number of codes that can be stored in a byte.

Number of bits in the byte	Number of different codes in each byte
1	2
2	4
3	8
4	16
8	256
16	65 536
32	4 294 967 296

Figure 2.7 *Each extra bit doubles the number of codes that can be stored in a byte*

The bytes in the BBC microcomputer have only eight bits, so we shall usually only discuss eight-bit bytes.

Codes and the computer

Computers are used to store data that is often in the form of words rather than numbers. The binary code is not the best way to store this data. Instead, computers use ASCII – the American Standard Code for Information Interchange. Figure 2.8 shows part of the ASCII code.

8-bit code	Letter	8-bit code	Letter
0100 0001	A	0100 1110	N
0100 0010	B	0100 1111	O
0100 0011	C	0101 0000	P
0100 0100	D	0101 0001	Q
0100 0101	E	0101 0010	R
0100 0110	F	0101 0011	S
0100 0111	G	0101 0100	T
0100 1000	H	0101 0101	U
0100 1001	I	0101 0110	V
0100 1010	J	0101 0111	W
0100 1011	K	0101 1000	X
0100 1100	L	0101 1001	Y
0100 1101	M	0101 1010	Z

Figure 2.8 *Representing letters in ASCII*

Other ASCII codes are used for the digits 1, 2, 3, etc. and also for commas and the arithmetical signs $(+, -, =, \text{etc.})$. Even a space has its own ASCII code – 0010 0000. Thus, to store the word HELLO!, the computer uses six bytes – one byte for each **character**. Figure 2.9 shows how the word is held in the computer's memory.

0100 1000	(H)
0100 0101	(E)
0100 1100	(L)
0100 1100	(L)
0100 1111	(O)
0010 0001	(!)

Figure 2.9 *How the word HELLO! is held in the computer's memory*

Teletext codes

In some microcomputers (such as the BBC microcomputer in **teletext** mode), other codes are used to represent picture blocks. Figure 2.10 shows some of these codes used to make up the picture of a rocket. These pictures are used by Prestel, Ceefax and Oracle and we shall look at these again in Chapter 12.

Figure 2.10 *Teletext codes*

	0	10	20	30	40	50	60	70	80	90	100	110	120
0	nothing	down	nothing	move cursor to 00									
1	next to printer	up	disable VDU	move cursor									
2	start printer	clear screen	select mode										
3	stop printer	start of line	reprogram charac's										
4	nothing	paged mode	nothing										
5	nothing	scroll mode	nothing										
6	enable VDU	nothing	nothing										
7	beep	nothing	nothing										back space & delete
8	back	nothing	nothing										nothing
9	forward	nothing	nothing										alpha red

Control systems

Because computers respond to digital (on/off) signals, they can be used for industrial control. One simple example is a fire alarm (Figure 2.11).

Only small computers are needed for control systems. Even an eight-bit byte can sense eight different temperature switches at the same time. It can also switch eight different things on or off independently. Thus these small computers are found in many places in the factory and home (Fig. 2.12). Here are a few examples:

central heating systems
coffee pots
digital watches
door chimes
electric cookers
electronic organs
electronic toasters
motor cars, such as the 'Maestro'
'pacemakers' for patients with heart problems
robots in production lines
toys like 'Bigtrak'
washing machines

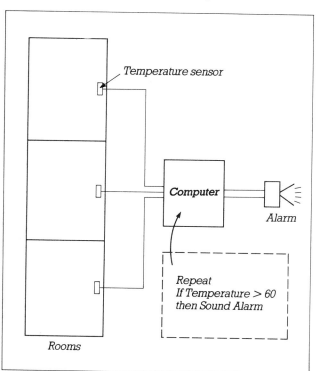

Figure 2.11 *Fire alarm. If the temperature in the room becomes too high the temperature switch comes on. The computer senses this and switches on the alarm bell*

Figure 2.12 *A modern microcontroller*

Analogue data

Some data cannot easily be represented by digital data. For example, a computer could be used to measure the temperature of a patient in intensive care. A single bit can only be on or off, so it would be no good for the thermometer. (It could only tell if the patient was alive or dead!) Quantities that can vary over a whole range of values (such as temperature) are called **analogue** quantities.

Figure 2.13 shows two different ways of showing time. The hands of the analogue watch move continuously. The numbers on the digital watch 'jump' from one number to the next.

Figure 2.14   *The analogue position of the joystick is sent to the computer in digital code*

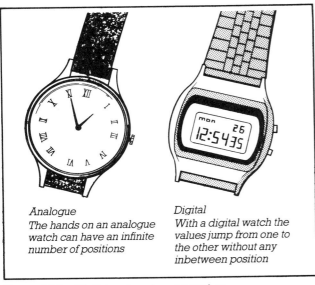

Analogue
The hands on an analogue watch can have an infinite number of positions

Digital
With a digital watch the values jump from one to the other without any inbetween position

Figure 2.13   *Digital and analogue watches*

Analogue quantities can easily be turned into voltages, which also vary over a whole range. They are easily converted into a set of on/off bits, that is into digital data, using an analogue-to-digital converter (ADC). The BBC microcomputer has its own built-in ADC. Some computer games need a joystick to be able to move, say, a 'spaceship' to any part of the screen (Fig. 2.14). Such joysticks are usually plugged into the analogue socket of the microcomputer. As the joystick is moved, the output voltage changes and the ADC converts this into digital data. This is used in the computer program to alter the position of the spaceship on the screen.

An ADC allows the computer to measure analogue quantities. A computer-controlled heating system has sensors in each room to measure the actual temperature. It has potentiometers to set the desired temperature. If the desired temperature is greater than the measured temperature, a digital output switches on the heater. This is an example of a system with analogue inputs and digital outputs.

Test yourself

Using the words in the list below, copy out and complete the sentences A to G. Underline the words you have inserted. The words may be used once, more than once, or not at all.

analogue   ASCII   binary   code
bit   byte   code   control
data   digital   infinite   teletext

A _____ data consists of on/off signals; by using a_____, these on/off signals can be used to send information.

B The_____ can be used for counting whole numbers.

C *The code used for storing characters, i.e. letters or numbers in a computer is called_____.*

D _____ codes are used for sending pictures along a telephone line.

E *A watch with hands is an_____ device, because the hands can have an_____ number of positions.*

F *Most ordinary computers are_____ computers.*

G *Analogue data can be turned into digital data with an_____ to_____ converter.*

Things to do _____

1 _Make a table, as in Figure 2.9, to show how a microcomputer stores the message HELLO FRED!_

2 _Convert the following binary numbers to their hexadecimal equivalents:_
  a _1010 0111_
  b _0000 0001_
  c _1111 0010_
  d _0010 0010 1001 1110_
  e _0110 1011 1000 1101_

3 _Sort out the following into analogue or digital quantities._
  a _The brightness of the sun_
  b _An electric light switch_
  c _A person's sex_
  d _A person's age_
  e _A mathematical statement, such as a = 5_
  f _A heart valve_
  g _Temperature_
  h _Weight_
  i _The loudness of a radio_
  j _The pitch or frequency of a musical note_

4 _In the BBC microcomputer a single byte stores the code 0101 0010. What **three** different things could this code represent?_

3

Communications

Visual signalling

Figure 3.1 *American Indians used to send messages over long distances by making signals*

Figure 3.2 *Ben Lomond – the 'Beacon Mountain'*

An important human need was (and still is) to communicate over a distance (Figure 3.1). In early times this was done by lighting a beacon on top of a high mountain. Near to where one of the authors lives is Ben Lomond, the highest point for miles around. On a clear day, it can be seen fifty miles away (Figure 3.2). What better place for signalling the approach of an enemy! 'Lomond' is a Scottish word, meaning 'beacon', and so aptly describes this mountain. It dominates, and has given its name to, the more famous Loch Lomond below it.

You should read the exciting poem 'The Armada' by Macaulay, which tells how news of the approach of the Spanish Armada was spread throughout England by this method. More recently the Royal Wedding of Prince Charles and Lady Diana was celebrated by lighting these old beacons once again.

In the days before radio, an admiral would give instructions to his commanders through flags flown from the top of the ship. This is the way that Lord Nelson sent his famous signal at Trafalgar, 'England expects every man will do his duty'. What Nelson wanted to say originally was, 'England **requires** every man will do his duty', but the flag officer pointed out that there was no flag for 'requires'. This meant that the word would have to be spelled out letter by letter. He suggested the word 'expects' instead and Nelson agreed. This story shows how difficult it was to use this means of communication (Figure 3.3).

Figure 3.3 *Flag signals could give communication problems!*

Where a sailor is near enough to be seen, messages can be sent by **semaphore**. The arm positions of the sailor represent different letters or words. Clearly, this method is much faster than hoisting flags. During the Napoleonic war with Britain, two French brothers, Claude and Ignace Chappe, built special towers with wooden arms to send signals over large distances with semaphore (Figure 3.4). This was very useful for giving details of the positions of the British ships enforcing a blockade. C.S. Forester tells an exciting tale in one of the *Captain Hornblower* books, where the hero led a raid to blow up one of these Chappe towers. The word used by the Chappe brothers to describe their invention was 'telegraph' – Greek for 'words at a distance'.

Figure 3.4 *The Chappe telegraph*

Electric telegraph and telephone

Telegraph

Up to about a hundred and fifty years ago, all long distance communication depended upon being able to **see** the signals. The discovery of electric current changed this. Almost immediately, inventors tried to make electric current carry messages. But electric current is invisible, so how could the message be received? The answer was to make use of some of the visible effects of electric current. Helmholtz knew that electric current passed through water causes it to break down into hydrogen and oxygen. Small bubbles of gas could be seen rising from the electrode when the current was switched on. Helmholtz arranged twenty-six pairs of wires, so that each pair could carry a current to a different jar of water. Each of these represented one letter of the alphabet and the jar where the bubbles were rising showed which letter was being transmitted (Figure 3.5). As you can imagine, this method didn't work very well!

Much better results were obtained with the **magnetic** effect of the electric current. When electric current is passed through a coil of wire, the coil becomes magnetic. This can be used to attract a piece of iron, called an **armature**. When the armature is pulled in, it breaks the circuit, so the current stops.

Figure 3.5 *The Helmholtz telegraph*

Now, the coil is no longer a magnet, so a spring pulls back the armature. The allows the **contacts** to meet again and the current is restored. You can see that this process goes on continuously. It is, in fact, how an electric buzzer works (Figure 3.6).

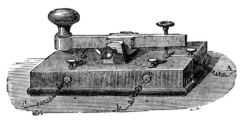

Figure 3.6 *The electric buzzer*

With this system Samuel Morse was able to send messages just by pressing the switch at one end of the pair of wires (Figure 3.7). At the other end, the buzzer sounded. In the USA, as we saw in Chapter 2. Morse developed a special code representing the different letters of the alphabet – the Morse code. His system, called the electric telegraph, was essential for opening up the American West, by linking towns and villages to the state capitals. Details of an Indian raid could be spread throughout the countryside within minutes and the army called out at once.

The Morse telegraph suffered from one major defect. If the wire was too long, its resistance was high. This resulted in the current being too weak to operate the buzzer at the other end. The solution to this problem was to split a long wire into several parts. At the end of the first stage, a **relay** replaced the buzzer. This relay had a coil of wire and an armature, but when the current passed through it, the contacts **closed** (Figure 3.8). When they closed they switched on a new current to the next stage. So this new device picked up the signal from the first stage and passed it

to the next, as if in a 'relay' race. A long line could thus be split into several stages, with a relay station every few kilometres.

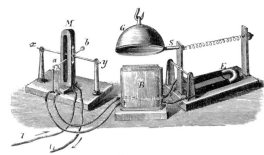

Figure 3.8 *An electric relay*

Telephone

The next advance came when Alexander Graham Bell discovered how to make the telegraph 'speak'. His **telephone** overcame the problems of having to learn the Morse code. This allowed everyone to communicate with one another. Note that the telegraph is a **digital** device, while the telephone is **analogue**. In the telegraph, the current is simply switched on and off. Even if the current is reduced by a long wire, it is still a current. Provided it is strong enough to operate the relay or the buzzer, it can still be useful.

When speech is turned into electric current, the size of the current varies very rapidly, thousands of times a second. The number of changes per second is called its **frequency**. (Frequency is measured in hertz, after Heinrich Hertz, who discovered radio waves.) The frequencies associated with each spoken letter of the alphabet are all different. To transmit sound, these different frequencies must all be faithfully reproduced in the receiver (Figure 3.9).

Figure 3.7 *Samuel Morse's electric telegraph*

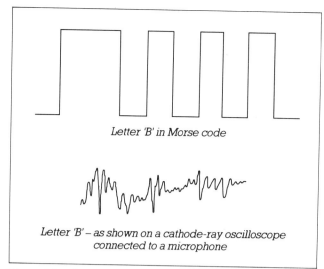

Letter 'B' in Morse code

Letter 'B' – as shown on a cathode-ray oscilloscope connected to a microphone

Figure 3.9 *Letter 'B' in Morse, voltage variation for spoken letter 'B'*

At that time, scientists thought that these rapid variations could not be transmitted along the wires. But Bell was not a scientist. He persevered until one day his assistant heard him say through their system, 'Watson, come at once, I need you.' (Figure 3.10). The reason for this call was that he had just spilt acid from the battery over his trousers. Both men were so excited by their discovery that they forgot all about the acid and constantly changed places to speak to each other.

Figure 3.10 *Bell and Watson with the first telephone*

We know now the tremendous effect that the telephone has had on everyday life. You can lift the receiver, dial a few numbers and speak to your friend next door, in the next town or even thousands of miles away. Have you ever wondered how the telephone system works? How does it find your friend's

telephone out of the millions of other telephones in the world? Figure 3.11 shows a relay with **two** pairs of contacts. One pair is normally closed, but opens when the armature is pulled in. The other pair is normally open, but closes when the armature is pulled in. When the armature is pulled in, A is connected to B. When the armature is released, A is connected to C. This allows the telephone system to choose between two alternatives. There would have to be many more relays to allow A to be connected to more people (Figure 3.12). Two relays would allow four different connections, three relays would allow eight different connections, and so on.

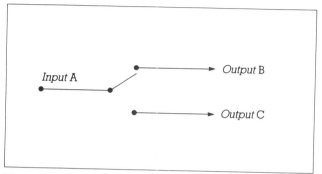

Figure 3.11 *A single relay can choose between two alternatives*

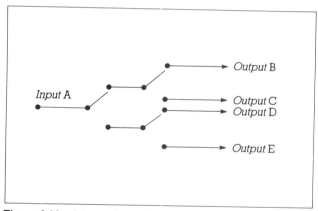

Figure 3.12 *More relays offer more alternatives*

You can see that this method will not work in practice. Connecting A to 1000 different telephones would need a relay with far too many contacts. Although this isn't the method actually used, it helps to explain the principles. In Figure 3.12, each of the three relays can be operated by switching its coil on or off. We can represent 'switched-on' by 1 and 'switched-off' by 0. The binary number 010 means that relay I is switched off, relay II is switched on and relay III is switched off. This binary number will therefore connect A to telephone number 2. Significantly, 010 is the binary equivalent of the decimal number 2. These binary numbers are called **addresses**. Our simple picture shows how binary addresses are used in a simple switching system.

This picture also helps to explain why computers start counting from 0. When all the relays are switched off, the binary address is 000. This is just as good as any other address, so it is usually taken as the starting point. Thus, addresses go from 0 to 7, rather than 1 to 8 as you might expect.

The telephone line can be used to transmit codes as well as speech. **Telex** (Figure 3.13) is such a way of sending messages. The sender types the message into an electric typewriter; the message is encoded and transmitted along the telephone line. At the receiving end a **teleprinter** prints out the message. Nowadays, even pictures can be sent and received in the same way, on a **facsimile** machine.

Figure 3.13 *Telex*

Radio and television

Radio waves

The telegraph and the telephone need wires to connect the sender to the receiver. In 1888, the young man Guglielmo Marconi was able to combine the telegraph with the new discovery of electromagnetic waves to send signals without wires.

Because the waves used by Marconi are invisible, it is difficult for us to 'picture' them. A good analogy is sound waves. These spread out from the source of the sound until they enter your ear (Figure 3.14). The fact, that you can hear your friend calling even when out of sight, shows that sounds waves bend round corners.

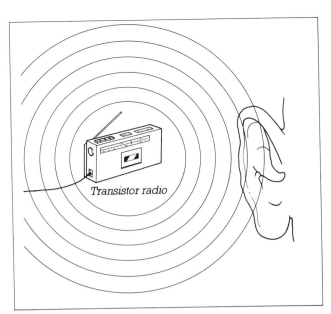

Figure 3.14 *Sound waves spreading out from a source*

Sound waves can also pass through the walls and floor of a room. You may also have had the experience of shouting at a cliff face and hearing the echo as the sound waves are reflected back (Figure 3.15). Radio waves have the same properties, although they are not the same as sound waves. Radio waves bend round corners, they can be reflected and they can pass through the walls of a building.

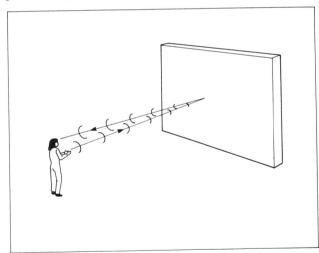

Figure 3.15 *Sound waves being reflected from a wall*

Sound waves affect the eardrum, causing vibrations inside the ear which the brain interprets as sound. Radio waves have no effect on the human body, but they do affect the electrons in a metal rod. The radio wave causes the electrons to oscillate up and down and this generates a small electric current. This small current can be **amplified** until large enough to drive an electric buzzer. Marconi pressed the switch in Newfoundland and made the buzzer sound in Cornwall (Figure 3.16).

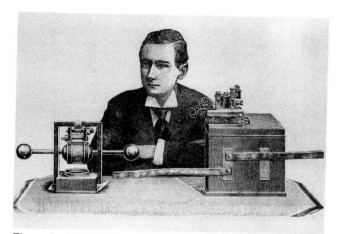

Figure 3.16 *The Marconi system*

'Wire-less' communication (as it was called) was immediately seen as a tremendous advantage. In 1922, the British Broadcasting Company (later Corporation) was set up and was soon sending information right into people's homes. The revolution in communications had begun to affect everyday life in a big way.

Amplitude modulation does not give very good reception. Hence new ways of modulating the radio wave were tried, in particular frequency modulation (F.M.). This needs higher frequency radio waves than for A.M. – around 100 million hertz, called very high frequencies (V.H.F.).

Transmitting speech is more difficult, because it is an analogue quantity. Little progress was made until the invention of the valve amplifier in 1904 (Figure 3.17). Instead of just switching the radio wave on and off, it could now be **modulated** with the speech being transmitted. The frequency of some radio waves is measured in millions of hertz. Speech or music (called **audio** signals) has frequencies of less than 20 000 Hz. Modulation thus consists of making the radio wave fluctuate at the frequency of the audio signal. One way of doing this is to alter the size (or amplitude) of the radio wave (Figure 3.18). The radio wave is said to be **amplitude-modulated** (A.M.) At the receiver, the A.M. wave is **demodulated** to extract the audio signal from it. This is then amplified until it is big enough to produce sound in a loudspeaker.

Figure 3.17 *An early Fleming valve*

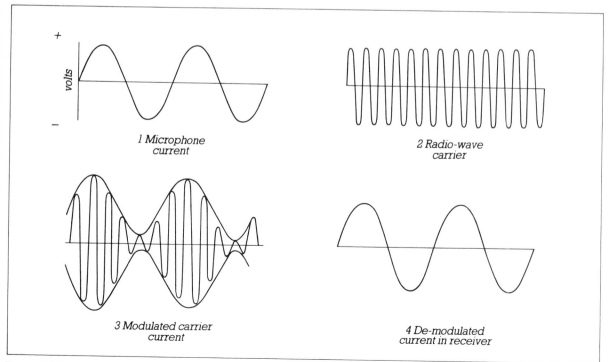

1 Microphone current

2 Radio-wave carrier

3 Modulated carrier current

4 De-modulated current in receiver

Figure 3.18 *A modulated carrier signal*

Television

Even before radio broadcasting, some technologists saw that the transmission of pictures would also be possible. A picture could be split up into a set of lines and each line into a series of dots. By transmitting each dot as black, white or various shades of grey, a complete picture could eventually be sent. John Logie Baird used a mechanical system of rotating discs to split up a picture into its component dots (Figure 3.19). By 1937, an electronic method of doing this had been perfected and this is the basis of modern television.

Figure 3.19 *The Baird television system*

The information about each dot is analogue, since it can be any shade of grey from black to white. Since there are 625 lines on the television screen, it is sensible to have at least 625 dots on each line (although more dots would give a better picture). A picture of 625 × 625 dots needs around 400 000 dots altogether. This picture changes twenty-five times a second to give the appearance of movement, so the picture information must change about 10 000 000 times a second (25 × 400 000). This is higher than the frequency of A.M. radio waves, so they cannot be used to transmit television pictures. Even V.H.F. waves are not high enough; ultra high frequency (U.H.F) waves are used instead. These cannot travel as far as radio waves, so television stations have to be set up all over the country (and even then, there are places that get very poor reception) (Figure 3.20).

Microwaves and cables

We have already noted that radio waves, like sound, can be reflected. In the 1930s, it was realized that this would be a good way of detecting aircraft or ships and this led to the development of **radar** (radio detection and ranging). Frequencies up to 1000 million hertz were used, because very little bending of the waves could be allowed. This is higher even than the U.H.F. used for television, and the waves were so short they came to be called **microwaves**. Higher frequencies can carry more information and ways were soon found of modulating microwaves to transmit thousands of telephone calls at the same time. This means that expensive telephone wires could be replaced by microwave links (Figure 3.21).

Figure 3.20 *Television masts, like this one at Crystal Palace have been set up all over the country*

Figure 3.21 *A microwave 'dish' on the Telecom Tower, London*

Microwaves 'bend' very little and certainly not enough to follow the curvature of the earth's surface. Thus, for communicating between different countries, microwaves are transmitted into space. Here they are picked up by satellites and retransmitted back to a receiver on another part of the earth (Figure 3.22). If each house had its own microwave receiver, it would be possible to get television pictures from any part of the world in the same way.

Figure 3.22 *A communications satellite*

At still higher frequencies, even more signals can be sent at the same time. The highest frequencies considered at the moment are around 750 000 000 000 000 Hz – which is in the region of visible light. Instead of transmitting them through space, they are sent down specially constructed light tubes, called **optical fibres**. Soon, cables of such optical fibres may be connected to every house. We will then be able to choose from hundreds of different television channels and still have enough left for individual radio, telephone and computer signals too (Figure 3.23).

Cable television will allow for mass communication on a scale that has never before been possible. It will dramatically alter our whole way of life, but even that is not the end of the story. Greater changes are on the way, because we are beginning to combine the technology of communications with computers. This could cause problems. The effects of the telegraph, the telephone, radio and television have occurred over a period of a hundred years. The new changes will occur over about ten years only, which may be too fast for ordinary mortals to cope with. We shall have to run very fast to catch up.

•ᴊ Test yourself _____

Using the words in the list below, copy out and complete the sentences A to G. Underline the words you have inserted. The words may be used once, more than once, or not at all.

analogue   code   data   digital   electricity
frequency   microwave   modulating
Morse   relay   telegraph   satellites

A *Before the discovery of_____long-distance communication was through sight only.*
B *The electric telegraph used the_____code to transmit data.*
C *A_____is used to boost the telegraph signal so that it can be sent over large distances.*
D *Radio, television and the telephone transmit_____data.*
E *The more the amount of data, the higher the_____of the carrier must be.*
F *Microwaves can be transmitted from one country to another with communication_____.*
G *Radio communication is obtained by_____the radio wave with speech or music.*

Figure 3.23 *The new London Teleport in the Docklands. It transmits cable-TV programs to Europe.*

Things to do

1 Find out why Helmholtz didn't use electric lights, instead of bubbles of gas, to show when the current was switched on.

2 A picture is sent by a satellite as a set of white or dark squares. These can be represented by the binary digits 1 and 0. Below is a simple picture and the way it is represented in binary. The satellite sends out these binary codes to the ground station.

Make up some pictures of your own and write down the binary codes needed to send the pictures from a satellite.

3 Make a simple radio receiver. Tandy shops sell inexpensive radio kits which are easy to construct.

4 The book **Telecommunications in Practice** published by British Telecom and the Association for Science Education (1985 – ISBN 0-86357-018-6) contains excellent descriptions of the ideas in this chapter and gives many ideas for practical projects – including setting up an optical communications link.

5 Arrange a visit to your local telephone exchange. Ask to see the old mechanical switching gear if they have any, as well as the modern equipment (see Figures below).

```
0 0 0 0 0 0 0 0 0 0 0 0 0 0 0 0 0 0 0 0 0
0 0 0 0 0 1 1 1 0 0 0 1 1 1 0 0 0 0 0 0 0
0 0 0 0 0 1 1 1 0 0 0 1 1 1 0 0 0 0 0 0 0
0 0 0 0 0 1 1 1 0 0 0 1 1 1 0 0 0 0 0 0 0
0 0 0 0 0 1 1 1 0 0 0 1 1 1 0 0 0 0 0 0 0
0 0 0 0 0 1 1 1 0 0 0 1 1 1 0 0 0 0 0 0 0
0 0 0 0 0 1 1 1 1 1 1 1 1 1 0 0 0 0 0 0 0
0 0 0 0 0 1 1 1 1 1 1 1 1 1 0 0 0 0 0 0 0
0 0 0 0 0 1 1 1 1 1 1 1 1 1 0 0 0 0 0 0 0
0 0 0 0 0 1 1 1 0 0 0 1 1 1 0 0 0 0 0 0 0
0 0 0 0 0 1 1 1 0 0 0 1 1 1 0 0 0 0 0 0 0
0 0 0 0 0 1 1 1 0 0 0 1 1 1 0 0 0 0 0 0 0
0 0 0 0 0 1 1 1 0 0 0 1 1 1 0 0 0 0 0 0 0
0 0 0 0 0 1 1 1 0 0 0 1 1 1 0 0 0 0 0 0 0
0 0 0 0 0 0 0 0 0 0 0 0 0 0 0 0 0 0 0 0 0
```

Representing a picture in binary

Boys operating a manual switchboard in Sutherland, 1886

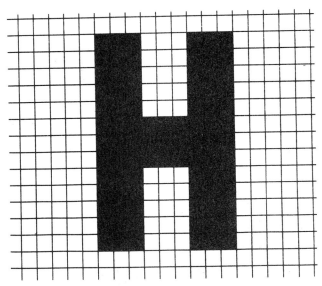

The picture

A modern System X exchange

4

Microelectronics

Digital electronics

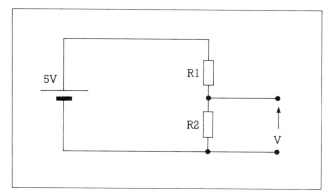

Figure 4.1 *Resistors in series*

Figure 4.1 shows two resistors in series connected to a battery. The battery voltage is shared between the two resistors. The voltage (V) across R2 depends on how big its resistance is, compared with R1. If R2 is large and R1 is small, then V will be large and the voltage across R1 will be small. Use your knowledge about electric circuits to convince yourself that this is true.

The switch

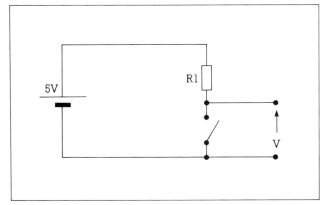

Figure 4.2 *The switch*

In Figure 4.2, the resistor R2 is replaced by a switch. When the switch is closed, its resistance is very small. The output voltage V will then be at 0 V. When the switch is open, its resistance is very large and the voltage will be near to 5 V. The output will thus be high or low, depending on whether the switch is open or closed. We can represent this with a **truth table** (Figure 4.3).

Switch	V
Open	HIGH (5 V)
Closed	LOW (0 V)

Figure 4.3 *The switch truth table*

Notice that we use the words 'HIGH' and 'LOW' to describe the voltage. This is quite normal in electronics.

The transistor as a switch

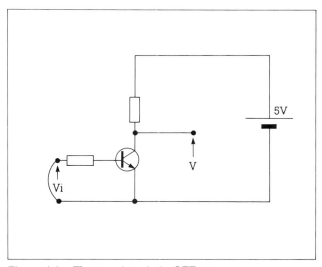

Figure 4.4 *The transistor in its OFF state*

A simple way of thinking about the transistor is to treat it like the simple switch. The 'switch' is controlled by the size of the input voltage Vi. If the input is connected to the 0 V line, as in Figure 4.4, then the input voltage is LOW. This makes the transistor have a high resistance. It then behaves like a switch that is open, so the output voltage is HIGH.

Figure 4.5 shows the input connected to the + 5 V line, so it is HIGH. This makes the transistor have a low resistance. Now it behaves like a switch that is closed, so the output voltage is LOW. This is described by its truth table (Figure 4.6).

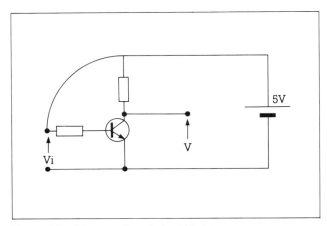

Figure 4.5 *The transistor in its ON state*

Input voltage	Output voltage
LOW	HIGH
HIGH	LOW

Figure 4.6 *The transistor truth table*

In digital electronics we are not interested in exact voltages, only if they are HIGH or LOW. We call these the **states** of the transistor.

In digital electronics we only have two states: the ON (or HIGH) state and the OFF (or LOW) state.

Digital logic

So far we have seen how information can be coded as ON and OFF signals and how transistors can be switched into their ON or OFF states. Thus it is possible for transistors to handle information. This is the way that digital computers work. For example, in banks, information about money is passed back and forth all day as a set of ON and OFF signals. Yet, if there are many computers, how does one particular computer know which other one it is talking to?

The same problem occurs when you want to speak to your friend on the telephone. How does the telephone system connect the right telephones together? In Chapter 3 we saw that this problem can be solved with relays, which are either switched ON or OFF. In modern telephone exchanges, transistors do the same job as these relays. The transistors are combined into **logic gates**.

What is a logic gate?

Once there was a man who became rather lazy. He did not like getting out of his car to open the garage doors, so he mounted a switch by the side of his garage drive. This switch was a photocell, which is operated by light. (If something passes in front of a photocell, the switch comes on.) He used this switch to open the garage doors automatically whenever he drove his car past the photocell. Unfortunately, he found that the garage doors also opened when the postman walked past to deliver letters!

After thinking about this for a bit, he realized that he would need two photocell switches spaced about two metres apart. He arranged that the garage doors would open only if both photocells were operated at the **same** time. His car was long enough to do this, but the postman was not. He first walked past one photocell and then past the other, not both at the same time. So the garage doors no longer opened when the postman walked up the drive (Figure 4.7).

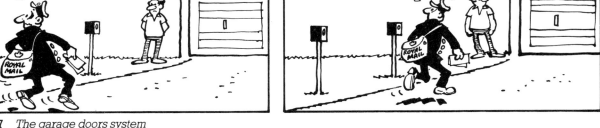

Figure 4.7 *The garage doors system*

The system used by this man includes an AND gate. This has two inputs and one output. The output is used to operate the garage doors and each input is connected to one of the photocells. When the car (or postman) passes in front of a photocell switch, it comes on. So each switch can be on or off. Hence there are four cases to consider (Figure 4.8).

Switch A	Switch B	Garage doors
OFF	OFF	SHUT
OFF	ON	SHUT
ON	OFF	SHUT
ON	ON	OPEN

Figure 4.8 *The AND truth table*

Note how the truth table (Figure 4.8) is written out. This is the standard way of presenting such tables.

In electronics, we often use the names HIGH and LOW to describe the state of each input, instead of ON and OFF. Figure 4.9 shows two more ways that are sometimes used.

Switch A	Switch B	Switch A	Switch B
L	L	0	0
L	H	0	1
H	L	1	0
H	H	1	1

Figure 4.9 *Alternative ways of writing a truth table*

These are called **logic levels**.

ON, HIGH, H and 1 all refer to the logic 1 state.
OFF, LOW, L and 0 all refer to the logic 0 state.

The AND gate switches its output ON only when both of its inputs are ON. An OR gate is used when **either** of two inputs is needed to give an output. For example, a bell might ring if you pressed the bell-push at the front of the house or the one at the back of the house (Figure 4.10).

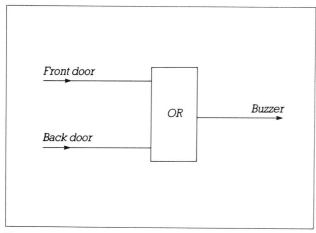

Figure 4.10 *The OR gate bell-push*

An electronic calculator

Since each transistor in a circuit is either ON or OFF, a set of, say, eight transistors side by side can represent a binary number (Figure 4.11). Basically, this is what a byte of computer memory consists of. Counting and adding are all carried out with logic states like these.

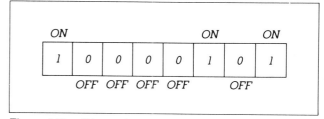

Figure 4.11 *A byte of memory holding the binary number 1000 0101*

By combining different gates together, any logical problem may be solved. Figure 4.12 shows a circuit with many different logic gates inside. It has two sets of inputs, each consisting of eight lines. Each of these passes a set of logic levels to the circuit. The binary numbers represented by these logic levels may be added, subtracted, multiplied, divided or combined in some other way.

Such a circuit is called an arithmetic and logic unit (or ALU). To choose which operation is to be performed on the input numbers, special control codes are sent to the control lines of the ALU.

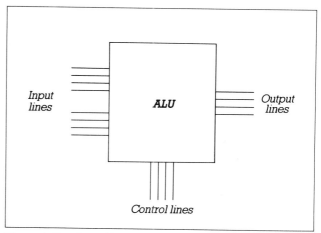

Figure 4.12 *An arithmetic and logic unit*

The silicon chip

Complicated logic systems were once made by inserting individual components into a printed circuit board and soldering them together (Figure 4.13).

But connecting components together like this is expensive. The resulting equipment is bulky and requires much power. Computers built in the 1950s used this technique. A computer of the same capability as the BBC microcomputer, if made from individual components, would fill the average classroom. It would also generate so much heat that it would need to be cooled all the time.

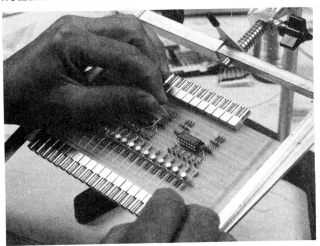

Figure 4.13 *A printed circuit board being assembled*

In 1959, in America's Silicon Valley, the way was found to combine many transistors on a single slice of silicon. The need for soldered interconnections could now be eliminated. The size of circuits and their costs and power requirements could be reduced dramatically. This was the beginning of microelectronics.

Description of the silicon chip

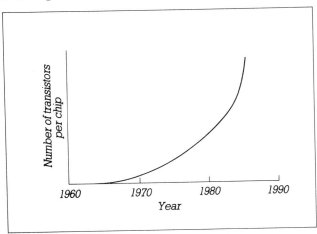

Figure 4.14 *Number of transistors on a chip*

As the distances between the transistors on a chip were reduced, their numbers could be increased (Figure 4.14). But this created new problems. Two circuits which are **nearly** the same, still require different chips to be made. Since electronic engineers have so many different applications, a very large number of chips needed to be constructed and this made them expensive. The solution was to make one chip that could be **programmed** for different purposes.

One such chip is the uncommitted logic array (ULA) (Figure 4.15). This contains a very large number of logic gates, but these are not connected together. The interconnections between the gates can be made later. A customer asks for a particular set of interconnections between the gates. This information is put into each chip, which is then sealed; it has been **customized**. The advantage to the customer is that he has chips made exactly to his requirements. The advantage to the supplier is that most of the manufacturing process is the same for all customers. One disadvantage is that this method of production is expensive. However, this cost is absorbed if a large enough number of chips is ordered.

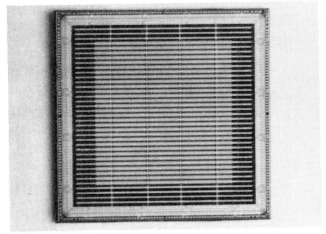

Figure 4.15 *The ULA in a Sinclair ZX81*

This technique is too expensive for a small number of customized chips. This means that an engineer can no longer try out many different designs and pick the best one. To solve this problem, designers turn to the computer (Figure 4.16). They build their electronic circuits on the computer screen itself and even test them there. The computer is programmed to behave in exactly the same way as the finished circuit, although it will probably be much slower.

Figure 4.16 *Computers help designers to create new circuits*

Microprocessors

Another technique used in the microelectronic industry is the microprocessor. Instead of a large number of interconnected logic gates, this device uses an arithmetic and logic unit (ALU) and some switching logic. The logic states to be combined are stored in memory bytes. Under the control of a **program**, bytes are collected from the memory and presented to the ALU. The program decides what process is to be performed and sends the proper instructions codes to the ALU at the same time. The ALU stores the result in the **accumulator** of the microcomputer. Further program instructions take this result from the accumulator and store it in a byte of memory, ready for further processing.

Figure 4.17 *A microprocessor*

Figure 4.18 *Inside a microprocessor*

Microprocessors are used extensively in control systems (Figures 4.17 and 4.18). These contain a small amount of memory, which stores the program that the microprocessor executes. This program is itself a set of digital codes. Here is an example of the way a microprocessor works.

Task Sound the alarm when two push-button switches are both pressed at the same time.

The **program** to carry out this task is a set of binary codes. These are stored in the program memory of the computer. The microprocessor contains a special counter, called the program counter. This points to each code in turn. When the microprocessor has executed one instruction code, the program counter points to the next instruction code, and so on.

In this way, any complex numerical or logical task can be carried out by the microprocessor. Each different task needs a different set of instruction codes. It is the job of the **programmer** to write the correct codes for each task. Since one microprocessor can be made to do almost anything required, only a few types of microprocessor need be made. Also, because they are so useful, very large numbers can be made; so microprocessors are inexpensive. These are the reasons for the microprocessor being so important in information technology.

Software and hardware engineering

The general name for computer programs is **software**. Thus, solving problems in electronics with a microprocessor is called **software engineering**. It is a very important way of using microelectronics; much of the rest of this book is devoted to it. However, it is not the only method used in industry. Connecting logic gates together is also very important. Although the microprocessor can do anything, most of its time is taken up in finding out what it has to do. The task problem just described takes three to five microseconds on the BBC microcomputer. Although this is fast for us, atomic particles can travel several metres in this time.

In one experiment, scientists need to know if two particles are produced at the same time. They need to know if particle detector A is activated at the same time as detector B, which needs an AND logic gate. This logic test has to take place within a tiny fraction of one microsecond, so clearly the microprocessor is much too slow. Logic gates constructed from transistors work thousands of times faster, so they are used instead of a microprocessor.

Here is another example. Electrons travel the length of a television tube in less than one millionth of a second. The microprocessor is far too slow to control these electrons. A ULA is much faster, which is why Sinclair uses one in his flat screen television set. It is also why the BBC microcomputer uses a ULA to run its screen display. Where speed is important, hardware engineering is still an essential branch of electronics.

✔️ Test yourself

Using the words in the list below, copy out and complete the sentences A to G. Underline the words you have inserted. The words may be used once, more than once, or not at all.

hardware   instructions   logic gates
microprocessor   program counter   software
transistor   uncommitted logic   instruction

A Microelectronic chips contain thousands of_____ switches.

B _____ engineers connect logic gates together to solve problems, _____ engineers solve similar problems using the_____.

C The_____ array is a set of_____ which are customized after manufacture.

D The_____ of a_____ program are digital codes stored in order in the memory.

E The microprocessor contains a_____ to point to the next_____ to be executed.

F Devices that have to work very fast are usually based upon the_____ or the_____ array.

G _____ usually have only two output states – HIGH or LOW.

≫ Things to do

1 Explain the difference between an AND gate and an OR gate.

2 Write out the truth table for the OR gate and the AND gate, using the symbols 1 and 0.

3 Find out which microprocessor is used inside each of the following computers:
   a ZX 81
   b ZX Spectrum
   c BBC microcomputer
   d Sinclair QL computer
   e IBM PC computer

4 What do the following abbreviations stand for?
   a K   d BBC
   b ULA   e Hz
   c ALU

5 Imagine a set of traffic lights; '1' means that a particular lamp is ON, '0' means that it is off. If the code 100 means 'Red ON, Amber OFF, Green OFF', complete the set of codes that describes the normal **sequence** of the traffic lights. By the side of each code, write down its meaning to the motorist. The first code is done for you.

Code	Meaning
110	STOP
???	?
???	?
???	?

Codes for traffic lights sequence

5

Computers

Figure 5.1 *Some people still think of computers as huge machines with lots of whirling reels and flashing lights!*

Computers today

If you think a computer is an unreliable beast that takes up a lot of space, has lots of flashing lights, whirling reels, and likes to live in an air-conditioned room, then you are out of date (Figure 5.1)!

Today, computers are compact systems – they don't take up much space. They are extremely efficient and reliable and are as much a part of our everyday life as washing machines and television sets.

Unfortunately, science fiction writers have given a lot of people the wrong impression about computers. Some people still think of them as electronic brains that can make things up and know what you are thinking. But this is not true. A computer is a machine. It can only do what it is told to do. It can only carry out instructions. It can't think up things for itself.

When people stop thinking of computers as mystery objects they can see how essential computers are. Now, most people don't see computers as a threat. Instead they realize that they are useful tools that can do many mundane tasks for them.

The human brain is an expert at collecting, storing and processing information. No computer can store as much information as our brain. Our brains can think intelligently – computers can't. Figure 5.2 shows some storage capacities. (A character is a letter of the alphabet, a number from 0 to 9, any punctuation mark or a space.) Computers are much faster than our brains, but as you can see from Figure 5.2, their storage capacity is much smaller.

Storage type	Capacity (millions of characters)
Human brain	125 000 000
USA National Archives	112 500 000
Magnetic (hard) disk	313
Encyclopaedia Britannica	260
Floppy disk	2.5
Book	1.3

Figure 5.2 *Types of information storage and their capacities*

The uses of computers

Today, computers are used far more than they were 20 years ago. It would be hard now to imagine a world without them. Many jobs that we take for granted today would have been impossible without computers. Two examples are travel in space and the use of credit cards.

In the United Kingdom, computer manufacture will soon be a larger industry than car manufacture. Computers are used for more and more tasks because they have become smaller and cheaper over the last 10 years. Computers are found in many unlikely places such as cars, washing machines and children's games.

None of this would have been dreamt of in the 1960s. The computer power in pocket calculators and small computers would have needed the space of a whole room then!

Computers have got smaller because of the silicon chip. All the components that are needed in a computer can now be etched onto a tiny piece of silicon. Every year the number of components we can put onto a chip doubles. Chip technology is responsible for all the things we now take for granted in computers: smaller size, larger storage capacity and reliability.

What is a computer?

A computer is a machine that processes information. What we mean by 'processes' is that the information put into the computer has something done to it. Sometimes the computer is asked to do calculations with the information. Sometimes we ask the computer just to store the information so that it can be easily found when we need it.

Information and computing

Information is extremely important in our everyday lives. Our brains collect information all the time. They have to analyse it quickly so that we can make decisions depending on the information we have received. For example, supposing you are riding your bicycle along the road. Suddenly, the door of a parked car opens. You brain receives this information from your eyes. Then it processes the information and decides what you should do. It will probably decide that you should either stop, or swerve out to avoid the door.

As the world about us gets more complicated, we have to process more and more information. This has become an enormous job. It is now not practical for people to do all the tasks and so computers are used instead. Today many of the jobs we take for granted such as weather forecasting, space travel, and clearing cheques would be almost impossible without

computers. Without a computer these jobs would need so much paperwork and so many people that they would be very expensive and impractical.

Hardware and software

You have probably heard the words 'hardware' and 'software' used when people are talking about computers. **Hardware** is the part of the computer that you can touch and handle. It is the name given to all the devices that make up a computer system. These devices include the **input devices** (how we get information into the computer) e.g. disk drives, tape drives and keyboards. They also include the **central processing unit (CPU)** and any extra storage, and the **output devices** (how we get information out of the computer) e.g. visual display units (VDUs) and printers. Figure 5.3, shows how these are linked in a simple computer system. Magnetic tapes and disks are also hardware.

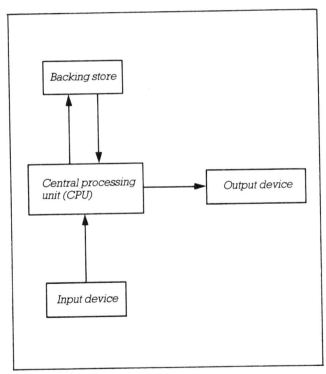

Figure 5.3 *A simple computer system*

Software is the name given to the actual programs that allow the hardware to do a useful job. Without software, hardware is useless. Software is programs made up of series of instructions that tell the computer what to do.

To understand the difference between hardware and software, think of a tape recorder and a blank tape. The tape recorder and the tape would both be the 'hardware' because we can actually pick them up. But if we recorded some music onto the tape, then the music would be the 'software'.

Why use computers?

Computers are extremely fast

Computers can process information very fast. For example an IBM computer used at the weather forecasting centre at Bracknell could do 1 million calculations every second. Computers used by the Electricity and Gas Boards work so fast that they could produce all the bills for their customers in a few days so that they could all receive their bills at the same time.

Computers are very accurate

Figure 5.4 *Computers don't make mistakes – they only do what they are told to do!*

You may have read in the newspapers, stories such as: 'Computer sends housewife 1 million pound gas bill' (Figure 5.4) or 'Computer pays headteacher her annual salary in monthly pay'! Although these stories are true, they don't happen as often as they used to. Now most people realize that computers don't make mistakes – they only do what they are told to do. In computing there is a saying 'garbage in, garbage out' or GIGO for short. What it means is that if some information is put into the computer incorrectly the computer won't realise that it is incorrect so it will give out a strange answer. If the computer is given the right information, it will always come out with the right output.

Computers can keep large amounts of information in a very small space

Keeping all the information we need written on paper in files is an enormous task. Once you have gone through the tedious job of making up the files and cataloguing them, you then have the problem of finding the file you want – sometimes you may have millions of them to hunt through! But if you use computerized storage you can keep millions of files in a very small space and can get the information from them in seconds. You can also have a spare copy in case of accidents – imagine having duplicate written files!

Computers can work continuously for 24 hours a day

Computers don't become ill and they don't have to take time off. They don't take lunch breaks or tea breaks and they don't go on strike (Figure 5.5).

Figure 5.5 *Computers don't have tea breaks and they don't go on strike!*

Instead, if necessary, computers can work continuously, 24 hours a day. They also work at the same rate throughout the day – they don't have 'off days' like we do. So for some tasks computers are better than people. But there are of course many things that computers can't do, for example house painting, hairdressing and nursing (Figure 5.6).

Figure 5.6 *Some jobs are better done by people!*

Computers can do some jobs that would be impossible without them

A lot of services that we take for granted would not be possible without a computer. One example is teletext. Another example is the use of cash dispensers and credit cards. These are only possible because computers can control how they work 24 hours a day. Space travel and successful weather forecasting would also be impossible without computers.

Input, process and output – the three stages of computing

All jobs can be split up into three stages whether they are being done by a computer or not. These stages are input, process and output. **Input** is all the information and materials you need to be able to do the job. What you do with the information or materials is the **process**. The **output** is the finished item or information. For example, suppose you want to make a cake. For the input you will need the ingredients and recipe. The process will be mixing the ingredients together in the correct way and then baking it. The ouput will be the finished cake.

In a computer the central processing unit (**CPU**) does the processing. Hardware can be connected to the CPU to input information. Some of the hardware devices can be used for output too. Figure 5.7 shows the three stages of computing.

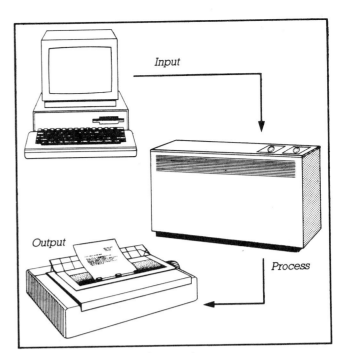

Figure 5.7 *The stages of computing*

Computers and memory

The central processing unit in a computer has a certain amount of memory. But the memory capacity is limited. Memory capacity is measured in kilobytes (K). The bigger the number of K a computer has, the more memory it has. So, for example, a Sinclair Spectrum microcomputer with 16K has less memory than one with 48K.

Usually the memory in the computer is used for the programs and the data that the computer is using at a particular time. But if more memory is needed then **backing storage** can be used. In most computers this is on magnetic tape or disk (Figure 5.8).

Figure 5.8 *Types of backing storage*

Where have computers come from

There have always been scientists who dreamt of creating calculating machines. To begin with, these were beads on rods (the abacus). Later, interconnecting cogs and wheels were used, the most famous of these machines was the Analytical Engine invented by Charles Babbage in 1834 (Figure 5.9). The first calculating machine driven by electricity was developed by Hermann Hollerith in 1890.

Figure 5.9 *Babbage's Analytical Engine*

The first electronic computer is said to have been Colossus, built in 1943. However, this was not a general purpose computer, but was designed for the specific task of cracking the German's secret codes during the war. The credit for inventing the first computer, in our sense of this word, is generally given to Von Neumann. He decided that certain criteria should be met by all computers:

1 Data and instructions should be represented as binary codes. They should be treated identically and stored in the same way.
2 The computer should be able to process both data and instructions.

Until about 1954, computers used electronic valves as the main processing devices; a typical machine might have 20 000 valves. They were unreliable and most commercial computers spent longer being repaired than being used. Today, we call these the First Generation of Computers. The Second Generation began when transistors were used instead of valves. This is the era when computers started to assume great importance in industry and when IBM (International Business Machines Corporation) grew to become the most important manufacturer.

The development of the chip

In 1959, engineers in what is now called 'Silicon Valley' in California developed the idea of an **integrated circuit**, with several transistors connected together on the same slice of silicon. The Third Generation of Computers arrived when these so-called 'silicon chips' were used to replace transistors and electronic valves. At once computers became cheaper, smaller, more reliable and more powerful – the IT revolution had begun.

It is hard now to imagine life without the silicon chip. They can be produced cheaply and in vast quantites, so they are found in all sorts of equipment. Cars, televisions, washing machines, record players, toys and many other machines can all work more efficiently if chips are used to control them.

Minicomputers and microcomputers

Computers up to the development of the chip, were very expensive and large. Today we would call them **mainframe** computers. Most were made by IBM. However, silicon chip technology has allowed computers to become smaller so that today's **minicomputer** is far more powerful than a mainframe of the 1960s.

The reason for this is the microprocessor (see Chapter 4). This device first appeared in the USA in the 1970s. Throughout Britain and the USA, enthusiasts then began to use this chip to make their own computers. These were called **microcomputers**. In 1976, the first microcomputer kit became available for hobbyists. This was the SC/MP from National Semiconductor (called the SCAMP). It could only be programmed in machine code and there were only 192 bytes for the user's program. It cost £120. Later it became possible to add a very elementary BASIC language to it, but even that used only 1K of memory. It was soon replaced by more powerful machines.

Figure 5.10 *The RM Nimbus PC – one of the most up-to-date microcomputers available*

Another of the first microcomputers was the Apple I, which had integer BASIC (it could not handle decimals). It was rapidly followed by the Apple II, which had an enormous (for those days) 16K of memory and ran a fuller BASIC. This has become the world's most famous microcomputer and is very popular in schools throughout the world.

Around the same time, a company called Commodore produced their first personal microcomputer, the PET (Personal Electronic Transactor). The first PET had 4K of memory, soon increased to 8K. The PET was the first microcomputer to come into British schools in any great numbers and the first to be used for microcomputer-assisted learning. Two years later, the PET was followed by the VIC20, aimed at the home market, closely followed by the C16 and the C64. One of their latest products is the Amiga, a powerful sixteen-bit machine with one megabyte of memory. It costs about the same as the original 4K PET, yet it has 250 times as much memory. If motor cars had been developed at the same rate as microcomputers over the past ten years, you would now be able to travel for 100 000 miles on one gallon of petrol!

In 1982, IBM entered the microcomputer market with their PC (Personal Computer). This was aimed at small businesses and became very successful. IBM's influence was so great that most other manufacturers have since tried to make their machines 'IBM-compatible'. This represents a change of direction because, previously, different microcomputers were not compatible. The C64 would not run programs written for the VIC20 and neither would run programs written for the PET – yet all three machines were made by Commodore within five years of one another. In future, we can expect every machine to run programs developed for a different one.

Computers in schools _____

Figure 5.11 *The BBC microcomputer dominates in British schools and colleges*

In Britain before 1982, the main microcomputers in schools were the PET and the Apple II. Then the British Government decided to help schools to buy their own microcomputers and, around the same time, the BBC launched a computer literacy campaign. The computer, commissioned by the BBC from Acorn computers, was called the BBC microcomputer (Figure 5.11). With the publicity given through television broadcasts (and because it was a very good machine), the popularity of the BBC micro grew very rapidly, until it now dominates in British schools and colleges.

The 'home' market, however, went for cheaper machines. The first to break through the £100 'barrier' was Sinclair's ZX81, more than one million of which have been sold. The ZX81, though, lacks colour and high resolution graphics. It was succeeded in 1982 by the ZX Spectrum, which continues to dominate in British homes.

'Fifth Generation' computers _____

We can safely predict that future computers will be faster, consume less power (already some can run from batteries) and will contain larger memories. The size of a microcomputer's memory is one measure of its power. Looking at the table (Figure 5.12), you can see that the cost of computer memory has halved every year, which means that, for the same cost, microcomputer power has doubled every year. If this continues (the signs are that this trend will **accelerate** rather than slow down), by the year 2000 the personal microcomputer will be more powerful than the biggest mainframe computer in the world today.

Microcomputer	Memory size	Cost	Year
Commodore PET	4K	£ 800	1977
Commodore PET	8K	£ 700	1978
Apple II	16K	£ 900	1980
Commodore 64	64K	£ 350	1982
Apple IIe	128K	£1000	1983
ACT Apricot	256K	£1000	1984
Atari 520ST	512K	£ 700	1985
Atari 1040ST	1024K	£ 700	1986
?????	16 000 000K?	£ 800?	2000

Figure 5.12 *Comparative memory costs of microcomputers*

At the same time that memory is becoming cheaper, the microprocessors used in it are becoming faster. More importantly, the newer microprocessors are able to work **in parallel**, with each one doing a part of the work. With these new devices, some countries are trying to build computers that are far more powerful than any built with third generation technology – the 'Fifth Generation of Computers'. What they will be able to do can only be guessed at, but it is a safe bet that they will affect all our lives to a very great extent. The prospect of every home having at least one powerful computer is not an impossible dream. This is why it is so important for everybody to know something about them and what they can do.

✓ Test yourself

Using the words in the list below, copy out and complete sentences A to L. Underline the words you have inserted. The words may be used once, more than once, or not at all.

outside   input   space   software   backing hardware   output   K   GIGO   processes information   fast   programs   continuously   IBM

A A computer is a machine which_____ information.
B The computer consists of two parts:_____ and_____ .
C The_____ is the_____ which allows the hardware to perform a useful task.
D A simple computer system usually consists of a CPU, input and output devices and some external storage called the_____ store.
E Gas boards use computers to produce bills because they are extremely_____ .
F A computer will only give the right result if you feed it the correct information to start with. This is often referred to as_____ .
G Computers can hold lots of_____ in a very small_____ .
H Another advantage of using computers is that they can work_____ .
I The three stages of computing are_____ process and_____ .
J Memory size of the computer is measured in_____ .
K Backing storage is used_____ the CPU.
L The largest computer company in the world is_____ .

≫ Things to do

1 a What does 'computer' mean?
b Give **three** examples of the sorts of jobs computers can do.
c For the **three** examples above, say why you think computers are suited to doing the jobs.
d Computers process information. What does 'process' mean?

2 a There are two parts to a useful computer system: hardware and software. Explain the difference between hardware and software.

b Draw a diagram of a simple computer system showing the following devices: backing store, central processing unit, output device and input device.

3 Why are computers useful? Choose from these answers:
a They can think for themselves
b They can solve any problem
c They can operate without a power supply
d They never go wrong
e They can make decisions when correctly programmed

4 Which of the following does computer hardware refer to?
a The compiler
b The program
c The data
d The electronics and casing
e The output result

5 The diagram shows a typical computer system. Write down the missing names a to d.

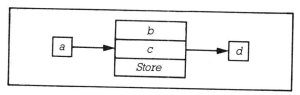

6 List **three** everyday sources of information with which you are familiar.

7 a What are the three stages of computing?
b Think of a simple task and divide it up into those three stages.

8 The essential procedures in the use of a computer are: input – process – output. An example of this with a micro-electronic device in everyday use could be a pocket calculator. The input of numbers and instruction is via the key pad, the process is the internal calculation, the output is the answer display.
Give **two** more examples of a device using microelectronics stating the input, process and output stages as in the example.

9 What is meant by the following terms which are commonly used in connection with computing?
a CPU   **c** GIGO
b VDU   **d** Backing store

10 Give **four** reasons for using computers and detail the advantages that they have over corresponding manual methods.

11 How would you describe to a person not familiar with computers the difference between a simple pocket calculator and a computer?

12 You have been asked to write an article for the school magazine describing the development of the computer since 1945. You decide to split your article into two equal parts:
   a the development of computer hardware, and
   b the development of computer software.
   Write a description of the main points you would include in your article.

13 The advent of chip technology and microprocessor systems has brought the world of computers nearer to the man in the street. Discuss this statement with reference to size, availability and cost of computers, their usage and other relevant information.

14 'Because of their cheapness and versatility, microprocessors and microcomputers are being used in an increasing number and variety of applications. It is likely that by the end of the 1980s, the large mainframe computer will have become extinct.'
   a Describe **four** ways in which microprocessors/microcomputers are being used. Indicate the effect, if any, which each of these applications is having on the use of large mainframe computers.
   b Comment on the suggestion, made in the quotation above, that by the end of the 1980s no large mainframe computers will be in use.

15 Make a survey of your school or college. Find out what proportion of your fellow-students own a home microcomputer. Make a bar chart of the most popular makes.

6

Flowcharts

What are flowcharts?

Flowcharts (or **flow diagrams**) are used to break a task down into lots of different steps arranged into a logical order. The steps are written inside boxes. Some of the more common flowcharts boxes are shown in Figure 6.1. There are others, but these will be dealt with later on in the book.

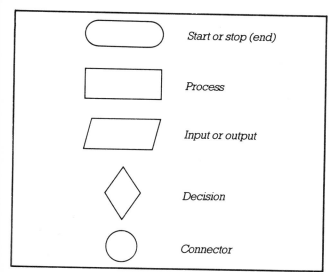

Figure 6.1 *Flow diagram symbols*

Stop or start boxes

These symbols are used at the start and end of the flow diagram (Figure 6.2). There is only ever one start symbol but there can be more than one stop or end box. The line with the arrow going into or out of the box shows whether it is stop or start box. There is always only one line of flow (line of arrow). The name of the box is placed inside the box (Figure 6.3).

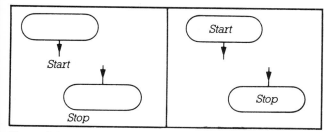

Figure 6.2   **Figure 6.3**

Process boxes

Process boxes have two arrows, one going in and the other going out. Sometimes they are called activity boxes, because something is done. A process is something which is done with the information. Quite often it will involve a calculation, but it could be just doing something e.g. hit a nail, pay some money etc. Anything that you have to do is put in a process box. The process is written inside the box. Figure 6.4 shows some typical process boxes. When we write flowcharts to write a program we usually put calculations in process boxes.

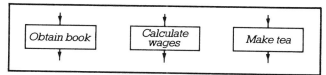

Figure 6.4

Input and output boxes

Input is what is required for the process to be done. If a calculation needs to be done, then the input will be some figures. If you are writing after a job, your input could be the job advertisement. The input box also has an arrow going in and one coming out. What the input is, is written inside the box. Figure 6.5 shows some typical input and output boxes.

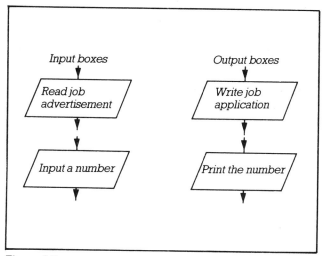

Figure 6.5

Decision boxes

These boxes are used to ask questions to which there are two answers: yes or no. The answer will always be either yes or no – never 'don't know'! Yes and no must be written alongside the paths to show which path is being taken (Figure 6.6).

One flow line goes into the decision box and two lines leave it once the decision inside the box has been made. The question inside the box must be one which has the answer yes or no. Some examples of decision boxes are shown in Figure 6.7.

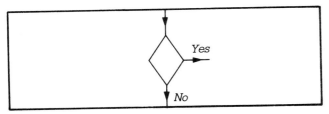

Figure 6.6

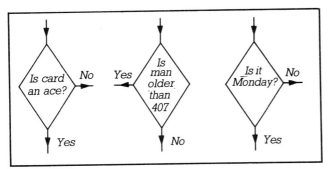

Figure 6.7

In decision boxes one of the flowlines can come out of the decision box to either the right or the left. This is useful in flowcharts where there are lots of decision boxes, because it stops the flowchart from becoming cluttered. The line coming out of the right or left of the flowchart eventually joins up at a place along the flowline going downwards. Figure 6.8 gives an example of this. This example forms what is known as a loop. If the answer to the question in the decision box is yes then one thing happens, if the answer is no then something else happens.

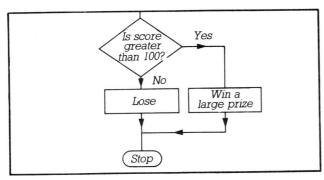

Figure 6.8

Connector boxes

These circular boxes are used to connect the flowlines when you have to turn over a page (Figure 6.9). They are usually numbered in case there is more than one flowline. When you first start drawing flow diagrams, it is best to start at the top of a clean page in order to avoid confusion.

Figure 6.9

Connectors can be useful in flow diagrams where there are lots of loops, because they make the diagram look neater.

Example 1 Draw a flow diagram to apply for a job that you have seen in a newspaper.

The steps involved are:
1 Deciding what input is required.
2 Deciding what needs to be done with the input material.
3 Deciding what output is required.

These can be summarized as:
1 Input   2 Process   3 Output

In this example the input is the job advertisement. You need this for the description of the job and the address to which to write. You need to read the advertisement. The process is deciding what to write, and the output is actually writing the job application. Figure 6.10 shows how the flowchart could be drawn.

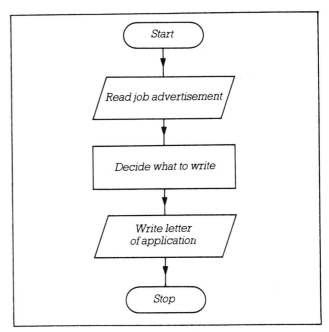

Figure 6.10   *Writing a job application*

Example 2 Draw a flowchart to show how you would play the following game.

First you must answer a question correctly. Then a coin is tossed. If it is heads you choose a number between 1 and 12. Each number wins a prize. If the number has been selected, then you must select again. If the number is 7 you win a booby prize. Figure 6.11 shows a flowchart for this. You could play a series of games by asking, just before the stop sign, if the player would like another game.

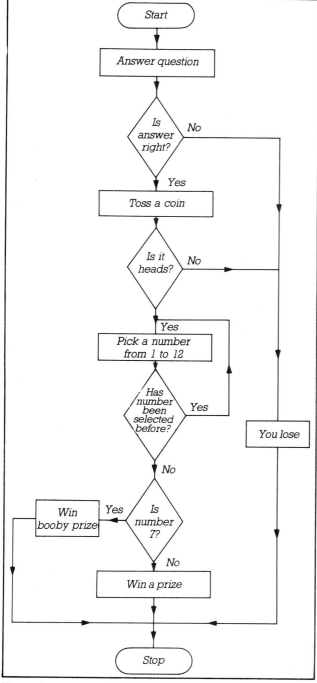

Figure 6.11 *Flowchart for a game*

Computing flowcharts

In the previous section we looked at non-computing flowcharts. These were flowcharts for doing various tasks that we have to do. It would be impossible for the computer to use them, but they show how a task can be broken down into a series of logical steps.

Now we will look at the way in which flowcharts can be used to help write computer programs. These computing flowcharts quite often involve numbers and the process boxes quite often contain arithmetic processes.

Steps for writing a computer flowchart

1 Deciding what output is required. It is very important to decide what output you require and the way it is set out. Also, you need to decide whether you require a hard copy (a printed copy).
2 Deciding on the method of solution. This involves deciding on the calculations you will use, headings, totals and loops.
3 Drawing a draft flowchart. This is just a brief sketch which shows the general flow of logic. You can tidy this up or alter it for the final flowchart.
4 Drawing the final flowchart. You need to draw a neat and accurate flowchart.
Remember that a flowchart should be capable of being used by other people. It must be easy to understand with clear statements inside the flowchart boxes.

Dry runs

Once you have drawn a flowchart you need to check it for logical errors. You do this by performing what is called a **dry run**. A dry run is a check to make sure that the flowchart is correct. Test data is put into the flowchart and each instruction in the boxes is obeyed in turn. When the data has been processed by the flowchart, we make sure that the output is correct. If it is not correct, then a mistake has been made in the drawing of the flowchart.

Quite often, it is best to choose several numbers in turn and test each by doing a dry run. When performing a dry run, it is a good idea to keep track of what is happening by drawing a table.

Figure 6.12 *A dry run!*

✔ Test yourself

Using the words in the list below, copy out and complete sentences A to G. Underline the words you have inserted. The words may be used once, more than once, or not at all.

arithmetic   task   decision
dry run   steps   process
test   logical   table

A Flowcharts are used to break a_____ down into a series of logical_____.

B A_____ box is used when something is done.

C The flowchart boxes which have questions to which there are either yes or no answers are called_____ boxes.

D In computing flowcharts the process boxes often contain_____ processes.

E After a flowchart has been drawn it should be checked for_____ errors.

F A_____ is performed to check the flowchart.

G _____ data is put into the flowchart and the outputs are written in a_____.

⋙ Things to do

1 The flowchart symbol shown is used to represent which of the following?

a The input of data
b Decision making
c The start
d Assigning of a value to a variable
e A calculation

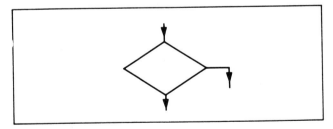

2 What is indicated by the following flowchart symbol?

a Input/output
b Process
c Repeated loop
d Decision
e Data from a backing store

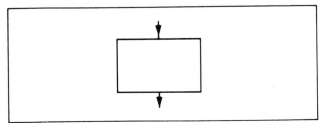

3 A 'dry run' is which one of these?

a A program to test that the computer is working correctly.
b The first time a program is processed on the computer.
c A program RUN which produces no results.
d A manual check of the program using test data.
e A program RUN which produces incorrect results.

4 Copy the following boxes, and write a suitable statement in each one:

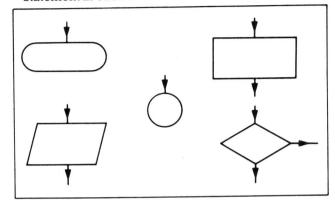

5 Give **four** reasons for using flowcharts.

6 Two boys play the game of marbles according to the following rules. The first player flicks his marble. The second player then has to hit the first player's marble. If he hits the marble then he wins, but if he misses then the other player takes his turn to hit his opponent's marble. The game goes on until one of the players wins. Arrange the following flowchart symbols to produce a flowchart to play the above game until one of the players becomes bored and wants to stop playing.

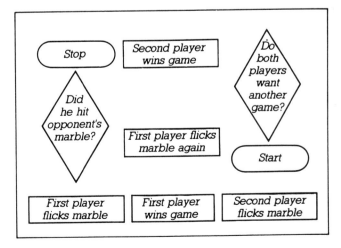

7 Draw a flowchart to make a pot of tea for four people.

8 Draw a flowchart to cross a road using the Green Cross Code.

7

Computer peripherals

Peripheral devices

To get data in and out of the computer, we need **peripheral devices**. These are devices that are attached to, and controlled by, the central processing unit. They are not contained inside the central processing unit (CPU). The world 'peripheral' means 'on the outside of'. So a peripheral device is a device on the outside of the CPU.

The peripheral devices provide the two way communication between the computer and the person using it, the **user**. Peripheral devices include devices for putting data into the computer (**input devices**) and devices for getting something out of the computer (**output devices**). There are some devices that are able to do both. Figure 7.1 shows some peripheral devices you might find in a modern office.

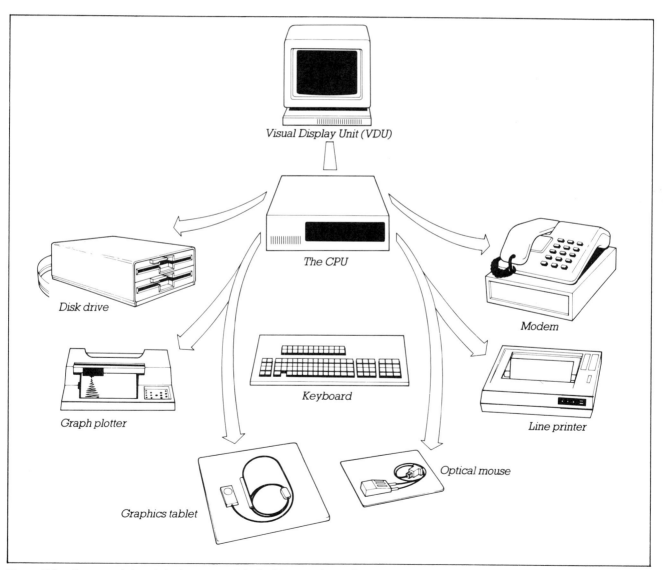

Visual Display Unit (VDU)

Disk drive

The CPU

Modem

Graph plotter

Keyboard

Line printer

Graphics tablet

Optical mouse

Figure 7.1   *Some peripheral devices you might find in a modern office*

VDU and keyboard

This is the commonest combination of input and output devices. Data can be input into the computer via a **keyboard** and output on a screen called a **visual display unit** (VDU). Figure 7.2 shows 6th-formers using VDUs and keyboards.

Figure 7.2 *6th-formers using VDUs and keyboards*

Paper tape and punched card readers

These are now obsolete methods of inputting data into the computer. They were both wasteful and time-consuming.

Document readers

A **document reader** can read off data from specially prepared documents. There are two types of

document reader. One is a **mark reader**, which can understand marks made at a certain place on a document. The other is a **character reader** which can read actual letters.

Mark readers

Marks on documents can be read in two ways. One method is **mark sensing**. This brushes electrical contacts across the paper. If the contacts touch a pencil mark then a current can flow between them because the pencil lead conducts electricity. This method is used, for example, for marking multiple-choice question papers.

A newer method involves directing a thin beam of light on to the document and sensing the light reflected by the document. If there is a dark part (pencil mark) then very little light is reflected. The method is called **optical mark recognition (OMR)**. Mark reading is ideal for documents such as meter-reading sheets, which the Gas or Electricity man marks in when he comes to read the meter (Figure 7.3). No other data preparation stage is needed, so fewer errors are introduced. Documents are read at very high speeds, much faster than typing speed.

Optical character readers

Optical character readers can recognize actual letters and numbers. The process of reading is called **optical character recognition (OCR)**. Sometimes the documents read in this way are typed, but they can also be handwritten. If the document used is handwritten then, just like humans, the reader can only read it if it is very neat. OCR is used for producing bills and is a very quick method of getting information into the computer.

	CUSTOMER ACCOUNT NUMBER	PREVIOUS READING	PRESENT READING
142071983 Mr M. Mouse 10 Disney Drive Anytown	0 0 0 **0** 0 0 0 0 0	0 0 **0** **0** **0**	0 0 0 0 0
	1 1 1 1 1 **1** 1 1 1	**1** 1 1 1 1	**1** 1 1 1 1
	2 2 **2** 2 2 2 2 2 2	2 **2** 2 2 2	2 2 2 2 2
	3 3 3 3 3 3 3 3 **3**	3 3 3 3 3	3 3 **3** 3 3
	4 **4** 4 4 4 4 4 4 4	4 4 4 4 4	4 **4** 4 4 4
PREVIOUS READING — 12000	5 5 5 5 5 5 5 5 5	5 5 5 5 5	5 5 5 5 5
EXPECTED HIGH — 20000	6 6 6 6 6 6 6 6 6	6 6 6 6 6	6 6 6 6 6
EXPECTED LOW — 14000	7 7 7 7 **7** 7 7 7 7	7 7 7 7 7	7 7 7 **7** 7
PRESENT READING — 14378	8 8 8 8 8 8 8 **8** 8	8 8 8 8 8	8 8 8 8 **8**
	9 9 9 9 9 9 9 **9** 9	9 9 9 9 9	9 9 9 9 9

Figure 7.3 *A meter reading sheet with mark sense boxes. Information is coded by shading-in the boxes*

Magnetic ink character readers (MICR)

These readers can read the characters printed in magnetic ink on cheques. They are extremely fast and can handle large amounts of work accurately.

Bar code readers

These peripheral devices can understand the pre-coded data in a bar code. There are two types of bar code reader. In one type, a light pen called a **wand reader** is passed across the bar code. In the other type, a laser scanner is fixed into a disk and the object is passed across the screen.

Bar code readers are excellent devices for data capture because they are very quick and they enable several jobs to be done at once. They are used extensively, for example in shops and libraries.

Printers

Printers provide the user with a hard copy (permanent copy) of the information that can, for instance, be posted. Bank statements, invoices, reminder letters, stock lists, pay slips etc. are all examples of information that may need to be output on a line printer.

There are two types of printer: **line printers** and **character printers**. Line printers can type a complete line at a time whereas character printers can only print a single character at a time. An ordinary typewriter is a character printer.

Line printers

These are the most common type of printer. They work at much faster speeds than character printers because they print a whole line at a time. Some line printers print the lines backwards on the return journey and save even more time.

Character printers

Character printers produce one character at a time and, as a result, are generally slower than line printers. However, what they lose in speed they generally make up for in print quality. The print produced by these printers looks as if it has been produced by a good quality typewriter rather than by a computer.

Dot matrix printers

Some **dot matrix printers** are line printers, printing an entire line at a time. The majority of them are character printers, printing each character in turn. Dot matrix printers are mainly used with microcomputers because they are fairly cheap. They consist of seven or nine hammers that can be struck individually, under computer control, against an inked ribbon to make a dot on the paper. By striking the right hammers at the right times they print numbers and letters (Figure 7.4).

By going over each character twice and moving the print head slightly, it is possible to produce near letter-quality print. Obviously this takes longer.

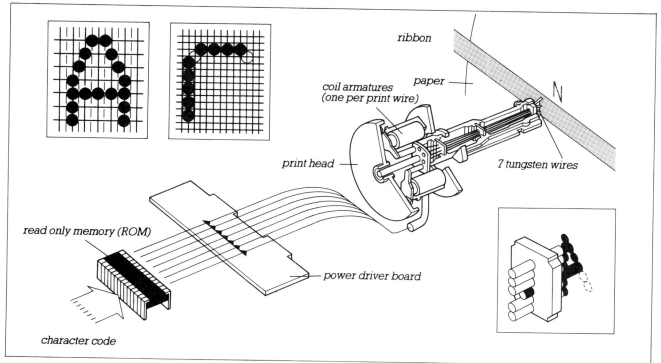

Figure 7.4 *How a dot matrix printer works*

Daisy wheel printers

The **daisy wheel printer** consists of a wheel with lots of arms attached to it, rather in the way petals are attached to a daisy. At the ends of these arms are two characters, one above the other. The daisy wheel rotates and a hammer presses the carbon and paper against the arm.

Daisy wheel printers are slow but produce high quality print. They are used mainly for producing business letters in conjunction with wordprocessors. Figure 7.5 shows a daisy wheel printer with a sheet feeder.

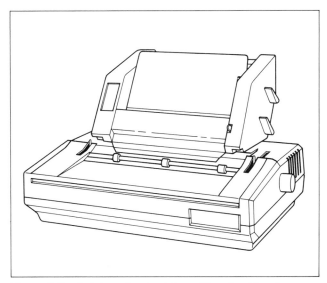

Figure 7.5 *A daisy wheel printer with a sheet feeder*

Laser printers

Laser printers are extremely fast and are used for producing Giro cheques, gas and electricity bills. The laser printer uses a similar principle for its use to that used by a photocopying machine. Laser printers are quite expensive, but are ideal where large quantities of bills need to be sent out in a short space of time.

Ink jet printers

In an **ink jet printer**, tiny drops of ink are sprayed on to the paper to form characters. The new ink jet printers are able to print graphics as well as use several coloured inks. Ink jet printers can be expensive but they are very quiet.

Comparison of printers

Figure 7.6 shows a comparison of the various types of printer.

Mouse

A **mouse** is a device with wheels underneath and, as you push it over a flat surface, the computer moves the cursor in the same way on the screen. There are usually three buttons on the mouse. One of these buttons is pressed when the cursor has reached its desired position.

A mouse provides a quick way of using the computer and is ideal for novices who can't type. A lot of software has now been written for use with a mouse and it is only necessary to move the cursor to select your options. It can also be used for tracing shapes and has buttons to tell the computer when to start and stop drawing.

Light pen

A **light pen** is a penlike input device that is used with a screen. It can be used to point to areas on the screen and thus indicate a selection from a displayed list, or it can be used to draw shapes. When the light pen is placed on the screen, the computer detects the light and finds its position.

When drawing lines on the screen, the pressing of a button on the light pen tells the computer when to start or stop drawing. Architects and car designers, for example, often make use of light pens in their work.

Type of printer	Advantages	Disadvantages	Typical speed
Dot matrix	Cheap and quick	Noisy Not quite letter-quality print	200–600 lines per minute
Laser	Extremely fast. Quiet because it is non-impact	Very expensive	10 000 sheets of paper per hour
Ink jet	Different-coloured inks can be used together. Quiet and fast	Expensive	100–400 characters per second
Daisy wheel	Letter-quality print. Relatively cheap	Noisy Slow	40–65 characters per second

Figure 7.6 *A comparison of printers*

Graph pad/tablet

One type of graphics pad has a pen (or a pointer) supported in a jointed arm. When the printer or pen is moved over the surface of the pad, the picture appears on the screen.

Another type of pad uses the pad for drawing and has lots of commands on the tablet itself, thus avoiding the need to use the keyboard. Using this pad it is possible to draw and print in different colours, copy, invert, mirror and flip any part of the picture.

Graph plotters

A **graph plotter** allows the computer to draw pictures on paper. These pictures may be graphs, pie diagrams, maps, three-dimensional drawings etc. As well as drawing the outline of the diagram, the plotter can also shade in diagrams and some plotters can use different coloured inks.

A computer with a graph plotter is a very useful system for an architect, draughtsman or engineer, because drawings on the VDU can be altered on the screen without having to redo the whole drawing. When the drawing is correct it can be printed out. The photographs (Figures 7.7 and 7.8) show examples of the types of plotter in common use.

Joysticks

Joysticks are mainly used by microcomputers and are almost essential if you want to play quick action arcade-type games on your home computer. The stick is used to control the movement of a shape on a screen. The movement of the joystick is transferred to the movement of the shape and provides a faster response than the normal keyboard.

Sometimes two joysticks are used so that the game may be played by two different players.

✓ Test yourself

Using the words in the list below, copy out and complete sentences A to S. Underline the words you have inserted. The words may be used once, more than once, or not at all.

*character   dot matrix   document reader   laser
CPU   keyboard   line   hard
bar code   daisy wheel   light pen   characters
wand reader   OMR   mark reader   word
CAD   bar code reader   joysticks   peripheral
input   punched tape   mouse*

A *A_____ device is a device which is under the control of the_____ but outside it.*

B *These devices can be divided into two: output and_____ devices.*

C *The most common combination of input and output devices is the VDU and_____.*

D *Card readers and_____ readers are not used much nowadays because they are very wasteful.*

E *A_____ can understand letters placed in boxes on a specially prepared document.*

F *Marks placed on a document can be read by a_____.*

G *This form of reading is called_____.*

H *An OCR can understand_____ on a document.*

I *A_____ is often seen in large supermarkets. The shop assistant uses a_____ to pass a beam of light across a_____ on the goods.*

J *A_____ printer can be used to obtain a_____ copy.*

K *A_____ printer prints one line at a time, but a_____ printer only prints a single character at a time.*

L *The_____ printer produces characters made up of a series of dots.*

M *For high quality print, it is best to use a_____ printer.*

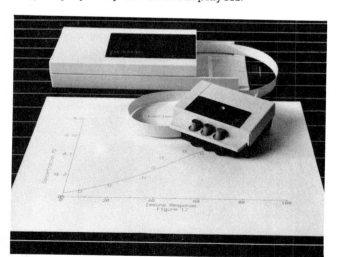

Figure 7.7   *A type of plotter that moves over the paper to draw a diagram*

Figure 7.8   *A plotter being used to produce a high-quality engineering drawing*

N A_____ printer is slow but produces very high print quantity. It is often used in conjunction with a_____ processor.

O If large quantities of printed material are needed very quickly, such as electricity bills etc., then a_____ printer can be used.

P A_____ has wheels underneath it and is pushed around on a flat surface so as to move a cursor on the screen of a VDU.

Q It provides a way of using the computer for those people who don't like using the_____.

R A_____ can be used to read bar codes as well as for selecting items from a menu on a screen or drawing diagrams.

S _____ are often used as input devices for playing games on microcomputers.

≫ Things to do _____

1 Explain the meaning of the following terms:
   a Peripheral device
   b Input device
   c Output device
   d User

2 Give the name of a peripheral device that would help to do the following tasks.
   a Play a game on a microcomputer.
   b Draw a map of England.
   c Scan a bar code on a grocery item.
   d Read the magnetic ink characters on the bottom of a bank cheque.
   e Enable an executive who doesn't like typing, to use the computer.
   f Help a car designer to design a new car.
   g Mark a multiple-choice answer sheet.
   h Print a list of pupils in a form.
   i Print out the quarterly gas or electricity bills.

3 What do the following abbreviations stand for?
   a OCR
   b OMR
   c MICR
   d VDU

4 Describe which type of printer you would use to do the following jobs. For each one you have chosen, explain your choice.
   a Suitable for typing out pupils' programs on a microcomputer in a school.
   b Producing high-quality typed letters on a wordprocessor.
   c Printing a very high volume of material i.e. all the bills for the water rates at once.

8

Backing storage

Backing storage is the name given to the storage outside the central processing unit. Backing store is needed because the main memory inside the CPU is limited in storage capacity and is volatile, which means the data stored is lost when the computer is switched off. Backing storage medium (material) is usually chosen on the basis of cost and storage capacity. We shall, now, look at some of the more common storage media.

Magnetic tape

Magnetic tape is used mainly by the large mainframe computers. Cassette tape will be dealt with later in this chapter. The tape is made of plastic coated with an iron oxide, and this can be magnetized to represent a code. The storage capacity of tape is very large but it has the disadvantage that it only allows **serial** or **sequential access** (see also Chapter 10). This means that, to get to one part of the tape, it may be necessary to run through all the tape if the information is at the end. If can be a time-consuming process and could take several minutes.

Magnetic tape is recorded and read using a magnetic **tape unit**. This is very similar to an ordinary tape recorder. The tapes can be taken off the units when not in use and stored in a **tape library**. Tape is mainly used for applications that need a high storage capacity and where quick access to data is not required.

Magnetic (hard) disk

These disks are made of thin metal coated with magnetic material on both sides. Magnetic disk storage is more expensive than tape, but is a much better way of storing information and data that is needed regularly. Disk is ideal for applications which use **real-time processing** because disk provides a **random access medium**. This means that the data held on the disk can be found almost immediately, because you don't need to go sequentially through the data before the item you want is found. Using magnetic disk, you go straight to the data. This method of access is referred to as **random** or **direct access** (see also Chapter 10).

Figure 8.1 shows the arrangement of a magnetic disk that enables data to be found very quickly. The first track containing the directory tells the disk drive where the read heads should move to in order to read the data. Hard disks hold much more information than floppy disks, typically from 10 to 100 megabytes.

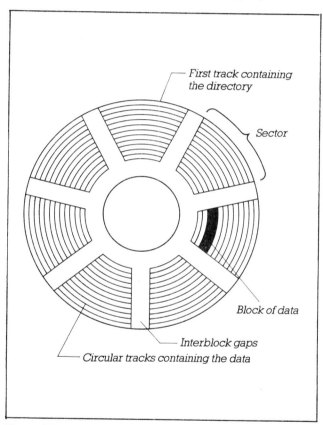

First track containing the directory

Sector

Block of data

Interblock gaps

Circular tracks containing the data

Figure 8.1 *The parts of a magnetic disk*

Disk drives

A **disk drive** is the hardware device that records information on to, and reads information off, the disk. The read/write heads move on arms, reading or writing information. The **disk operating system (DOS)** is responsible for the storage of information on the disks and allows the computer to gain access to the information in as short a time as possible. The disk operating system is an actual computer program which co-ordinates all the functions of the disk drive.

Disk packs

Disk packs are used when large quantities of data need to be stored. Disk packs usually contain about eleven disks in a single plastic case. Disk packs that can't be removed from the drive unit are called **fixed disks**. When the packs can be removed they are called **exchangeable disk packs**.

Floppy disks (diskettes)

Floppy disks are the commonest type of backing storage media used mainly by microcomputers. The disks are made of a flexible plastic that has been coated with iron oxide.

There are three sizes of disk: 3½ inch, 5¼ inch and 8 inch diameter. Most microcomputers use either of the two smaller disks. The disk is contained inside a cardboard envelope. Inside the envelope there is a liner which removes any debris on the disk surface and also lubricates the disk as it rotates. To read and write the data off and on to the disk, a **floppy disk**

drive unit is used. The read/write head moves along the short cut in the cardboard envelope towards the centre. It can find, read and write data at extremely high speed.

Like hard disks, floppy disks are a random access medium. Since the floppy disks have to be small, the data needs to be packed together very closely. Because of this, floppy disks can be very sensitive to dust and changes in temperature so, for some computer systems, floppy disks would not be reliable enough for storage.

The amount of storage capacity depends on the recording density (how near the tracks and sectors are to each other). A typical disk drive with a disk of 5¼" diameter can hold between 150 and 500 kilobytes of information. Some disks can hold information on both sides. The **write protect notch** at the side of the disk can be covered with tape to prevent erasure.

Figure 8.2 shows the parts of a floppy disk, whilst in Figure 8.3 a floppy disk is being put into a disk drive. Figure 8.4 shows how to look after your floppy disks.

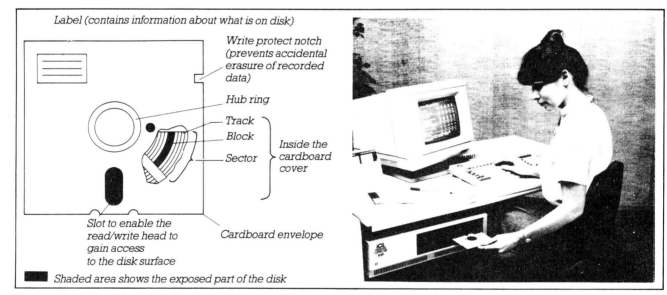

Figure 8.2 *Inside a floppy disk*

Figure 8.3 *Putting a floppy disk into a disk drive*

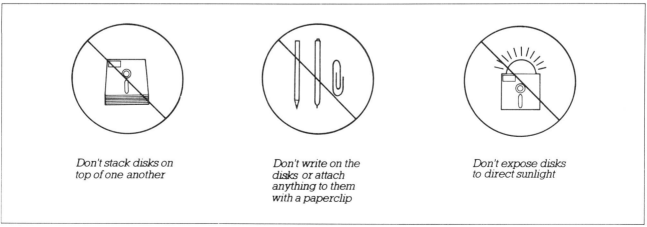

Don't stack disks on top of one another

Don't write on the disks or attach anything to them with a paperclip

Don't expose disks to direct sunlight

Figure 8.4 *How to look after your floppy disks* (contd.)

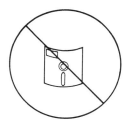 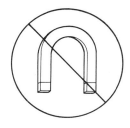 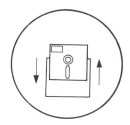

Don't bend disks

Don't place near magnets or magnetic materials

Always replace the disk in its paper envelope after use

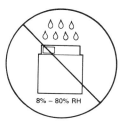 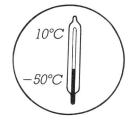 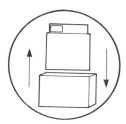

Don't expose disk to moisture (Note: RH means relative humidity, which is the percentage of moisture in the air)

Avoid extreme temperatures, hot or cold

Always replace the disk in its envelope in the plastic case

Figure 8.4 (contd.)   *How to look after your floppy disks*

Floppy disk drive unit

The **floppy disk drive** is the unit which rotates the floppy disk and enables the read/write head to put information on or take information off the disk. Most disk units contain two disk drives because one of the units can be used to record information off the other.

Quite often the disk drive units will be used to store information in the form of files. These file stock lists, names and addresses, payroll information etc.

The disk operating system (DOS) keeps a directory of the files on the disk. It controls the information storage and retrieval.

Cassettes

Cassettes can be used as a cheap alternative to disks with microcomputers (Figure 8.5). The cassettes are the same as those used in an ordinary cassette recorder. The trouble with using cassettes is that the loading of a program takes quite a long time. Also the reliability of loading is not always what might be desired. Because of the slowness and the unreliability, their use is usually restricted to home computers. Figure 8.6 shows the similarities and differences between the main types of backing store.

Figure 8.5   *Data cassettes for microcomputers. They are like ordinary cassettes but are made to a higher standard and are usually shorter in length*

Magnetic tape	Magnetic disk	Floppy disk	Cassette tape
Cheap	Expensive	Fairly cheap	Very cheap
Serial (sequential) access	Random (direct) access	Random (direct) access	Serial (sequential) access
Very large storage capacity (10–60 megabytes)	Very large storage capacity (2–60 megabytes)	Medium storage capacity (0.25–1.5 megabytes)	Very small storage capacity
Slower access time	Fast access time	Fast access time	Very slow access time
Fast transfer rate	Very fast transfer rate	Fairly slow transfer rate	Very slow transfer rate
Exchangeable	Exchangeable or fixed	Exchangeable	Exchangeable

Figure 8.6 *Comparison between the main types of backing store*

Video discs (laser discs)

Great advances in magnetic disk technology have been made in the last few years. A few years ago, 240 kilobytes (1 Kbyte = 1000 bytes) of data on a single disk was thought to be impossible, but now, 10 megabytes (more than 40 times as much) is fairly ordinary. But even that is small compared to people's real needs. For archives and large databases or any application where huge amounts of information need to be kept, the storage capacity of magnetic disks is inadequate. Magnetic tape could be used for its huge storage capacity but the fact that it is a serial access storage medium means that it is very slow, and prevents its use in a lot of applications.

Laser discs (videodiscs) were invented to overcome these storage capacity problems. They are read by a machine that uses technology similar to that of a compact disc player. The main advantages of these discs are that a lot of information can be stored in a small space, and the access is random so that the information is found quickly. The information stored on videodisc is permanent and not easily destroyed.

Videodiscs need a special disc player, a suitable computer, a tracker ball or mouse and a colour monitor (VDU). They are made of plastic and contain information on both sides. However the machine cannot automatically read the reverse side, so the disc must be turned over.

The signals that store the information are recorded as pits arranged in a special track on the reflective plastic disc. As the disc rotates, the spiral track is scanned by a finely focussed laser beam; the light is reflected at the surface of the disc and is picked up by a sensor.

The pits in the disc can carry either moving video pictures in an analogue form or sound, text, graphics, still pictures and computer programs, all contained on digital pulses.

Laser or videodiscs are used by the Domesday Project (see Chapter 18) and also for interactive training programmes (Figure 8.7).

Figure 8.7 *A videodisc being used for training*

Videodiscs are really only **ROM (Read Only Memory)** so it is impossible to change the information on them or to record information over them. There is, however, some research going on at the present time, to develop a videodisc that can be altered.

To make the Domesday equipment easy to use, a tracker ball is used to select an option on the screen. The tracker ball is a little like a mouse and is used to move the cursor around the screen to select an option.

Microfilm and microfiche

Offline information can be stored in the form either of sets of photographic slides (each set called a **microfiche** Figure 8.8) or of photographic film in the form of a reel (called **microfilm**). Pages of print taken off the screen of a VDU can be greatly reduced in size.

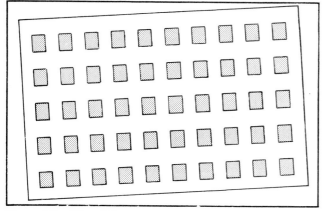

Figure 8.8 *Microfiche*

Computer output on microfilm (COM) is ideal for situations where information is kept that doesn't go out of date quickly, such as catalogues of books in a library or bookshop.

Another advantage of using microfiche or microfilm is that information can be posted easily and cheaply. Many banks use COM to hold details of the balance (amount of money) in customers' accounts.

Softstrip

Softstrip is a paper-based backing storage system. Information, software, graphics and sound can be stored on data strips printed on plain paper. A softstrip is shown in Figure 8.9. Datastrips can be printed in magazines, newsletters and other published material. This means that instead of tediously typing in the listings of programs that you find in computer magazines and books, you could simply use the special softstrip reader to read the programs directly into your computer.

Softstrips can be of variable length and printing density. A typical strip printed with high density on a laser printer has a storage capacity of approximately 3500 bytes, which is about that required to hold three pages of A4 text.

Softstrips can be produced by nearly all the popular dot and laser printers.

Softstrip reader

The reader plugs into the cassette i.e. serial part of the computer and when the reader is placed over a strip it scans the pattern on the strips and transmits it into the computer. The reader takes about 30 seconds to read the longest strip which is quite a long time when compared to disk.

The reader has a big advantage in that it can read the strip through general dirt and can even read a crumpled strip. The greatest advantage is that the strip can be photocopied. If you want to protect a strip against photocopying, you simply scribble over the strip with a felt tip pen in red or blue ink. If this is done, then the scribble comes out as black on a photocopy, thus rendering it useless for reading.

Since the strips are on paper they can easily be posted, and because the softstrip uses the ASCII code, it can be produced and read by different makes of computers.

◝ Test yourself

Using the words in the list below, copy and complete sentences A to O. Underline the words you put in. The words may be used once, more than once, or not at all.

serial   magnetic   floppy disk   laser   real-time disk pack   write project   disk operating system random access   exchangeable   slow   microfilm microcomputers   backing   microfilm   COM magnetic tape   unreliable   Domesday   microfiche softstrip

A _____ *storage is storage outside the CPU.*

B _____ *is a type of storage media that is used by the larger mainframe computers.*

C *There are two types of access to data, _____ access, which means the information is accessed sequentially and _____ where the information is accessed immediately.*

D *A _____ disk is a random access medium whereas _____ is a serial access medium.*

E *Magnetic disk is a reliable storage medium for applications which use _____ processing.*

F *A series of magnetic disks contained inside a plastic case is called a _____. Sometimes these packs can be removed. They are then called _____ disk packs.*

G *A flexible magnetic disk is called a _____. They are generally used by _____ and the smaller mainframes.*

H *Floppy disks have a _____ notch which is covered up with tape to prevent accidental erasure.*

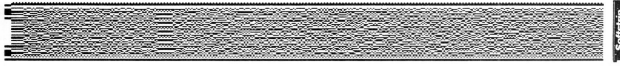

Figure 8.9 *This strip contains an IBM Basic program to calculate roots of numbers*

I The _____ keeps a directory of the files and controls the information storage and retrieval on the disk.

J Cassettes can be used as a cheap alternative to disk for home computers, although they are too _____ and _____ for serious use.

K Videodiscs or _____ discs are a new type of backing store which are able to hold huge amounts of information in a small space.

L Videodiscs are used as storage media in the _____ project and for interactive training programmes.

M Information can be kept offline in the form of a set of photographic slides called a _____ or photographic film on a reel called _____.

N _____ is used in libraries, bookshops and any situation where lists need to be displayed without going to the expense of having an online terminal.

O _____ is a new type of backing storage media that uses a pattern on a strip of paper to store data.

⟫ Things to do _____

1

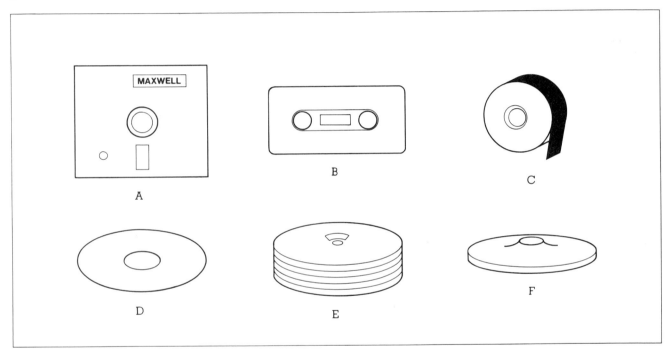

a Name the backing storage media in the diagrams A to F.

b Select the backing storage media that would be the most suitable for doing the following. Give reasons for each of your choices.
   i Storing games programs for a home computer where a limited amount of money is available.
   ii Storing pictures and computer programs for an interactive training program.
   iii Storing letters and documents for a wordprocessor.
   iv Storing a program to be printed in a computer magazine.
   v Storing out-patient records in a hospital where they may not be needed for several years, if ever.
   vi Storing in-patients records in a hospital where the medical staff may need the information immediately.
   vii Storing information about how much money a bank customer has in her account.

2 a i What is a sequential access file?
   ii Give an example of a medium suitable to hold a sequential access file.
   iii Give an example of an application where a sequential access file would be appropriate.

b i What is a random access file?
   ii Give an example of a medium suitable for a random access file.
   iii Give an example of an application where a random access file would be appropriate.

3 A computer uses two types of store: main store and backing store. Why do computers need backing store as well as main store?

4 *John hasn't much of a clue when it comes to looking after his programs held on floppy disks. Look carefully at the cartoons and write down a list of all the things he is doing wrong.*

5 a *The diagram shows part of a school's pupil file held on magnetic tape. Write in the empty circles the correct letters to show each of the following.*
   A *A block*
   B *A record*
   C *A field*
   b *What does the circle labelled D show.*

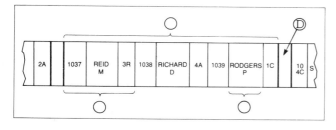

6 *The diagram shows a cross-section of a magnetic disk store.*

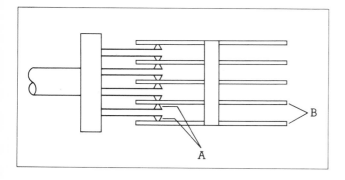

a *What are the parts labelled A and B called?*
b *What three items of information are needed by the computer to enable it to find data stored on a disk?*
c *Why are magnetic disks often preferred to magnetic tape as a means of storage?*
d *Although many people prefer disks, why do most computer installations use magnetic tape as well?*
e *Describe **two** methods of making sure that data stored on magnetic tape is not accidentally lost.*

7 a *Compare magnetic tape storage with magnetic disk storage. In your answer discuss methods of data access, speed of data retrieval, the amount of data stored and a typical application implemented on each storage medium with reference to the suitability of the chosen storage medium for each application.*
b *Name the different types of magnetic tape and disk storage media commonly used as backing store. Indicate which are used as backing storage for mainframe and which are used for microcomputers.*

8 a *What are the advantages of computer output on microfilm (COM) over printed output on paper?*
b *Give one application of COM, stating **two** reasons for your choice.*
c *Why isn't microfilm usage more popular?*
d *Distinguish between microfilm and microfiche.*

9

Errors and how to avoid them

Figure 9.1 *Computers need to be accurate as well as fast*

Computers can't make mistakes but the people who put the data into the computer can (Figure 9.1). When computers first arrived they were blamed for all sorts of mistakes. You may remember we mentioned, in Chapter 5, the newspaper story, 'Computer pays headteacher her annual salary in monthly pay' (Figure 9.2).

Data capture

Data capture means getting the information (**data**) into the computer. Data capture techniques include key-to-disk, mark sensing, optical character recognition, bar codes and magnetic ink character recognition. Direct methods of data capture avoid having to type any information in at a keyboard and so are less prone to errors.

Figure 9.2 *Computers have been blamed for all sorts of mistakes*

Most computer applications involve data preparation with staff keying in information contained on specially prepared documents called **source documents**. This is where most of the errors are likely to occur.

Transcription errors

These are errors which happen when the source data is input into the computer. Transcription errors include the misreading of the source documents, entering the wrong values and the transposition of digits (putting numbers in the wrong order) e.g. 1021503 instead of 0121503 (Figure 9.3).

There are various checks that can be performed to detect or reduce these errors.

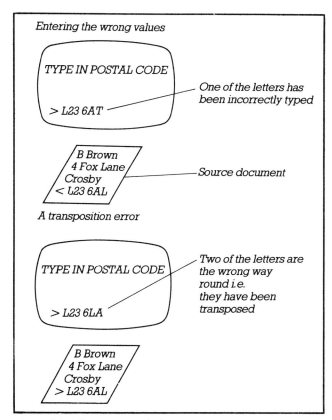

Figure 9.3 *Some transcription errors*

Verification check

These check the data before it is accepted into the computer, and can be done in a number of ways. Two people could each copy the data from the source document and the two versions could be checked against each other. If the two sets of data don't match then the information is rejected. Sometimes the same person is asked to type a long number, such as an order number, twice so that this type of check can be made. Unfortunately, verification is costly in terms of time.

Validation checks

These checks are performed by the actual computer program as the data is being input into the computer. The program looks at the data to see if it is of a certain type or of a certain range. If the data isn't valid then the computer will ask the person inputting the information to recheck it.

Here are some validation checks that are usually made.

Range check

A range check is used to see if numbers are too high or low (Figure 9.4).

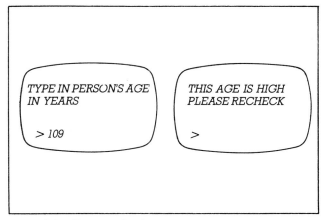

Figure 9.4 *A range check*

Field or data type check

Field or **data type checks** detect numbers where letters should be, and vice versa (Figure 9.5).

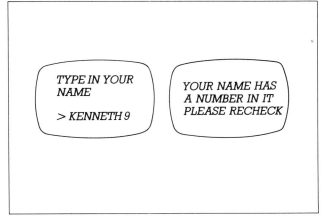

Figure 9.5 *Field or data type check*

Check digits

Most computer applications use code or account numbers. These numbers are meaningless to the person typing them in, so it is very easy to make a mistake. This could, for example, mean the wrong account was processed.

Check digits are an extra digit or digits, placed at the end of a series of numbers, which can be used to check them. There are many different ways of calculating check digits, here is just one of them.

This system is used in the International Standard Book Number (ISBN) which can be seen on the cover of any book published, including this one. This is how the check digit works. Suppose a book has the ISBN 0 7195 2844 5. The check digit is the 5 at the right hand side. Working from the far left hand side and ignoring the check digit, the first number we come to is zero. This is multiplied by 10. The second number is a 7. This is multiplied by 9. The third number is multiplied by 8 and so on.

$0 \times 10 = 0$
$7 \times 9 = 63$
$1 \times 8 = 8$
$9 \times 7 = 63$
$5 \times 6 = 30$
$2 \times 5 = 10$
$8 \times 4 = 32$
$4 \times 3 = 12$
$4 \times 2 = 8$
Total = 226

The results of the multiplication are added up and then divided by 11. The remainder of this division is subtracted from 11 and, if the ISBN is correct, the result gives the check digit.

$226 \div 11 = 20$ remainder 6
$11 - 6 = 5$ which is the check digit

When the ISBN number is typed into the computer, the computer performs these calculations and checks the calculation result against the check digit. If there is any discrepancy, then the computer will ask for the number to be keyed in again. The ISBN check digit systems uses weighted modulus 11. 'Weighted modulus' means that each digit in the ISBN, excluding the check digit, has a certain weight depending on its position. This is a bit like place values in number bases. Each number is multiplied by its weight – the value of its position. So the left hand number has a weight of 10, and is multiplied by 10, and so on. Then the total is divided by the modulus, 11. Finally, the remainder is subtracted from the modulus, 11.

Hash totals

Hash totals are the totals of numbers input into the computer. This is how the check works. Suppose we want to input the numbers 6 and 7 into the computer. Using this check we would also input the number 13 which is the hash total. The computer will automatically check the input numbers with the hash total. If the two numbers are different then they must be rechecked.

Batch totals

If a larger number of data numbers are input it is easy to make a mistake. To try to avoid these mistakes the numbers can be added up and the total input as well. If the computer adds up the numbers and doesn't get the same total as the input one, then one of the input numbers must be incorrect.

Limitations of error checking

Despite all these checks some errors will occur. It is very easy for example, for a typist to type letters or numbers in the wrong order, especially if she is working at high speed. Most computers cannot distinguish between correctly and incorrectly spelt words although some wordprocessors can do this. Probably the best way of ensuring that as few mistakes occur as possible, is to type in the data twice.

·˙ Test yourself

Using the words in the list below, copy out and complete sentences A to J. Underline the words you have inserted. The words may be used once, more than once, or not at all.

verification transcription range program batches field hash check source valid

A _____ *errors happen when the source data is input into the computer. They involve the operator misreading _____ documents, entering the wrong values and putting the digits the wrong way round.*

B _____ *is a pre-input check on data. It involves typing the information into the computer twice.*

C *Validation means checking the data to see if it is _____.*

D *Validation is performed by the computer _____.*

E _____ *checks make sure that the data is in a certain range.*

F *A check which could detect numbers where letters should be is called a _____ check.*

G _____ *digits are used to detect errors after the verification stage.*

H *In an International Standard Book Number (ISBN) the last number is a _____ digit.*

I _____ *totals are totals of numbers input into the computer.*

J *Batch totals are totals of _____ of numbers that are input into the computer.*

⠿ Things to do ──────────

1 *Explain in detail what is meant by verification and validation. Suggest appropriate checks to ensure correct input of:*
   a *Dates of birth of pupils in your school*
   b *Surnames*
   c *Bank account numbers*

2 *Explain how the following are used as data validation methods to check data:*
   a *Batch totals*
   b *Range checks*
   c *Field checks*
   d *Check digits*

3 a *What is meant by a 'check digit'? Give two circumstances in which check digits are used.*
   b *Briefly outline some of the limitations of error checking.*

4 a *Below is an ISBN (International Standard Book Number).*
      ISBN 0 903 885 19 0
      Explain how a check digit may be used to detect a transcription error in the above code number.
   b *Explain what a hash total is and how it is used.*

5 *The flowchart gives a simple method for calculating a check digit for a given account number:*
   a *Use the method in the flowchart to calculate a check digit for this account number: 4629*
   b *Why are check digits used?*
   c *Name an application which would make use of check digits.*

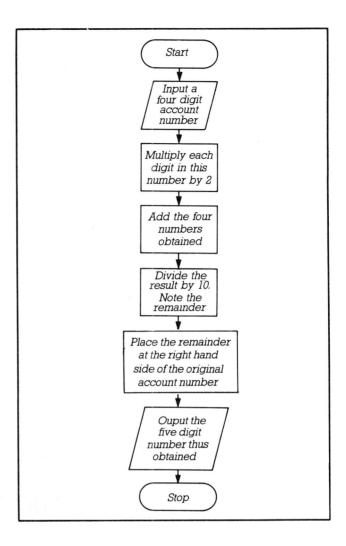

10

Files

Filing systems

If you were going to keep a large amount of information, you would probably keep it in some sort of order. You might use a filing system. A filing system lets people store information in a manner that means that it can be accessed easily and quickly. The system should be able to allow new information to be added without altering the whole filing system.

What is a file?

A file is an organized collection of related data about a certain subject. When a large number of files is placed together, these form a **database**. Databases often contain a great deal of personal and secret information, so here security requirements will be very high (Figure 10.1).

Figure 10.1 *Databases often contain personal and secret information*

How do we look at the information?

To get the information out of a file an **information retrieval system** is used. This is a program that is used to deal with files held on a computer.

These systems can be used to add new information to a file (called **file creation**) or to look up information that has been placed on the file by someone else (called **file interrogation**).

Figure 10.2 *Interrogating a file!*

Manual filing systems

The simplest filing system you will have come into contact with is a telephone directory. A telephone directory is arranged in alphabetical order. Think about how you use the book to find a phone number.

One of the snags with a phone book is that it is always out of date as soon as it is published. It isn't easy to add new names or delete old ones. You have to wait for the next year.

Other types of filing system are, for example, a library system and a name and address book.

Suppose you wanted to create (make up) a file about all the pupils in your school. You could use a manual system using cards, with a card for each pupil, as in Figure 10.3.

Surname .... Other Names ....

Address ....

.... Postcode ....

Telephone No ....

Name of Parents/Guardians ....

....

Date of birth ....

Form ....

Figure 10.3 *A record*

Each of these cards is called a **record**. A record is used to contain information about a person or object.

Figure 10.4

Each record holds information under a number of headings (e.g. Name, Address, Age etc.). These headings are called **fields**. A group of records is joined up to make a **file** (Figure 10.5).

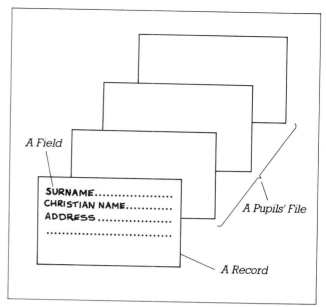

Figure 10.5 *Part of a card system which has fields, records and files*

Why use a computerized filing system?

Here are some reasons.

1 It is much easier to find the information you want – with a manual system you rely on the fact that the file has been put back in the correct place. Finding a file that has been put back in the wrong place can be an awesome task.

Figure 10.6 *In a manual filing cabinet everyone relies on the files being put back in the right places. This is not necessary with a computerized filing system*

2 It saves space. This can be an important consideration, especially with large databases.

3 File processing is much easier – this processing could include:
a Sorting into a specified order.
b Searching for related items. Unlike a manual system you can search using any of the fields. It is also possible to narrow the search down by using more than one field for the search.
c You can merge files together.

4 It is easier to maintain security. Files held on computers are more difficult to break into.

A typical information retrieval system

You will probably be using an information handling package in your course. **GRASS** is an example of such a package. The letters in GRASS stand for (**GRAphics Searching and Sorting**). This package contains many files, containing information about Butterflies and Moths, Pond Animals, Kings and Queens, Birds and Volcanoes. The author particularly likes the one on Monarchs. Basically this file contains all sorts of information about Kings and Queens of England. It contains sixty-one records, because that is the number of Kings and Queens there have been.

Figure 10.7 shows what is on one of the screens. It contains all the fields that are used.

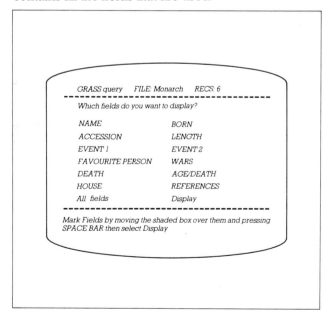

GRASS query   FILE: Monarch   RECS: 6

Which fields do you want to display?

NAME   BORN
ACCESSION   LENGTH
EVENT 1   EVENT 2
FAVOURITE PERSON   WARS
DEATH   AGE/DEATH
HOUSE   REFERENCES
All fields   Display

Mark Fields by moving the shaded box over them and pressing SPACE BAR then select Display

Figure 10.7   *A Monarch screen containing all the fields*

If you want to, you can select each individual's record. The record will contain all the details about a particular King or Queen.

Let us look at the record on William the Conqueror (Figure 10.8).

GRASS query   FILE: Monarch   RECS: 61

NAME: William the Conqueror
BORN: 1027
ACCESSION: 1066
LENGTH: 21 years
EVENT 1:   Domesday Book
EVENT 2:   Philip I of France
F-PERSON   King Harold
WARS: Battle of Hastings 1066
DEATH: Murdered
AGE/DEATH: 60
HOUSE: Norman

Press SPACE BAR for more   Press ESCAPE to finish

Figure 10.8   *A Monarch screen showing the record on William the Conqueror*

Many file handling packages will also draw graphics and diagrams for you. The diagrams include pie diagrams, histograms and scatter diagrams.

The two types of access – random and serial

File processing is an extremely important aspect of nearly every computer application. The type of access used depends on what backing storage is used (see Chapter 8). The choice of the backing storage depends on factors such as cost and time of access (speed).

Magnetic disk and magnetic tape are the two most common mediums (Figure 10.9).

Figure 10.9   *Tape is one common backing store medium; disk is another*

Serial access

Serial access is the type used to access files held on magnetic tape. What it means is, that to get to one part of the tape, it may be necessary to run through all the tape if the information is on the end. This can be a very time consuming process, since the search for data could take several minutes.

Because of the delay, it makes this form of access unsuitable for applications such as airline booking and on-line enquiry systems.

Some of the applications, such as payroll, are very suitable for this type of access. With a payroll you need to go through each employee's record to work out how much he or she is to be paid. Preparing bank statements for customers is another application.

Magnetic tape is often chosen because it is cheaper than disk and holds a lot more information.

Random access

Random access is provided by magnetic disk. This means that the data or information held on the disk can be found almost immediately, because you don't need to go through the data before the item you want is found. Using magnetic disks, you go straight to the data.

Comparison

To understand serial and random access more clearly, we can look at the following example.

Suppose you had an LP record and a cassette tape of the same piece of music. If you wanted to find the fifth piece of music on the LP it would be easy. You would just put the stylus down at the fifth track. This is an example of **random access**.

If you wanted to find the fifth piece of music on your cassette though, it would not be so easy. You probably would have to go through the other pieces to get to the fifth one. This is an example of **serial access**.

Security of information held on files

Putting information into computer files takes a lot of time and effort. Large databases can contain huge amounts of information that people have keyed in. Some of the information may be personal or secret. It is essential that the information is kept secure. There are two ways that the security can be breached: **deliberately** and **accidentally** (Figure 10.10).

Deliberate breaches of security

Unauthorized access (hacking)

This means that people look at information, who are unauthorized to do so. To prevent this, the file name

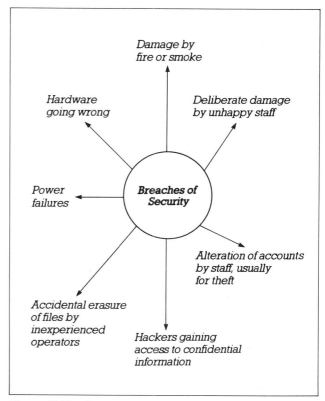

Figure 10.10 *Some of the problems with security*

can be kept secret or a secret code can be used. In order to gain access to the file you need to type in the correct file name or code. Despite these measures, you still hear of young people gaining access to large company or Government databases on their home computer.

Figure 10.11 *Some pupils look on breaking computer security codes as a challenge!*

63

You could keep the computer disks in a safe, but it is sometimes inconvenient to do this. In a lot of cases you have to rely on the honesty of the computer staff.

Accidental damage

Accidental erasure

You have probably experienced losing a program you have written; it can be very frustrating. In a large computer installation steps need to be taken to stop people wiping disks or tapes. A **write-permit ring**, when fitted, allows data to be written onto a reel of magnetic tape. When the ring is removed, it is not possible to write new data onto the tape. On a floppy disk there is a **write-protect notch** that is used for the same reason (Figure 10.12).

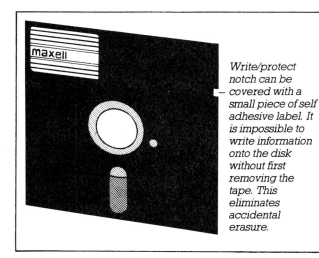

Write/protect notch can be covered with a small piece of self adhesive label. It is impossible to write information onto the disk without first removing the tape. This eliminates accidental erasure.

Figure 10.12 *The write-protect notch on a floppy disk*

Other types of loss and damage can happen because of fires, floods etc.

Safeguarding files

Back-up copies

All organizations that use computers make sure that they have spare copies (called **back-up copies**) of all their files. Where possible, the back-up files are kept in another building.

The ancestral file system (grandfather–father–son principle)

Another way we can safeguard files is by using the **ancestral file system**. Here, one file is used with a transaction file to produce a new file. The original file is called the **master file** and this is the **father file**. The father file along with a **transaction file** (which contains recent changes) is used to create a new master file called the **son file**. The father file and the transaction file are kept together and stored in a safe place. If the son is lost or corrupted (altered incorrectly) then the father and transaction files can be used to produce a new son file. The son file can now be the father file to produce another new son file. The original father file is now referred to as the **grandfather file** (Figure 10.13). In this way we can produce generations of files. It is usual only to keep three generations, and all the old files can be used again.

Figure 10.13 *The ancestral file system!*

Test yourself

Using the words in the list below, copy out and complete sentences A to J. Underline the words you have inserted. The words may be used once, more than once, or not at all.

deliberate protect back-up ancestral transaction hacking databases permit recreated son father

A _____ *contain huge quantities of information.*

B *There are two ways that security can be breached:_____ and accidental.*

C *Another name for unauthorized access is_____.*

D *To stop people writing over magnetic tape, a write_____ ring is used.*

E *Floppy disks use a write_____ notch to prevent people accidentally erasing a disk.*

F *A spare copy is called a_____ copy.*

G *The_____ file system is used to ensure that, if a file is lost, then it can be recreated.*

H *If a master tape or disk is destroyed, then it may be_____.*

I *The recent changes are kept on a file called a_____ file.*

J *Three generations of files are kept along with the transaction files. They are called the grandfather,_____ and_____ files.*

⊱ Things to do _____

1 Explain the meaning of the following words that have been used in this chapter.
   a Database
   b Information retrieval system
   c File creation
   d File interrogation

2 Your local youth club decided to computerize all its members records. It is decided that the source document shown below should be filled in by all the members.

```
Surname  ........................... Other Names  ...............

Address  ...................................................................

...................................  Postcode  ..............

School or College  .................. Phone No.  ...............

Date of birth  ...........................................................

Interests or Hobbies  ...............................................

...................................................................
```

   a With reference to the above source document, explain the meaning of the following terms:
      i   File
      ii Record
      iii Field
   b It is likely that some of the fields will be used as key fields to look up certain information. Write down **three** fields which you think will be important for making searches, and explain your choices.

3 Give **three** reasons why a computerized filing system is more efficient than a manual one.

4 Describe an information retrieval system that you have seen being used. Describe the information on each record and how the package was used.

5 Explain what precautions you could take in order to protect valuable data files from the following:
   a Destruction
   b Theft
   c Unauthorized access

6 Mrs Jones is a patient at a large hospital. She has to visit the hospital each month. After each visit, details are written out on paper and added to her already bulky file, which is returned to the appropriate place in the hospital records department. This department takes up a whole floor of rooms with shelves from floor to ceiling in each room, each shelf crammed tight with files similar to Mrs Jones's. Explain how the introduction of a computer might help hospital staff and benefit the patient.

7 Barclaycard keep records of all their customers on magnetic tape in the form of <u>customer files</u>. On each <u>master file</u>, details such as name, address, amount owed, minimum payment and date due are kept. The customer pays a certain amount of money each month and every month the computer centre receives a tape called the <u>transaction file</u>, which contains details of all the payments that have been received from all the customers.
The transaction tape is <u>processed</u> with the master tape to produce a new <u>up-to-date</u> file which now has all the new amounts on it.
   a Explain what is meant by the following words which are underlined in the above passage:
      Customer file
      Master file
      Transaction file
      Processed
      Up-to-date
   b Often computer systems make use of the grandfather–father–son system. What does this mean?
   c Why is the above system used?

8 A computer print-out of a section of an employee's file in a large factory has been copied in the table below.

NAME	SEX	AGE	DEPARTMENT
WATKINS J.	F	25	TYPING
WATKINS J.	F	32	TYPING
WATKINS J.A.	M	43	MACHINE SHOP
WATKINS J.L.	M	27	MACHINE SHOP

   a Describe this file in terms of fields and records.
   b In the interrogation of this file, how could confusion between the four surnames be avoided?

Computer programming languages

The programs for computers can be written in many different languages, just as humans can communicate with each other in different languages. The language used by most microcomputers is BASIC. Some other computer languages are COBOL, FORTRAN and ALGOL.

Why we need computer languages

Computer languages have been developed at the same time as the hardware. This has made programming computers a lot easier. Computer languages are needed because they allow the person using the computer to tell the computer what to do. The very early computers such as ASCC amd ENIAC had the program stored in the electrical components. They were only able to do one job. To program the computer to do a different job it would have been necessary to completely rewire it.

The earlier computers were used mainly by scientists for performing millions of complicated calculations. As a result of this the computer languages used to supply instructions to the computer were for scientific uses. They were not much use for business uses such as file handling.

When computers got a lot cheaper, business languages began to be developed. These languages had facilities such as extensive file handling and scheduling of processing which were not needed in the scientific languages. Also in the business world, less experienced staff would be using the computers, so the languages needed to be simpler.

High-level languages

A **high-level language** is a language geared towards solving problems. This means that, rather than taking notice of how the computer was designed to solve the problem, we take more notice of the type of problem to be solved. So high-level languages are **problem orientated**. The low-level languages take account of design features of the computer and are **machine orientated**.

High-level languages are much easier to write than low-level languages because the program instructions are similar to instructions written in English. 'High' in the term 'high-level language' doesn't mean that it is more complicated. It means that the language is more problem orientated. One statement in a high-level language can be used for several instructions in a low-level language. So it takes less time to write a program using a high-level language.

Because high-level languages work independently of the machine, it is fairly easy to modify (adapt) the program so that it will run on a completely different computer.

There are many high-level languages. Which one is chosen really depends on the sort of job that you want to do. High-level languages are usually either business languages or scientific languages.

Most business programs are written in a language called **COBOL (COmmon Business Orientated Language)** because of its extensive file handling ability. Other business languages include **RPG II** and **BASIC (Beginner's All-purpose Symbolic Instruction Code)**. Scientific languages include **ALGOL (ALGorithmic Orientated Language)**. **FORTRAN (FORmula TRANslation)** and **BASIC**.

BASIC is a high-level language with which you are probably familiar. It is an ideal language for people who are learning programming. It can be used for writing business and scientific programs but it takes longer and has some limitations which the other languages do not have.

Low-level languages

Low-level languages are usually machine dependent. This means that one computer's low-level language is different from another's. Consequently it is not easy for a programmer (someone who writes programs) to move from one machine to another as he or she will have to learn a completely new language. Low-level languages are machine orientated and one low-level program instruction has to be written for every machine instruction. This tends to make the programs very long and tedious to write. So low-level languages are seldom used commercially nowadays, and easy to understand high-level languages such as BASIC are used instead.

You may be asking, 'If low-level languages are so difficult to use, why do they still exist?'. The answer is, 'Because they are much faster.' Imagine talking to a group of Russians. You would need to employ an interpreter. Everything you said would be translated into Russian. Everything they said would have to be translated into English. The conversation would be far quicker if you learned Russian yourself. Similarly, if you give instructions to the microprocessor in its language, it will carry them out much more quickly.

Machine code

Machine code is a **machine language** with instructions in a binary code that can be understood directly by the computer hardware. No other programs are needed.

The main problem with programming in machine language is that codes are very difficult to memorize and having to look them up every time can be very tedious. Also, understanding what the series of 0s and 1s mean is almost impossible (Figure 11.1).

Programming languages

Programming languages, like BASIC on the BBC microcomputer, are **interpreted**. Each line of the program is translated into the binary machine codes before being executed. The time taken to do the translation is hundreds of times longer than the time to carry out the instruction. So interpreted languages are very slow.

On the other hand, writing languages directly in machine code is slow and many errors are made. Some of these might not be discovered until the program had been in in use for years. Engineers have thus developed **compiled** languages, to get the speed of machine code and the simplicity of written words. The simplest compiled language is called **Assembler**. As assembler program is turned directly into machine code on a line-by-line basis (Fig 11.2).

FORTRAN and COBOL are compiled languages. Here, though, each line of the program has to be turned into many lines of machine code, so these compilers are bigger and much more expensive in computer running time. It is also much slower to write in a compiled language. The **whole** program has to be correct before it is compiled, and this requires careful attention to detail when it is written. Because of this, programmers now prefer to write programs in small **modules**, each of which can be tested separately. All the time, newer and more powerful languages are being produced which support this **modular** approach. One very new language is actually called MODULA.

Others have tried to produce 'fifth generation' languages, which are nearer to the way humans think and speak. The most important of these at the moment is PROLOG. However, the situation changes very rapidly and we can expect even better languages to appear in the future.

Figure 11.1 *Machine language has very little in common with everyday English. A high-level language such as BASIC has easy-to-understand instructions*

```
        7859 78       .ch     SE\CHANGE VECTOR
785A AD 04 02         LDA     vector
785D 85 78            STA     vecstr
785F AD 05 02         LDA     vector + 1
7862 85 79            STA     vecstr + 1
7864 A9 00            LDA     #(rfrsh MOD 256)
7866 8D 04 02         STA     vector
7869 A9 78            LDA     #(rfrsh DIV 256)
786B 8D 05 02         STA     vector + 1
786E 58               CLI
786F 60               RTS
```

Figure 11.2 *An example of Assembler – the simplest compiled language*

✓ Test yourself

Using the words in the list below, copy out and complete sentences A to I. Underline the words you have inserted. The words may be used once, more than once, or not at all.

directly   BASIC   high-level   compiled languages   machine   COBOL   dependent FORTRAN   high   interpreted

A *Computer_____ enable humans to communicate with the computer.*
B *The language that is most commonly used in school is called_____.*
C *A_____ language is a problem orientated language.*
D *Low-level languages are said to be_____ orientated and machine_____.*
E *_____ is a common business language used because of its good file handling.*
F *ALGOL and_____ are scientific languages.*
G *BASIC is a_____ level language.*
H *Machine code consists of a binary code. It is understood by the machine_____.*
I *High-level languages are_____ or_____ to produce machine code.*

≫ Things to do

1 *Which of the following is not a computer language?*
  a *BASIC*
  b *RPG II*
  c *FORTRAN*
  d *CPU*
  e *COBOL*

2 *Which **one** of the following is a high-level language?*
  a *Compiler*
  b *Assembler*
  c *CESIL*
  d *ALGOL*

3 *The programming language specially designed for commercial work is which **one** of the following?*
  a *ALGOL*
  b *BASIC*
  c *COBOL*
  d *FORTRAN*
  e *PASCAL*

4 *FORTRAN is an example of which **one** of these?*
  a *A low-level language*
  b *An assembler code*
  c *A machine code*
  d *A high-level language*
  e *A compiler*

5 *Name two examples of high-level languages other than BASIC.*

6 **a** *Distinguish between high-level and low-level computer languages.*
  b *At a particular computer centre, certain programs are written in low-level language. Suggest why this might be so.*

7 *As a programmer I have the choice of writing my programs in a low-level language or in a high-level language. Each of them has its advantages and its disadvantages. In the table following, enter one advantage and one disadvantage of each.*

	Low-level language	High-level language
Advantage		
Disadvantage		

8 *There are various levels of programming used to communicate with a computer:*
Machine code   Low-level   High-level
Explain the difference between the above three levels referring to storage space required, ease of programming and debugging, ease of use and any other relevant information.

9 *Most programs are now written in high-level languages. Give **two** reasons why low-level languages are still used.*

10 *FORTRAN and COBOL are two widely used programming languages.*
  a *Explain where their main applications lie and why it is not easily possible to interchange their use.*
  b *Explain their relationship with machine code and briefly indicate why it is impracticable to use machine code as an everyday language.*

11 The following list is a list of computer languages:
COBOL   BASIC   FORTRAN
From the above languages, select which one
would be suitable for each of the following
applications:
a Teaching pupils in a school computer
   programming
b Calculating mathematical tables.
c A computerized catalogue of all books in a
   library
d Stock control in a factory
For each one, say why the language you have
chosen is suitable.

12 Older computers needed to be programmed in
'machine code'. The computers of today now use
easy-to-understand computer languages such as
BASIC, FORTRAN and COBOL. These languages
are called 'high-level languages'. They are easier
to use than 'low-level languages' because they
have statements which are very similar to English
statements.
a What is meant by 'machine code'?
b Why is it difficult to write a program in machine
   code?
c What do the following abbreviations stand for?
    i BASIC
   ii FORTRAN
  iii COBOL
d What is meant by 'high-level' and 'low-level'
   computer languages?

12

Computer communication systems

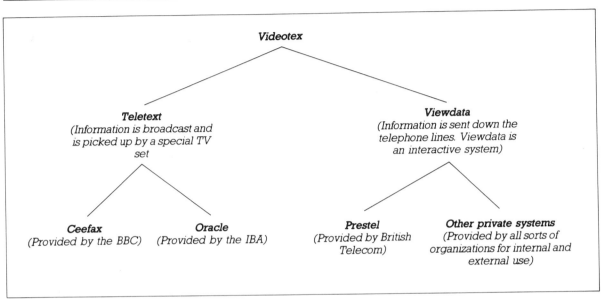

Figure 12.1 *Computer communication systems*

Videotex

Videotex is the name given to any information service which can display text on a screen of a television set. The information can be transmitted as a signal in addition to TV programs (**teletext**) or transmitted along the telephone lines (**viewdata**).

Viewdata

Viewdata was invented and set up by British Telecom to provide the world's first public fact-supplying service, called **Prestel**.

A VDU (or an ordinary TV set), a telephone, a **modem** (which converts the signal from the computer so that it can pass along telephone lines), a keypad or keyboard and a printer, make up what is known as a **videotex terminal**. Unlike teletext, viewdata is an interactive system, so you can put information in as well as get it out.

The terminal is connected via a modem (Figure 12.2) and the telephone lines to a large database (vast store of information). When the button marked **phone**, is pressed on the keyboard, the terminal automatically dials the number to the computer to be accessed. A code is input at this stage, so that the pages can be paid for.

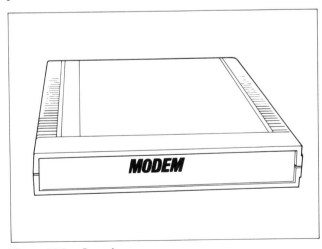

Figure 12.2 *A modem*

Using the system is easy. The users just select various options from menus, until they get to the information they want.

Prestel

Prestel (Figure 12.3) is the information service provided by British Telecom and this offers access to over a quarter of a million pages of information on all kinds of topic. Prestel offers open services that can be used by anyone with a telephone, on payment of a subscription. Closed user groups pay more than the ordinary subscription to gain access to specialist information.

Prestel also offers a **telesoftware** facility, that allows the user to **download** software via Prestel on to his/her own computer and store it on disk for future use.

Mailbox is a feature of Prestel and it allows short messages to be sent from one computer to another. Using Mailbox the user is limited to one 40 character-wide page and this tends to limit its use to short messages and memos rather than letters and reports.

The main Prestel computer is also able to communicate with other databases. Computers owned by various companies can be accessed in this way through the Prestel **gateway** service. Using this, you can book airline or theatre tickets and find information about nearly every service you can imagine.

Figure 12.4 *Just a few of the thousands of screens for Prestel*

Figure 12.3 *The Prestel network system*

71

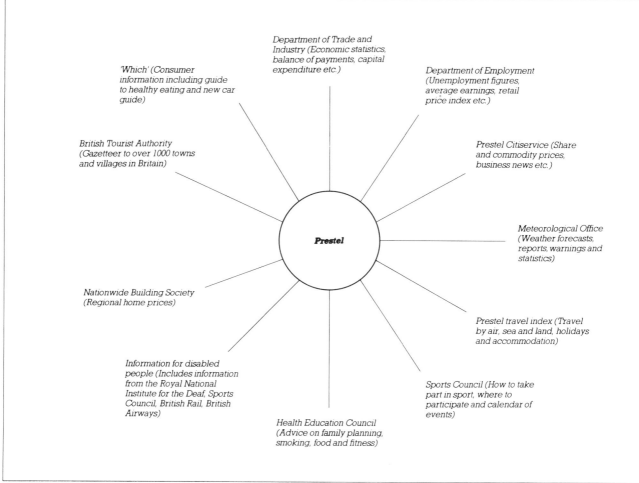

Figure 12.5 *Just some of the organizations who provide information on Prestel*

In the figure, radiating from a central circle labelled **Prestel**:

- 'Which' (Consumer information including guide to healthy eating and new car guide)
- Department of Trade and Industry (Economic statistics, balance of payments, capital expenditure etc.)
- Department of Employment (Unemployment figures, average earnings, retail price index etc.)
- British Tourist Authority (Gazetteer to over 1000 towns and villages in Britain)
- Prestel Citiservice (Share and commodity prices, business news etc.)
- Meteorological Office (Weather forecasts, reports, warnings and statistics)
- Nationwide Building Society (Regional home prices)
- Prestel travel index (Travel by air, sea and land, holidays and accommodation)
- Information for disabled people (Includes information from the Royal National Institute for the Deaf, Sports Council, British Rail, British Airways)
- Sports Council (How to take part in sport, where to participate and calendar of events)
- Health Education Council (Advice on family planning, smoking, food and fitness)

The Times Network for School (TTNS) ———

This is a viewdata system that has been provided by Times Newspapers, specifically for education. The **TTNS** mailing system is superior to that on Prestel. You can transmit a document of up to twenty-four pages to another user over the telephone lines. Like Prestel, TTNS also has a telesoftware facility.

As well as being able to access the main TTNS database, you can also join schools together to form a **closed-user group**. This allows the members of the group to communicate, via the telephone lines, with each other (Figure 12.6). Sometimes whole education authorities form a closed-user group, so that schools and colleges can communicate with each other and with the education office.

Teletext (Ceefax and Oracle) ———

Ceefax and **Oracle** are known together as **teletext**. Unlike the more sophisticated Prestel system, teletext does not operate through the telephone network. Instead it uses spare space in television transmission.

Figure 12.6 *'Hey! That's mine!' – Schoolchildren using TTNS*

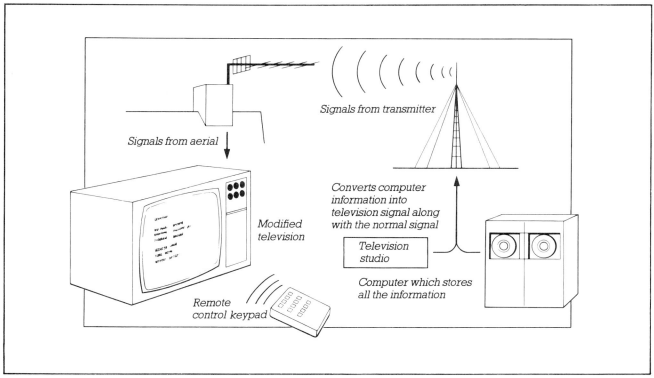

Figure 12.7 *The teletext (Ceefax and Oracle) network system*

Ceefax is the system operated by the BBC and Oracle is operated by the IBA. A modified television is needed to be able to receive teletext along with a special keypad. Teletext only works when TV programs are on the air (Figure 12.7).

The sort of information on Teletext includes pages of news, finance, hobbies, weather, food prices, recipes, cinema etc. Generally, the teletext system is of more interest to domestic users than business users.

The teletext system is simply an electronic magazine and it is impossible for the user to communicate over the system.

Telecom Gold (electronic mail)

Telecom Gold (electronic mail) is an extension to the Prestel system and provides users with an almost instantaneous transfer of information. A letter or document typed on a wordprocessor can be corrected or changed and then sent, via a satellite communications system, from an office in one country to a computer with a VDU in another country. For short distance links, the normal telephone lines are used. The letter or document is held in the computer memory until required, and then it can be answered in the same way.

Altogether, this system increases efficiency tremendously and the process of sending out a letter and receiving a reply can take minutes rather than, often, more than a week.

Another advantage is that users don't need to spend time looking for writing paper, envelopes and stamps. With the system, they are no longer needed. Also, letters received are automatically stored on magnetic disk or tape for future reference, and this type of storage takes up very little space.

Costs

Teletext is the cheapest system by far, but it is non-interactive and is really only an electronic magazine. The actual cost is that of a special TV set, i.e. about £50 more than a normal set.

Viewdata charges are quite complicated. Again you need a TV or a VDU as well as a computer, modem and telephone. It is also useful to have a disk drive so that you can download software. A diskdrive will also reduce the time that you need to be on-line to the main computer because, if you wanted to send a message, you could prepare your message first and store it on disk before sending it.

As well as the telephone rental and calls charges (most of which will be at the local call rate) you have a charge for the number of minutes you use the system. This charge, as with phone charges, will be more expensive in the peak periods.

⠂⠄ Test yourself _____

Using the words in the list below, copy out and complete sentences A to L. Underline the words you have inserted. The words can be used once, more than once, or not at all.

viewdata   teletext   interactive   Mailbox
modem   telesoftware   TTNS   Prestel
closed-user   Gateway   videotext   Oracle
Telecom Gold

A _____ is the name given to any screen based information service.
B _____ is the service transmitted along with TV signals and _____ is transmitted along telephone lines.
C The first public fact-supplying service was called_____.
D To work this system a TV, telephone and a_____ are needed along with the computer.
E Videotex is an_____ service whereas teletext is not.
F _____ is provided by British Telecom and it allows users to download software into their own computer. This software is called_____.
G Short messages and memos can be sent using the_____ feature.
H Prestel users are also able to gain access to some other databases using the_____ service.
I _____ is a viewdata system provided by Times Newspapers, specifically for education.
J Using this system, groups of schools can be joined together so that they can send messages and information. Such a group is called a_____ group.
K Ceefax and_____ are non-interactive information services which are known together as_____.
L _____ is the electronic mail facility provided by British Telecom.

⠿ Things to do _____

1 Which one of the following is an example of viewdata?
   a Teletext
   b Ceefax
   c Oracle
   d Prestel

2 Which of the following provides the Prestel service?
   a The BBC
   b The IBA
   c Teletext
   d British Telecom

3 Name *two* teletext services.
   Prestel is which of the following?
   a A telephone system
   b An information service
   c A television programme
   d A device that speaks
   e A foreign language translation device

4 Which of the following is not a television based information system?
   a Ernie
   b Oracle
   c Prestel
   d Ceefax
   e Teletext

5 Explain the meaning of the following words (if you get stuck, use the glossary at the end of the book).
   a videotex
   b modem
   c database
   d telesoftware
   e closed-user group

6 a A friend of yours is interested in having an information system in his home. Write an explanation of the teletext and Prestel systems. Outline the advantages and disadvantages of each of the systems.
   b Which system do you think he should buy? Give reasons.
   c If you friend were a stockbroker and wanted a system for work, which system would he now choose?

7 Teletext and viewdata are both information retrieval systems.
   a Give an example of a teletext system.
   b Explain how teletext is broadcast and received.
   c Name British Telecom's viewdata system.
   d Give *two* possible uses of viewdata:
      i in the home   ii in a business

8 Teletext is really only an electronic magazine. Do you think that magazines and newspapers will be replaced by computerized information systems?

9 a Write a list of the steps involved in the writing of a letter by hand.
   b Assume that you are the manager of a large company. Now, write a list of the steps taken to produce a letter, bearing in mind that you would have a secretary to type the letter for you.
   c From your answer in part b write down the steps which you would not need if you were using electronic mail.

10 Explain what electronic mail is and why its use is likely to escalate in the future. Do you see its introduction replacing the postman? Give reasons.

11 Write down the meaning of serial access and random access. The Prestel system uses a disk pack means of storage. Why would magnetic tape be an unsuitable storage medium for this system.

13

Information technology in control

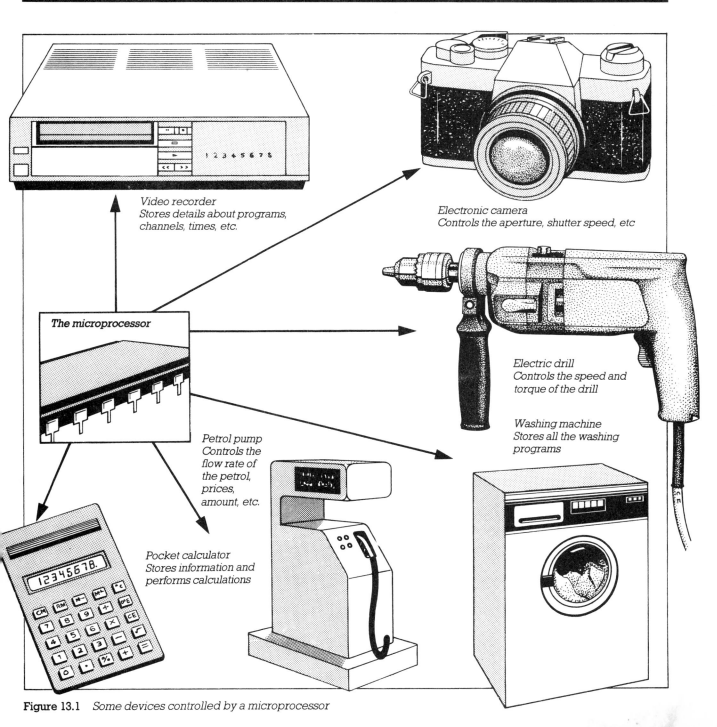

Figure 13.1 *Some devices controlled by a microprocessor*

Video recorder
Stores details about programs, channels, times, etc.

Electronic camera
Controls the aperture, shutter speed, etc

The microprocessor

Electric drill
Controls the speed and torque of the drill

Washing machine
Stores all the washing programs

Petrol pump
Controls the flow rate of the petrol, prices, amount, etc.

Pocket calculator
Stores information and performs calculations

Microchips (microprocessors)

More and more household devices now have microchips hidden away inside them. **Microchips (microprocessors)** help make the machine more 'intelligent'. Figure 13.1 shows some devices that are controlled by microprocessors.

All of these devices have one thing in common, they all need to go through a series of activities in a set order. Microchips in the devices tell them what to do.

A microprocessor is a **Large Scale Integrated Chip (LSI)** which is used to make up the Central Processing Unit (CPU) of a computer. A large scale integrated chip is a thin slice of silicon (a wafer) that has thousands of electrical components etched on it. Microprocessors are chips that contain the various parts that make up the CPU i.e. the ALU, the control unit and sometimes a limited amount of memory.

Unlike a computer, a microprocessor does not need to be loaded with a set of instructions or program before it can be used. The program is contained in the electronic circuits. This means that each type of chip is specially made for a particular application (use).

Automatic machines

Microchips are used to control **automatic machines**. An automatic machine is a machine that goes through a whole process without human intervention. It is able to obey a series of instructions. These machines do not need to be supervised because all the processes are done, in order, by the machine itself. An automatic washing machine is a good example of an automatic machine.

Automatic washing machines

Washing clothes manually can take a long time and needs constant supervision. So it is not surprising that an automatic washing machine was invented to get rid of the drudgery.

An automatic washing machine contains a series of **stored programs**. Each of these programs will carry out a series of processes in a particular order.

Depending on the type of wash you wish to do, you can select a suitable program to do the washing for you. Figure 13.2 shows a typical wash by an automatic machine.

Other automatic machines

Other automatic machines include juke boxes, video recorders, alarm clocks, central heating thermostatic controls, dishwashers, answering machines, programmable telephones and some children's games and toys.

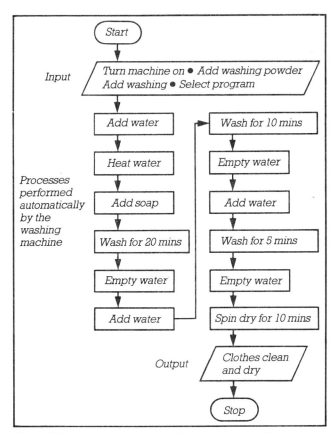

Figure 13.2 *An automatic washing machine wash*

Computer simulation

Figure 13.3

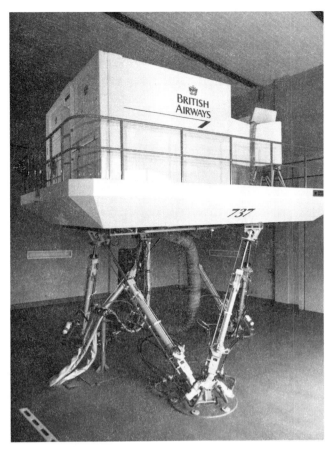

Figure 13.4 *A flight simulator*

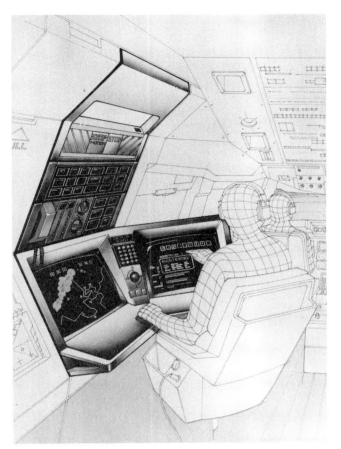

Figure 13.5 *Inside a flight simulator*

Computers are very good for imitating real situations on the screen. A mock situation set up by the computer is called a **simulation**. Simulations are often used for training or for carrying out mock-ups of situations that could prove too expensive or dangerous if carried out in real life. You can now buy computer programs for your home computer that involve simulation. So, you can now drive a Formula One racing car at Le Mans (Figure 13.3) or land a Harrier jump-jet on the flight deck of an aircraft carrier, all in your own home!

Flight simulators

Flight simulators are used to train both military and commercial pilots. The flight simulator consists of a computer-controlled model of an aircraft flight-deck. The aircrew and instructor sit in the simulator and the instructor can use the computer to set up various mock situations such as take-offs and landings. Simulators have the added advantage of being able to put the pilot in situations that would be far too dangerous in real life, such as engine failure etc.

To make the simulator more realistic it creates, physically, all the movements of a real aircraft – banks, climbs etc.

When you look out of the windows of the simulator, the view appears exactly as it would from a real aircraft. The instructor can even use the computer to simulate bad weather conditions, so pilots can have practice in flying in snow or fog.

Figure 13.4 shows a flight simulator from the outside and Figure 13.5 shows the inside of another flight simulator with, in the foreground, the instructor sitting at his console.

Robotics

Why use robots?

Robots, unlike people, don't become ill, don't have tea or lunch breaks and don't go on strike! They can also work continuously and at the same rate throughout the day. Robots are able to produce the same standard of work over and over again.

What is a robot?

In a dictionary you will find a robot described as 'a mechanical man' or 'a more than humanly efficient automaton'. An **automaton** is something that moves by itself. It acts because of a routine, rather than because it is 'intelligent'.

Robots at home

Most of us would like to have a robot as a personal servant to do some of the jobs we dislike doing. Just imagine having a robot to do all those unpleasant tasks, like tidying your bedroom or doing your homework (Figure 13.6).

Figure 13.6 *Robots are a girl's best friend!*

Unfortunately, the robots we have at the moment aren't capable of doing these jobs but who knows what the future might bring. The sort of jobs we would like a robot to do are quite complicated. At the moment the robots we have aren't clever enough to deal with all the problems which they might come across in the course of doing a simple job, like hoovering a carpet. The robot would need to be able to recognize that you have left a pair of slippers on the carpet before it went over them with the vacuum cleaner. A lot of jobs that seem simple to us, aren't so simple for a robot.

We do, however, have personal robots such as **Omnibot** and **Topo** (Figure 13.7) that can deliver goods and messages from one room to another.

Figure 13.7 *Omnibot and Topo, personal robots*

Robots in factories

The commonest type of robot is free standing and can be found in factories, working on assembly lines. Usually the robot consists of a flexible arm fixed to a stand. The arm is controlled by a computer, sometimes built into the stand. Many different tools can be attached to these arms, for example, paint sprayers, welding tips and soldering irons. Using robots in factories means that work can be done quicker, cheaper and better than it could be done by people. Unfortunately, though, it also means that people's jobs are taken over by machines. As more of these machines are used, more people may become unemployed.

Robots are mainly used for building cars and common household goods such as washing machines and fridges. We now even have robots building robots. (Figure 13.8).

Figure 13.8 *'What was it again, George? . . . If it takes one and a half robots one and a half days to build . . . how many robots?'*

Robots involved in dangerous work

Robots can work in dangerous or unpleasant conditions. It is much better to risk the destruction of a robot than to risk a human life.

The army use robots to investigate bombs and make them safe. Cars are often left that have been filled with explosives and booby-trapped. A moving robot can be steered by remote control and used to view the inside of a car. If necessary, it can then set off a small controlled explosion to defuse any bomb in the car. Figure 13.9 shows such a robot.

Robots are also used under water. Figure 13.10 shows a robot that can be operated at extreme depths. This robot can be used for inspecting underwater structures such as on drilling platforms. It is also useful for recovering wreckage from aircraft that have crashed into the sea.

Figure 13.9 *An army bomb disposal robot*

Figure 13.10 *An underwater robot*

Robots in schools

Because of its importance in industry, pupils can now gain experience of robotics in schools in their computer studies or CDT lessons.

Figure 13.11 shows a computer-controlled lathe. A piece of metal is placed in the lathe and the dimensions are then keyed into the computer. The lathe turns the metal to the correct size and produces a perfect result every time.

Figure 13.11 *A computer-controlled lathe*

Figure 13.12 shows a robot arm built out of Lego as a part of a CDT project for GCSE. Figure 13.13 shows a robot vehicle called **Trekker**, whose movement can be controlled by the BBC computer in the background.

Figure 13.12 *A Lego robot arm*

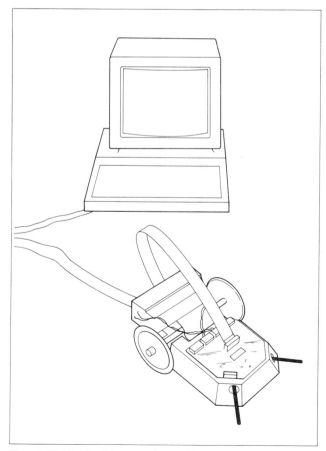

Figure 13.13 *Trekker, a robot vehicle*

Computers controlling a process

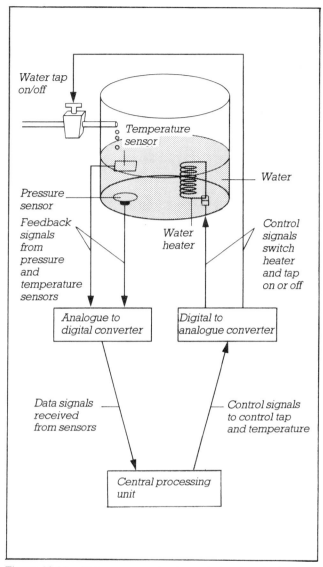

Figure 13.14 *Using a computer to control a chemical process*

Data for computers can be created by equipment or machinery. Data can be either **digital** or **analogue**.

Analogue data includes temperature, pressure, flow rate, current, voltage and depth. These quantities are continuous, which means that they have millions of values. They can be measured using special sensors. Because computers usually deal with numbers (digital data), the data is fed into the computer via an **analogue-to-digital converter**, which converts the analogue signals to digital ones. The computer then makes a decision, depending on to how it has been programmed. It can then control the process by outputting signals which alter the conditions. Sometimes, such a sequence is referred to as a **feedback loop**.

Suppose, in a chemical process, a container needs to be filled with water and heated up to 70°C. If we are using a computer to control the process, it will automatically turn the tap on to let the water into the container. Water pressure changes with depth. A pressure sensor will, therefore, relay data about the depth back to the computer. When the depth reaches a certain value, the computer will switch the tap off. A temperature sensor will relay temperature information back to the computer. The heater is switched on until the temperature reaches 70°C. The computer then switches the heater off. At any time when the temperature drops below 70°C, the heater is switched on again and so the temperature is always kept at 70°C. Figure 13.14 shows how this works.

In some situations, data will be in a digital form, for example, the number of units produced by a machine. In situations such as these there is no need for an analogue-to-digital converter.

✔ Test yourself _____

Using the words in the list below, copy out and complete sentences A to L. Underline the words you have inserted. The words may be used once, more than once, or not at all.

Feedback loop   automatic   free microprocessors   analogue   automaton microchips   digital   LSI   CPU   program intervention   simulation program   training

A *Many common devices are now_____ due to the introduction of_____ or_____.*

B *A microprocessor is an_____ chip that contains all the circuits of the_____.*

C *Microchips are used to control_____ machines.*

D *An automatic machine goes through a process without human_____.*

E *An automatic washing machine contains a series of stored_____.*

F *Computers can also be used to imitate a real situation. This is called a_____.*

G *Simulations are good for_____ people such as pilots.*

H *An_____ is something that moves by itself and acts because of a routine rather than because is it intelligent.*

I *A robot with a flexible arm attached to a stand is called a_____ standing robot.*

J *Data created by equipment or machinery can be of two types:_____ or analogue.*

K *To operate analogue control with a digital computer, you need an_____ to_____ converter.*

L *Computers can control processes by using a_____.*

➤➤ Things to do _____

1 a *Explain what a microchip or microprocessor is.*
  b *What type of devices benefit from having microchips in them?*
  c *Here are the names of four devices that can be controlled by a microprocessor. Explain what the microprocessor does in each of the devices.*
    i   Video recorder
    ii Electronic camera
    iii Pocket calculator
    iv Petrol pump
  d *What is the main difference between a microprocessor and a computer?*

2 a *A washing machine is an automatic machine. Explain what is meant by the term automatic machine.*
  b *Give **three** examples of automatic machines.*
  c *For one of the examples you have given, describe the steps that are done automatically by the machine.*

3 a *Explain what is meant by a simulation.*
  b *Explain how computer controlled simulation can be used to train personnel. Refer to a suitable application in your answer.*

4 a *Look up the word 'robot' in the dictionary you use and write down the definition.*
  b *Think of **two** industries that use robots and write down the benefits they have given these industries.*
  c *What disadvantages are there in using robots in assembly lines?*

5 a *Name **three** robots that you have seen in television programmes, films or advertisements.*
  b *Say whether the three robots you have chosen correctly portray the way the robots are used in real life.*

6 *Using an example which you have read about or seen, describe how robots can be used to improve efficiency in certain industries. Explain how the jobs were done before the robots were introduced.*

7 *Explain what is meant by the following terms.*
  a *Digital data*
  b *Analogue data*
  c *Analogue-to-digital converter*
  d *Feedback loop*

14
The electronic office

Figure 14.1 *The paperless office is nearly here!*

The office of the past depended heavily on paper. In a typical company an order would be received by post. The office clerk would type out several copies and send them to different offices. The finance office would type out an invoice. Copies of all the letters, orders and invoices would be kept in different folders in filing cabinets. The only storage medium was paper.

Today, this picture is changing rapidly. In the electronic office, orders are sent by electronic signals via a computer network. Words appear on the screen and are read by the office clerk. Copies are sent along the **local area network (LAN)** to the finance office. Invoices can be prepared and sent, letters written and information stored without the use of paper at all. The day of the 'paperless' office has nearly arrived (Figure 14.1).

Let us now look at some of the people who work in the electronic office and see what they do.

Sheila – a secretary who uses a wordprocessor

Sheila is a secretary for a group of people who need high quality letters. Her personal computer and its wordprocessing software make her correspondence work much more efficient.

At the moment she needs to edit (alter) a long letter. Her computer first produces a menu showing just what can be done (Figure 14.2).

```
-- Main menu --                        8/5/87 10.01

C =   Create a new letter or document

E =   Edit an existing letter or document

P =   Print a letter or document

I =   Index of letters and documents on file

D =   Delete a document

F =   Finished using the system

M =   More main menu selections

Type the letter and then press RETURN
```

Figure 14.2 *A typical menu for a wordprocessing system*

Sheila has already stored a version of the letter on the computer. To get it on the screen (**retrieve** it) she inserts a disk with her letters stored on it and types in the document's name. Almost instantly the letter is displayed.

One of her problems is that in this long letter there appears the name of a company that has just changed its name. She uses the **Global-Search-And-Replace** program. When a word or name needs to be changed throughout a document, then it is input once only and the program will alter it in every place it appears. Sheila also needs to move a sentence from the middle of a paragraph to the end. Using certain keys she selects the sentence to be moved. She then presses the CUT key and the sentence disappears. Then she moves the cursor to where she wants to put the sentence. By pressing the PASTE key, the sentence automatically appears in its correct place. The rest of the text adjusts itself to the new position.

Sheila looks at the VDU screen and she is satisfied that the letter is alright. She presses a key and the printer starts to print out the letter. This is a daisy wheel printer that produces high quality type. She doesn't need to wait for if to finish before starting her next job.

Her next task is to send out personalized invitations to a product demonstration. The invitation is to be sent only to the larger customers who have spent more than £40,000 with the company in the last year. A disk is picked out containing the names and addresses of all the customers. By specifying certain conditions she can send the invitations to the correct people. The printer is set up to print the invitations and then the address labels to stick on the envelopes. Sheila can send out a hundred personal invitations in less than an hour. Imagine how long this would take by hand!

Sarah – A busy executive who uses a personal computer

Sarah is an executive working for a large company and her job involves her in having to make many decisions during the day. Quite a lot of Sarah's time is taken up with meetings and appointments. With such a busy schedule her **personal computer (PC** for short) helps her to organize her day.

At the moment, Sarah is looking at a computerized diary on the screen of her personal computer. She suddenly realizes that she has a meeting with all her sales staff from all over the country. An agenda for the meeting needs to be prepared. Sarah types in the agenda on her PC using the wordprocessing facility to help her correct the odd mistake. When the agenda is correct she uses the electronic mail facility to send it to all the sales branches simultaneously.

Sarah now needs to prepare a report about the salesmen's expenses, which have been getting a bit out of hand lately. Her secretary has prepared a table of each salesman's expenses, using a spreadsheet program. Sarah feeds the disks into her PC and gets the table up on the screen (Figure 14.3).

Figure 14.3 *Sarah uses the spreadsheet program to show John, a salesman, his expense account*

The table shows the figures for the last 12 months expenses for each salesman. Some of the expenses for meals have been very large and what she would like to see is a reduction in these bills of around 20 per cent. She feeds in the reduction and the computer automatically recalculates each salesman's reduced monthly expenses. Instead of having to wade through hundreds of calculations with a pocket calculator, she can enter one figure and let the software recalculate all the others. She then looks at the spreadsheet and the total expenses of all the salesmen, and is satisfied that a 20 per cent reduction would be suitable. A copy of the table is printed out for her reference at the meeting.

John – a salesman who works from a branch office

John is a salesman who works from a branch office. At the moment, John is taking a customer's order over the phone. As the customer gives him the details, John types in the customer's name on his terminal. The information from the customer file is displayed on the screen and John notices that the customer hasn't paid his last bill and the amount is now two weeks overdue. John informs the customer that the account is overdue and the customer promises to put a cheque in the post to cover the amount.

John then types in the details of the new order and mentions that the goods should not be sent out unless a payment has been received by the accounts department.

By co-ordinating the work of the accounts and sales offices, the computer saves money by not sending goods to people who haven't paid their last bills. The computer is thus able to improve the **cash flow** of the company.

Videoconferencing (teleconferencing)

Videoconferencing is a way of a company holding a conference or meeting without everyone who is involved having to travel to the head office. Often meetings or conferences last only a couple of hours but involve many hours of travel, there and back, for the people who attend. This is wasteful in both time and money.

Instead of travelling to the meeting the staff involved can position themselves in front of a video camera and screen in their own branch office. The system can then be linked through the telephone lines to the meeting room in the head office which may be hundreds of miles away (Figure 14.4).

You may have seen this technique used on TV, where debates take place between people in different studios in different parts of the country.

At the moment, only very large organizations have this facility in their own offices. Most commercial organizations have to travel to their local videoconferencing studio.

Figure 14.4 *Videoconferencing*

Facsimile transmission

A **facsimile machine** (often called **Fax**) is a little like a long-distance photocopier. Instead of transferring the information on one piece of paper to another piece of paper, the information is changed into signals which are passed along telephone lines (and maybe by satellite) to another facsimile machine. This decodes the signals and converts the information into a hard copy. Diagrams and text can be passed in this way instantly (Figure 14.5).

Fax machines using analogue signals have been in use for some years. Fax using digital signals is now becoming widely used. With digital Fax, as well as providing a hard copy, the information can be displayed on a screen or stored on disk so that it may be recalled at a later date.

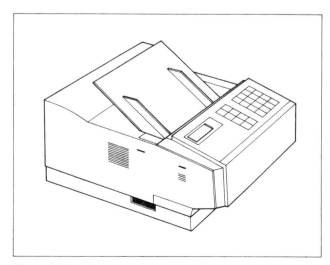

Figure 14.5 *A Fax machine*

The future

The developments we have mentioned, and others, have led some people to predict that the office of the future could be entirely electronic. Each secretary could have a wordprocessor linked to a powerful computer. Communication with the manager or with other secretaries would be via the network. If this becomes true, it may no longer be necessary for so many to travel to their offices every day; they may be able to work from their own homes. This would relieve the problems of commuting to a large city, such as London or Manchester. Instead, people may prefer to live in the country or near a holiday resort. This is just one more way in which microelectronics could dramatically alter the way we live.

Test yourself

Using the words in the list below, copy out and complete sentences A to G. Underline the words you have inserted. The words may be used once, more than once, or not at all.

wordprocessors   paper   videoconferencing
facsimile   daisy wheel   electronic office
personal computer

A The office of the past depended heavily on_____.

B We are now seeing the introduction of the _____.

C Secretaries now use_____ to prepare, edit, store and retrieve text.

D Wordprocessors usually use a special type of printer called a_____ printer that produces high quality type.

E Executives in large companies often use a_____ to help them organize their work.

F _____ is a way of holding a meeting without people having to leave the office.

G A long-distance photocopier, called a_____ machine is used to transmit text and pictures over large distances.

Things to do

1 **a** What do you understand by the term 'paperless office'?

b Give and explain some of the advantages of having a paperless office.

2 Wordprocessing is the application of information technology to typewriting.

a Where is the text stored as it is typed?

b Where is the text stored afterwards?

c Give **three** examples of the types of commands that are available to the operator.

d What type of printer do you think will be used to print the information out? Give reasons for your choice.

e The Minutes of a meeting have been typed on a wordprocessor and stored on a disk. The draft copy shows one mistake. In the middle of a long paragraph, the word 'the' has been typed in twice. Briefly describe how the operator would correct the Minutes.

3 Explain how a personal computer (PC for short) can help busy executives organize their day.

4 A company whose main office is in London but which has five branch offices situated in Dublin, Manchester, Glasgow, Birmingham and Bristol, often holds meetings in London. Explain how the following facilities could help them to run their business more efficiently.

a Videoconferencing (teleconferencing)

b Facsimile transmission

15

The social implications of computers

Computers, as well as bringing great benefits to mankind, also pose some problems. Figures 15.1 and 15.2 show some disadvantages and advantages of computerization.

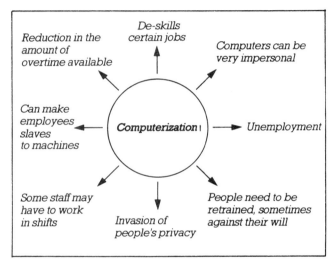

Figure 15.1 *Some of the disadvantages of computerization*

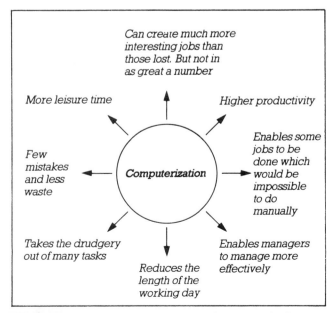

Figure 15.2 *Some of the advantages of computerization*

The threat to your privacy

A great deal of information about every one of us is collected and kept by many organizations. The diagram (Figure 15.3) shows organizations that would keep details about a baby in the first few years of her life. This information rapidly grows as more and more organizations become interested in her.

Here is a list of some of the organizations who might hold information about you:

Schools
Medical authorities
DVLC (Driver and Vehicle Licensing Centre)
Insurance companies
Inland Revenue
Building societies and Banks
Libraries
Credit Card companies
Electricity and Gas Boards
Water Boards
Credit referral agencies
Rates Departments

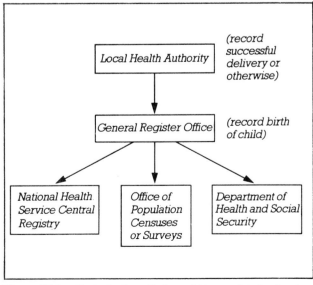

Figure 15.3 *Organizations that would keep details about a baby in the first few weeks of her life*

A lot of people think that information about themselves is private. They think of the information as belonging to them. Unfortunately, we live in the real world and we have to accept that some organizations need this information about us. Accepting this, we need to be assured that this information is only used for the purpose for which it was collected and that it is not divulged to anyone else.

Some people say that you needn't be worried about the information if you have nothing to hide. There's a certain amount of truth in this, but many people don't want to reveal things because they wish to keep them private.

One of the main fears people have about computerization is that it is much easier to access confidential files and copy them. Computers are also able to exchange information. The PNC (Police National Computer) regularly exchanges information with the DVLC (Driver and Vehicle Licensing Centre) computer in Swansea about the owners of vehicles. Figure 15.4 shows some database linkings that exist already.

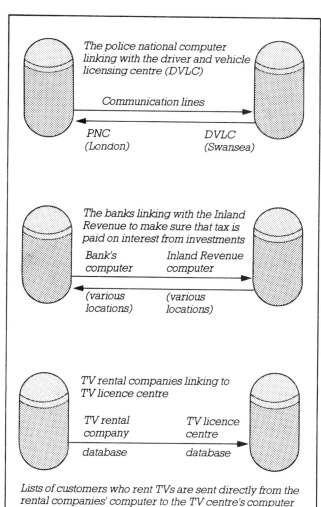

Figure 15.4 *Some database linkings that already exist*

The 1984 Data Protection Act

The 1984 Data Protection Act is a law to protect us against the misuse of information that is held about us. Before this Act, there were only guidelines about what should and shouldn't be done. Here are some of the main points in the Act.

1 The Act makes it an offence to disclose any information to outsiders.
2 Any companies that hold personal information have to be registered centrally with the Data Protection Authority.
3 Information collected for one purpose should not be used for another purpose.
4 People have the right of access to the files held about them to check that the information is correct.
5 Adequate security should be provided to prevent unauthorized access.
6 There are limits to the exchange of information.

Loss of jobs

Most inventions were supposed to cause unemployment. When the motor car first came out it was thought that it would cause widespread unemployment because horses needed so many people to look after them. Just think for a moment about all the jobs that have been created because of the car, from the people who make the cars to traffic wardens!

The first computers needed a whole array of people to keep them working. Nowadays the situation has changed. Modern computers are simple, need very little data preparation and don't break down very often.

Figure 15.5 *Some people will be replaced by the new technology!*

There is no doubt that computers have and will continue to cause unemployment (Figure 15.5). However, some of the jobs that the computer has replaced were dull and repetitive or even dangerous. The advertisement shown in Figure 15.6 is from IBM, the largest computer manufacturer in the world. It shows quite clearly how the statement, 'If we did not have computers, there would be more jobs' could be answered.

Two men were watching a mechanical excavator on a building site.

"If it wasn't for that machine," said one, **"twelve men with shovels could be doing that job."**

"Yes,"replied the other,"and if it wasn't for your twelve shovels, two hundred men with teaspoons could be doing that job."

There are two ways to regard technological development. As a threat. Or as a promise. Every invention from the wheel to the steam engine created the same dilemma.

But it's only by exploiting the promise of each that man has managed to improve his lot.

Information technology has given man more time to create, and released him from the day-to-day tasks that limit his self-fulfilment.

We ourselves are very heavy users of this technology, ranging from golf-ball typewriters to ink-jet printers to small and large computers, so we're more aware than most of that age-old dilemma: threat or promise.

Yet during 30 years in the UK our workforce has increased from six to 15,000. And during those 30 years not a single person has been laid off, not a single day has been lost through strikes.

Throughout Britain, information technology has shortened queues. Streamlined efficiency. Boosted exports. And kept British products competitive in an international market.

To treat technology as a threat would halt progress. As a promise, it makes tomorrow look a lot brighter.

IBM

IBM United Kingdom Limited P.O. Box 41 North Harbour Portsmouth PO6 3AU

Figure 15.6

The attitude of the Trade Unions

Generally the Trade Unions accept that we have to have the new technology in order to compete with other countries. In some industries, such as the newspaper industry, the Unions have tried to hold on to old outdated practices, and this has led to long drawn-out strikes.

Many hazardous jobs in industry are now performed by robots and many tedious jobs are now being performed by computers. This leaves the more interesting and higher paid jobs to the remaining workforce. It hasn't escaped the Unions' notice that industrial action (strikes) can be effective if just the computer staff are called out. The other staff in the company can still draw their pay but, because of the importance of the computer system, the company can be effectively crippled.

✓ Test yourself

Using the words in the list below, copy out and complete sentences A to E. Underline the words you have inserted. The words can be used once, more than once, or not at all.

compete   privacy   PNC   unemployment DVLC   Data Protection

A *Many people worry that a lot of personal information is held by computers. They worry that their_____ may be invaded.*

B *Information held on one computer may be exchanged with information from another computer. The PNC computer exchanges information with the_____ computer.*

C *The 1984_____Act ensures that certain guidelines about privacy are met.*

D *When computers were first introduced, people were convinced that their use would lead to_____.*

E *Trade Unions now accept that the new technology is essential in order to_____ with other countries.*

❯❯ Things to do

1 *'With the development and widespread use of computers, many new jobs have appeared and many older jobs have disappeared.'*
   a i *Discuss briefly this statement, giving **four** reasons why this has happened.*
      iii *Give **two** examples of new jobs that have appeared and two examples of jobs that have disappeared as a result of this development.*
   b i *How is the computer likely to affect the job situation in the next ten years?*
      iii *Give an example of a job where you expect computers to play a more important part.*
      iii *Give an example of a job where the impact of computers is not so great.*

2 *In a few years from now, a large computer will have lots of details about our private lives stored in it. This computer will be used by the Government for a variety of things. No longer will people be able to avoid paying National Insurance contributions and tax. They will know every detail about us. As in the book* Nineteen Eighty Four, *Big Brother is watching you. They will even be able to find out if you own a dog by information obtained from the Supermarket's main computer. Dog licence avoidance will no longer be possible if you want to buy dog food from the supermarket.*

   The above statement represents a rather pessimistic Nineteen Eighty Four *type view of the future. How far is this statement true? Give any instances where information used for one purpose is used for other purposes. Discuss whether you think* the statement is justified. Give some situations where the transfer of information is a good thing.

3 Imagine you are the owner of an engineering company which employs about thirty people. You are thinking of buying a computer to improve your company's efficiency. The Union is opposed to its introduction.

  a Write down and explain fully why the Unions would be opposed to its introduction. Give **three** reasons.

  b Write a short speech which could be read to the staff to try to dispel their concern. Try to emphasize how the computer will improve the business and their working conditions.

4 **a** It is generally accepted that personal data (data about people) which is stored in a computer system should be **accurate**, **secure** and **private**. With the help of examples, briefly explain the meanings of these three terms.

  b Computer systems used by government, local authorities and commercial organizations all store personal data. Describe **three** computer systems which use personal data and indicate any dangers which would arise if the data were not accurate, secure and private.

5 Mr Smith, a professional engineer, and his wife own their own home and have a teenage son who attends the 6th form of the local comprehensive school. Mrs Smith has had to take a part-time job as a shop assistant in order to meet the hire-purchase demand on their second car.

  a A number of computer files will refer to Mr Smith. Write down:

    i **one** held by a government department

    ii **four** financial files (excluding gas and electricity)

    iii **one** of interest to the police

    iv **one** held by the local authority

    v **one** held by his employer.

  b How are people's lives being affected by computers in:

    i recreation

    ii everyday life

    iii employment?

6 The above shows some of the items of information that could be held on a computer file by the personnel department.

  a Write down any of the questions which you feel would be an infringement of your privacy. Explain why you object and give reasons why you might not want the company to know the details.

  b Imagine you were the owner of the company and you were responsible for the design of the form. Write down some reasons for the inclusion of some of the more intrusive questions in the above form.

7 The Metropolitan Police (London-based police force) alone has access to computer files on more than 23 million of us, both in its 'C' computer and the Police National Computer. In the criminal computer there are 1.25 million Special Branch files on people who are not necessarily criminals or even suspected of a crime.

  Comment on the above passage saying whether you consider it is a good or a bad thing that so much information is held about us, bearing in mind that the population of Great Britain is approximately 55 million.

  Why do they need this quantity of information? Give reasons.

Full name	Address
Tel. No.	
Single/married/divorced/widowed	Years at above address
Religion	Politics
Any Union membership?	If yes, which one?
Is he/she an active member of the above Union, if applicable?	
If yes, give any details on any danger to company.	
Does he/she own his/her own house?	
If yes, how much mortgage outstanding?	
Bank account number	
Has he/she ever been bankrupt?	
Salary	Tax code
Mother's and Father's occupations	

16

Computers and banking

Banking was one of the first industries to use computers. A lot of banking services that we now take for granted, such as credit cards, would be impossible without computers.

Data capture techniques and hardware used by banks

Data capture means getting the information into a form that the computer can process (Figure 16.1).

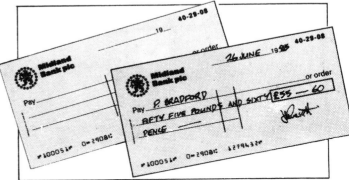

Figure 16.2 *Cheques use MICR for data capture*

When a cheque arrives at the bank there is only one group of figures that needs to be typed in. This is the amount of the cheque, since obviously this is not known during the printing of the cheques. When the cheques reach the clearing bank where all the cheques are sorted for all the banks, the magnetic characters are read by a **magnetic ink character reader**. This reader can read cheques at a rate of about 2500 per minute. MICR is chosen by banks because it is difficult for people to forge or alter the numbers. MICR is very expensive but, in one way, this makes it more suitable for banks, since few other people are likely to come into contact with it.

Magnetic encoding

Figure 16.1 *Data capture!*

MICR (Magnetic Ink Character Recognition)

In this form of data capture the computer can read certain numbers which are written in magnetic ink at the bottom of a bank cheque (Figure 16.2). About 6.5 million cheques are handled by the banks each day and the clearing process only takes about three days. Without **MICR**, cheques would take much longer to clear. Someone would have to key all the information contained on the cheque into the computer. You can imagine the work this would involve.

Figure 16.3 *Cash dispenser cards use magnetic encoding*

If you look at a bank credit card or a card that can be used in a cash dispenser you will notice that it has a dark band on it (Figure 16.3). The stripe on the card is of a magnetic material which can be used to hold information. This process is called **magnetic encoding.** A cash dispenser is a terminal that is connected by telephone line to a main computer. When the card is inserted into the cash dispenser the bank's computer can read the information in the magnetic stripe.

Cash dispensers

Many of you will have noticed the cash dispensers sprouting through the walls of High Street banks and building societies. A few years ago it was common to find queues inside the banks and building societies; now it is just as common to find them on the outside, especially at weekends and outside normal business hours.

The cash dispenser, or **automated teller machine system (ATMS)** as it is more correctly called, provides banking services for its customers 24 hours per day (Figure 16.4). As well as providing cash, it can also order statements, and customers can deposit cheques and cash. Some customers prefer the impersonal service that the cash dispensers offer. Unlike human cashiers, the cash dispenser can't think you might have stolen the cheque book or think that you are spending too much. It is not uncommon to find a queue outside whilst the bank is empty inside (Figure 16.5).

An advantage to the banks is that it is impossible for the customer to withdraw money from the cash dispenser that they haven't got in their account. Also, fewer staff and smaller premises are needed and this reduces the overheads.

Figure 16.4 *Automatic cash dispensers provide customers with banking services 24 hours per day and 7 days per week*

Figure 16.5

To get money from a cash dispenser you put a plastic card, like the one shown in Figure 16.6, into the machine. The card needs to be inserted the correct way round. A screen then lights up and displays messages to guide the customer through the series of steps.

You then type in your secret number called your **Personal Identification Number (PIN)** which is not displayed on the screen for security reasons. You then press one of the buttons for which service you require. If you want cash then you type in the amount of money you want, usually in multiples of £5. If you have the money in your account, the machine will dispense it.

For security reasons, if the PIN number is entered more than twice incorrectly, then no money is given and the card is automatically kept by the machine.

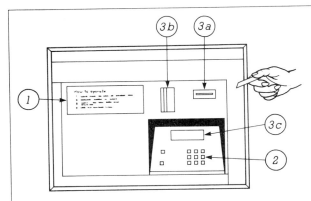

1 The customer is given step by step instructions on how to operate the cash dispensing machine
2 The keyboard (input device)
This is where the information is typed into the computer such as the customer's secret number (PIN)
3 a This is where the customer inserts the plastic card into the machine. The card must be inserted the right way round
  b From here the amount of money the customer has keyed in is released
  c This is the VDU screen where certain messages appear such as 'Enter personal number'. The screen gives instructions to the customer

Figure 16.6 *Using a cash dispensing machine*

Cheque clearing

Suppose Jane wants to buy a portable colour television from Comet Electrics and pay by cheque. Jane banks with Lloyds and Comet Electrics banks with Barclays. Figure 16.7 shows what happens to the cheque from when it is given to Comet Electrics to when the money is subtracted (debited) from Jane's account and added (credited) to Comet Electrics' account. This process is call **cheque clearing** and, because of the huge number of cheques cleared each day, computers are used for nearly all of the process.

1 Jane writes out a cheque for £240.00 made payable to Comet Electrics.

2 Comet Electrics pay the cheque into their Barclays branch.

3 Barclays bank types in the amount of the cheque in magnetic ink characters so that it can be read at the clearing bank using MICR.

4 All cheques, including this one, are sent to a bank in London called a **clearing bank**. Here, all the cheques are sorted into bank sorting code numbers.

5 The details of all the transactions (items of business) are sent on magnetic disk to the Bank of England from the clearing bank. The Bank of England transfers the £240 from Lloyds Bank to Barclays Bank.

6 The cheque is sent from the clearing bank to Jane's branch of Lloyds Bank, identified by the bank sorting code number, where the amount is deducted from her account.

7 Barclays Bank receives notification that the cheque has been cleared and credits Comet Electrics' account with £240.

8 The whole process of cheque clearing takes a minimum of three days.

Figure 16.7 *What happens to Jane's cheque*

Bankers' Automated Clearing Services (BACS)

Bankers' Automated Clearing Services Ltd was set up by the larger banks to deal with standing orders and direct debit payments. It is situated in Edgware, north-west of London, on the spot where the old De Havilland aircraft factory stood and where Amy Johnson's famous aeroplane was built in the late 1920s.

Security is very strict, bearing in mind that the computer equipment in the building cost a staggering £5–6 million. Every night some 6.5 million payments are processed, valued at over £1 500 000 000.

As well as processing transactions that take place in this country, BACS also houses the **Swift** computer for the UK which deals with international payments.

The BACS service is used to pay two thirds of all monthly salaries directly into employees' accounts. It is also used to pay regular bills and payments such as pensions, local authority rates, mortgages, loan repayments etc.

The BACS computers keep a diary of all the payments to be made. These payments are made and are transferred between the banks on magnetic tape. The fact that not many people have heard of BACS shows the system's reliability and success.

Figure 16.8

Electronic Fund Transfer (EFT)

This is a modern banking system that transfers money from one place to another. It works instantly, so it saves the time of filling in pieces of paper such as credit card slips or cheques and the delay in clearing cheques.

Electronic Fund Transfer is used by shops with a special **Point-of-Sale (POS)** terminal. The customer puts his card into a special till and the money is automatically, and instantly, transferred from the customer's account to the shop's account. No paperwork is involved and the shop benefits in not having to wait for the money.

The Nottingham Building Society and the Bank of Scotland have a system which allows EFT from home (Figure 16.9). Customers can transfer money from one account to another or pay bills automatically without leaving their home. You can even apply for a loan using the service (Figure 16.10)

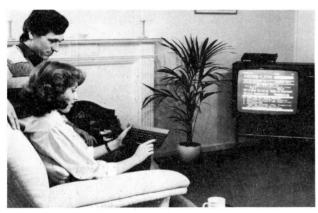

Figure 16.9 *Using the Homelink service. Information is keyed in using the remote control keypad. The modem on top of the TV set connects up to the Homelink computer via the telephone lines*

Figure 16.10 *You can apply for a loan using the EFT service from home!*

The social implications of a cashless society

A future without the use of any cash is unlikely, but in the next few years we will probably see more payments being made without using cash.

Advantages

A cashless society is far more convenient. Mortgage repayments, telephone, rates, electricity and gas bills, loan repayments – all these are automatically deducted from the amount in your bank. You no longer find that your phone has gone dead because you have forgotten to pay the bill. The computer does all these tedious chores for you and never forgets to pay a bill.

It will no longer be necessary to draw large sums of money out of the bank to make large purchases. This leads to less risk of being robbed. It also avoids the inconvenience of having to draw out money from the bank all the time.

Also, credit cards allow people to buy goods and then to decide whether to pay for them at the end of the month or obtain them on credit, paying a proportion off each month.

Disadvantages

One of the main disadvantages that a cashless society could bring is that it would be very easy to spend more than you can really afford. In the 'olden' days people were given their wage packet in cash. From this wage packet they gave their landlady or their parents a certain amount, bought a weekly ticket to get to work, and what was left was theirs to spend. They had to make sure that they had enough money to last them till the next pay day. If they did not have enough they had to do without for a few days. Borrowing money was very frowned upon. These simple rules of budgeting were summarized by Mr Micawber, a character in *David Copperfield*, written by Charles Dickens (Figure 16.11).

It is harder to relate to the money you have when you can't acutally see it. Money comes into and goes out of your account automatically, so it is much harder to know how much you have left. Most transactions would be done by credit card and since this money is 'money on paper' people might spend more on purchases than they would if they were using cash.

With the increased use of credit cards, more and more information needs to be kept about individuals by outside organizations. These details are needed so that a person's credit worthiness can be assessed. Inevitably some of the details may be incorrect and result in the person affected being refused credit.

Figure 16.11 *'Annual income twenty pounds, annual expenditure nineteen pounds, nineteen shillings and sixpence, result happiness. Annual income twenty pounds, annual expenditure twenty pounds, no shillings and sixpence, result misery'*

✔ Test yourself

Using the words in the list below, copy out and complete sentences A to G. Underline the words you have inserted. The words may be used once, more than once, or not at all.

cash dispensers   ATMS   magnetic   plastic PIN   data capture   BACS   magnetic ink   EFT

A *Collecting for processing is called_____.*

B *With cheques, the_____ characters are read directly and there is no need to type in all the information via a keyboard.*

C *Banks now use_____ which allow customers to obtain money at any time including weekends.*

D *Cash dispensers or_____ are also used for depositing cheques or cash or obtaining a bank statement.*

E *To use one of these machines a_____ card is inserted into the machine. The card has a_____ stripe on it. A secret number called your_____ is keyed in along with how much money you need. The machine then gives you your money and returns your card.*

F *_____ is a modern banking system which can transfer money from one place to another without paperwork.*

G *The_____ was set up by all the banks to deal with standing orders and direct debits.*

≫ Things to do

1 *Explain what the following abbreviations mean with reference to computers used in banking. For each one, explain how banking efficiency is improved using them:*
   a *MICR*
   b *ATMS*
   c *BACS*
   d *EFT*
   e *PIN*

2 *Colin the Conman finds himself in the following situation. Say, with reasons, whether you think he is likely to succeed with his crime.*
   a *He finds a cash card and goes round to the nearest cash dispenser and feeds it in.*
   b *He takes his cheque book and alters the account number with ordinary black ink to change the number to his friend's number. His idea is to get the money out of his friend's account.*

a

b

95

3 Explain in your own words all the processes that are involved in the clearing of a bank cheque.

4 You will have seen banking machines operating through the walls of the banks in our High Streets.
  a Explain what these machines do.
  b What do the initials ATMS mean?
  c In addition to dispensing cash, what other banking jobs can they do?
  d Do you think people prefer to use these machines? Explain your answer.
  e Outline the advantages which these machines have over the normal banking services offered inside the bank.

5 Draw a diagram of a cheque. Label on the cheque the following things:
  a The individual account number.
  b The name and address of the bank (make up an address).
  c The serial number of the cheque.
  d The sorting code number of the branch.
  e The space where the magnetic ink characters are placed.

5 Why aren't the magnetic ink characters placed on the cheque as are the rest of the other numbers? What information is contained within these numbers?

6 Some computer experts believe that, because computer systems are so successful in dealing with money transfers, it would be possible for society to completely do away with cash (coins and notes).
  a Name **three** different ways, other than cash, of paying for goods or services.
  b Describe what part the computer system plays in making money transfer in one of the ways you have named.
  c It is certainly possible to design computer systems which would enable society to do away with cash, but it is very unlikely that a 'cashless society' will occur in the near future. Give **two** reasons why this is so.

17

Computers in shops

Figure 17.1

Chain stores such as Sainsbury, Littlewoods, Marks & Spencer, Tesco, etc. are able to offer high quality goods at a reasonable price by bulk buying. The stock is bought centrally by head offices. Many small businesses have been replaced because they are unable to compete with the efficiency of the larger stores.

If a shop is to use a computer, then the computer must be able to help them order stock, pay for the stock, record when and what is sold and to reorder new goods. Shops are able to keep their prices lower by high productivity.

All of the above jobs can be very time-consuming and they involve handling large amounts of information. It is not surprising that many shops have looked for an easier way of doing these tasks. Computers are ideal because they can deal with such repetitive jobs very easily. All the larger shops use computers as well as some of the smaller ones.

Figure 17.2 *Running a shop*

Point-Of-Sale (POS) Terminals

A **Point-Of-Sale (POS) terminal** is a computer terminal situated where the conventional till used to be. The point-of-sale terminal is used to read machine-readable tickets. It saves time because less information needs to be keyed in at the keyboard. Figure 17.3 is a diagram of a point-of-sale terminal.

The machine-readable tickets can include bar codes, magnetic striped tags and kimball tags.

The POS terminal tells the main computer when an item is sold and the main computer automatically deducts this item from stock records. Some POS systems automatically reorder the items when they have fallen below a certain level.

Bar codes

Bar codes are the thick and thin lines you see on many goods you purchase. These lines contain a code that can be read by a laser scanner. Sometimes this scanner is on a wand (Figure 17.4), or it can be fitted inside a panel in the POS desk (Figure 17.5). The stripes in a bar code contain a 13-digit code number and the computer can understand this code.

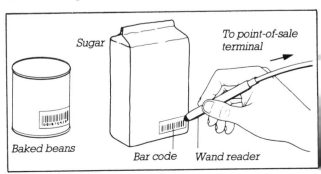

Figure 17.3 *A point-of-sale terminal*

Figure 17.4 *Using a wand reader to read bar codes*

Figure 17.5 *Using a bar code reader in the desk of a point-of-sale terminal*

Using the product code, the computer can link this code with the price of an article (Figure 17.6). To change a price, the computer needs to be told what new price the code is to represent.

Figure 17.7 shows some ways the use of bar codes helps to save time and money.

Here are some advantages for customers in the use of bar codes.

1 Due to an increase in speed there will be fewer queues at the tills. This means that the shopper won't have to wait so long.

2 With an increase in productivity, it may be possible to lower the prices.

3 The supermarket can offer a greater variety of items and is less likely to run out of goods because stocktaking is more efficient.

4 The shopper gets an itemized receipt showing the items and the prices.

5 The POS terminal reduces mistakes, because information doesn't need to be typed in.

There are, however, also disadvantages for customers. Some of these are:

1 It is easier for the shop to change prices, since it doesn't need to go around repricing each article. Only a few numbers have to be typed into the main computer to change the price.

2 There is no need to price individual articles so it is harder for the customer to keep track of how much he or she has spent.

3 Some customers, particularly older ones, might not like the system because they don't understand it.

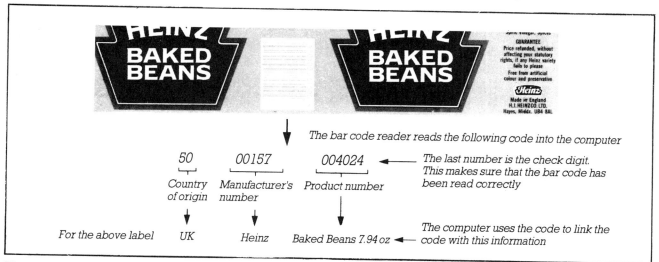

Figure 17.6 *How a computer uses a bar code*

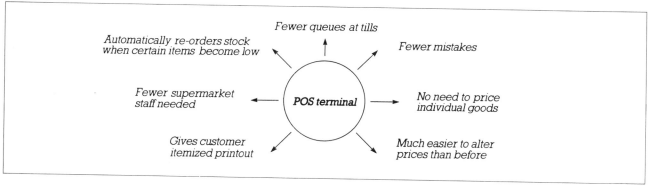

Figure 17.7 *How a point-of-sale terminal saves time and money*

Kimball tags

These are usually used by shops that sell clothing. They consist of tags with holes in them that contain information about the goods (Figure 17.8). The **Kimball tag** doesn't contain the price but it contains information such as colour, style, size etc. When an item is bought, the sales assistant removes the tag and at the end of the week sends all the tags to be processed. The computer then works out what the shop has sold and what should be reordered.

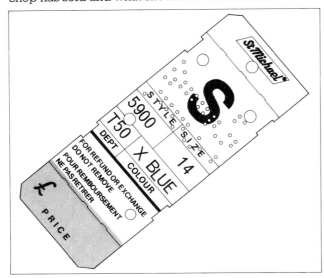

Figure 17.8 *A Kimball tag*

Magnetic stripe tags

Figure 17.9 *A magnetic stripe tag*

These tags contain the same information as held by the Kimball tags, except that it is coded into a magnetic pattern on a magnetic stripe. The information is read using a special wand reader.

Intelligent scales

These are microprocessor-controlled scales and can be seen in the large food supermarkets, for example in the fruit and vegetable section. Intelligent scales display the weight of the goods and the price per pound. A ticket is then automatically printed out for the cost of the goods and this is stuck on the bag containing them. The assistant at the scales only needs to type in the type of goods and the scales work out the total price automatically.

✓ Test yourself

Using the words in the list below, copy out and complete sentences A to N. Underline the words you have inserted. The words may be used once, more than one, or not at all.

computer   machine   deducts   point-of-sale
Kimball   reorder   bar code   wand reader
productivity   desk   priced   magnetic stripe
itemized   alter   intelligent   thirteen

A Supermarkets can keep prices lower by high_____.

B In the larger shops you now find_____ terminals.

C The POS terminals are connected to a central_____.

D Instead of typing in the price, quantity, etc. at the keyboard,_____-readable tickets are used.

E As well as bar codes, these tickets also include_____ tags and_____ tags.

F Using a POS terminal, when an item is sold, the computer automatically_____ it from stock records.

G When an item of stock becomes low, the computer will automatically_____ it.

H Many goods in shops now have a series of black and white lines printed on their labels. These lines are called a_____.

I A bar code reader is usually set into the_____ and the goods are passed across it. Sometimes a_____ is used instead.

J The lines that make up a bar code are used to represent a_____ digit code.

K An advantage to the customer of using a POS terminal is that the customer gets an_____ receipt.

L A possible disadvantage for the customer is that the individual article may not be_____, so it is harder for customers to keep track of their spending.

M Also, it is easier for the shops to_____ prices.

N Microprocessor-controlled scales that print out a ticket to stick on to the goods being weighed, are said to be '_____'.

⋙ Things to do

1 Many supermarkets are now using computerized tills, called point-of-sale terminals. Each point-of-sale terminal has a laser scanner connected to it, which is used to read the bar codes on the goods. The terminals are able to produce itemized receipts for customers. The terminals are connected to a main computer and, when an item is sold, the computer automatically deducts it from

stock records. The computer is able to produce important management information on which lines are selling well etc. Some systems automatically reorder goods from the suppliers when stocks are low.

a Where in a supermarket would you find a point-of-sale terminal?

b Other than a keyboard, what kind of input device might it use?

c What is a bar code and how is it used?

d The bar code reader is a direct form of data capture. What does this mean and what advantage does it have over indirect data capture such as key-to-disk where the information is keyed in?

e The above computer system deducts an item from stock records when it is sold. This might not give the true number of items left. Give two ways an article can be removed from stock without it being sold.

f Some customers are worried that it is far too easy to alter prices using this system. Explain why their fears could be justified.

g Give **two** jobs that the supermarket staff will not have to do, that the computer will do automatically.

2 Here is a bar code, such as will be found printed on the labels or packaging of nearly all the articles you find in supermarkets.

A bar code

a List **three** items of information which are contained within a bar code.

b Why is the products price not included in the bar code?

c Why is a check digit included?

d What are the advantages to management in the use of bar codes?

e What are the practical disadvantages to shoppers in the use of bar codes?

f What are the advantages to shoppers in the use of bar codes?

g List **three** things that the point-of-sale terminal prints out for the customer.

3 Here are three tickets which can be read directly by a machine.

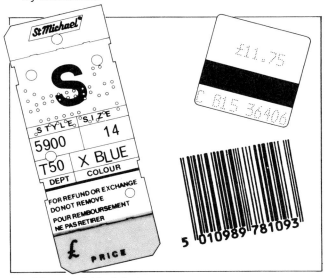

Machine-readable tickets

a Name each of the three tickets.

b Try to obtain as many different machine-readable tickets as you can and stick them into your books. For each ticket, explain how it is used.

18

Information technology in the community

As well as helping industry and commerce to become more efficient, information technology is also able to improve the quality of life of ordinary people.

Information technology is being used in hospitals, libraries, schools, old peoples' homes and in other areas of community life.

In this chapter we shall look at a few areas where ordinary people are benefiting from the use of IT.

Information technology and medicine

All hospitals make use of information technology and, because of the diverse nature of the work that hospitals do, the computer has many quite different uses.

Organ transplants

Computers are very good at looking at and comparing lists. When a person dies and their organs such as heart, kidneys etc. are donated, the computer can be used to match and identify a patient to receive them. This needs to be done extremely quickly and is why computers are really essential (Figure 18.1).

Figure 18.1

Computer diagnosis

Figure 18.2 *Computer diagnosis!*

Computers are used to diagnose many illnesses. Often the information is fed directly into the computer from machines attached to the patient, such as electrocardiographs (measure heartbeat) and body scanners.

Computers can be used to locate tumours at an early stage when, by other means, they cannot be easily and surely detected. Body scanners send rays into the human body (Figure 18.3) and the rays are picked up by a detector. Signals from the detector are analysed by the computer and are converted to a digital form which can then be displayed as a picture on a television screen (Figure 18.4). On the screen the tumour appears as a dark patch.

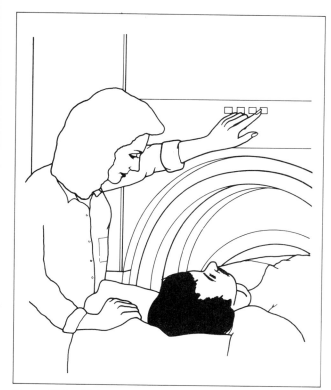

Figure 18.3 *Using a body scanner with computer diagnosis*

Figure 18.4 *Information from the body scanner is used, here, to build up a picture of the human brain, in sections. Any tumours can thus be precisely located*

Intensive care

In intensive care units, computers are used to monitor instruments which record important data about the patient. If the data moves outside certain limits, an alarm is sounded, so that immediate medical help can be brought.

The measurements constantly taken by the computer might include blood pressure, pulse rate, heart waveshape from an ECG, respiration rate and volume, and electrical signals from the brain. Previously, these measurements needed to be taken so regularly that a nurse was needed for each patient. Now, many more patients can be looked after by one nurse.

Computers are also used to monitor vital data during surgery in the operating theatre.

Keeping patients records

Computers can be used to provide a complete, accurate, up-to-date and readily available source of information about patients' health. Records of patients are usually kept for the duration of their lives so, in the past, a large amount of space was taken up by paperwork. There were also problems in locating a particular patient's file – especially if, say, the patient moved about the country a great deal.

Most hospitals now store patients' records on magnetic tapes or disks. The information can be found immediately by the computer. There are terminals at certain places in the hospital. The doctors or nurses can find details of a particular patient very quickly.

Inpatients' records are probably best kept on magnetic disk. This method allows quicker access because it is a random access storage medium. These records will be needed much more often than the outpatient records. Outpatient records contain a large quantity of information that may only be used, say, a couple of times in a patient's lifetime. So these records can be stored on magnetic tape which has slower access time.

New data can be added to the patient's records by keying this into the computer via a terminal. Thus the patient's record can be kept up-to-date with the latest information about his or her condition or circumstances.

Doctors and nurses used to spend about 30 per cent of their time processing information in files, but now this has been vastly reduced because of the introduction of computers.

One problem with using a computer in this way is that very confidential information is kept about the patient. Obviously, many patients would not like this information to be seen by just anyone. One way round this problem is to introduce a code or password which the user needs to type into the computer before he or she can gain access to the patients' files. Another way, used in some of the extremely complicated systems, is to only allow the terminals a certain amount of necessary information for different users. So, a nurse could obtain some information, and a doctor would be able to get further details.

Computers and the family doctor

A doctor's diagnosis of what is wrong with a patient depends a great deal on how good is the doctor's memory; in other words, how much information he can remember. Computers can help doctors make a better diagnosis because they contain more information than a doctor's short-term memory.

An average family doctor diagnoses correctly for about 50 to 60 per cent of the time. Using a computer, diagnosis is 70 to 90 per cent accurate. So when computers are used in doctors' surgeries, they help give more accurate diagnoses. This means that consultants (specialist doctors) are needed less.

Starting to use a computer in a doctor's surgery is not an easy task. In the average practice with four doctors there will be about 10 000 patients. To begin with, all the notes of the patients will have to be typed into the computer. An average record for a patient has about 1500 characters. So for 10 000 patients, the computer will need 15 megabytes of storage. This means removable disk packs or fixed disk packs will have to be used for storage. The system is still too expensive except for larger practices. Figure 18.5 shows a family doctor using a computer to keep his patients' records.

Figure 18.5 *A family doctor using a computer to keep his patients' records*

Use in the supplies office

Most hospital supply departments contain terminals which are linked to a central computer, usually situated at the Regional Health Authorities Headquarters.

All data about orders needed by the hospital and the deliveries received, are entered into the terminal from where they are transferred to the headquarters via telephone lines. Once the hospital stocks fall below a certain level, they are automatically re-ordered by a computer. This prevents the possibility, for instance, of running out of a certain drug, which could prove fatal (Figure 18.6).

Figure 18.6 *Nurses ordering medical and surgical supplies using a Videotex terminal*

Teleshopping for the old or disabled

In Bradford and Gateshead, computers are being used to help the socially disadvantaged people in the community, such as the elderly or disabled.

Generally the main problem that old or disabled people face when shopping, is getting back from the shops with heavy shopping bags. Shopping thus needs to be done regularly, because they are limited to what they can carry. The completely housebound people have to rely on others to do their shopping for them.

Figure 18.7 *Senior citizens at a Day Centre, ordering goods using a teleshopping terminal*

Teleshopping involves using a **Videotex** system with terminals situated in old peoples' homes, community centres, libraries etc. Ideally the terminals should be situated in the homes of those people who cannot get out easily, but instead they ring through to a centre where the operator keys in their order into the terminal. Each customer is given a catalogue so that he or she knows what can be ordered (Figure 15.7).

Each terminal is used to feed information about the goods ordered into the main stores' computer (Figure 18.8). The two main stores operating the service are Tesco and Mainstop, although some smaller shops, such as a bakery and a chemist, have also joined the service. The goods are delivered to the person's home by delivery drivers who have been funded by the Manpower Services Commission, using vans that are used for 'meals-on-wheels' services during lunchtimes.

Not only is the service a simple teleshopping service, it is also an information service that contains details of local events, welfare benefits and a range of other useful material.

Figure 18.8   *The teleshopping main computer which controls each Videotex terminal*

Information technology and the Police Force

Crime has become very sophisticated (Figure 18.9) and, as a result, harder to detect. To handle this, the police have very sophisticated methods of crime detection. '**Information**' is the key word in crime detection and this information must be accurate and obtained quickly.

To obtain immediate access to up-to-date information about crime and criminals, computers are used. The old manual systems were far too slow and, in 1968 the Police National Computer Unit was set up in Hendon to provide all the various police forces throughout the county with fast, up-to-date information.

Figure 18.9   *'Fred is very sophisticated! He uses a computer in all of our robberies!'*

The Police National Computer (PNC) and its background

The **Police National Computer (PNC)** now provides quick access, day and night information of national as well as local significance, to all the police forces in England, Scotland and Wales. The Police National Computer is situated at Hendon. It is linked to terminals in police stations all over the country. The linking is done via the telephone systems, using modems. There are a large number of terminals attached to the main computer so there is a fairly complex switching mechanism and this allows each terminal to obtain information from the main computer in as short a time as possible.

The information held on the PNC is separated into indexes. Each deals with a particular subject. It is possible for some crossreferencing of these indexes. By looking at a particular index, a policeman can obtain any relevant information and also find out where to get further information. We shall now look at some of these indexes.

Stolen and Suspect Vehicle Index

One crime which has increased tremendously over the last few years is car theft. Every day hundreds of cars are stolen. Some are taken only for joy rides and recovered by the police fairly quickly. Others are stolen permanently and are re-sold, and some are stripped down for their parts. Often, cars stolen are used in other crimes.

As soon as the owner reports that a car is missing, information such as registration number, make and colour are keyed into the PNC via one of the many terminals. Once this information has been obtained, it is transmitted via radio to the patrol cars who are then on the lookout for the vehicle.

The index is divided into two parts. Firstly, there is the index of registration numbers and, secondly, an index of engine and chassis numbers. The first index is used more often, but when cars are involved in crime, they quite often have false plates and so the second index is used to identify them. If only part of a registration number is known, it is possible for the computer to produce a list of possible vehicles. Details of stolen contractors' plant and marine engines are also contained in the index.

Vehicle Owner Index

The information for this index comes from the Driver and Vehicle Licensing Centre (DVLC) at Swansea. The index contains all the names and addresses of the registered keepers of motor vehicles, together with descriptions of the vehicles.

If the registation number is known, then the owner can be contacted if the car is stolen and he is not aware of the theft. Again, if the number is only partially known, it can still be traced.

It is possible for the Stolen and Suspect Vehicles Index and the Vehicle Owner Index to be searched together, using the registration number as the search key.

Fingerprints Index

The Fingerprints Index is a coded version of the National Fingerprint Collection which is held by the police at New Scotland Yard. Any person who has been convicted of a crime will have his fingerprints held on this index. It is used to check the identity of prints found at the scene of a crime with prints of people who have been previously convicted.

Names Indexes

The police have records in these indexes of people who fall into any of the following categories.
1 Persons convicted of serious offences.
2 Persons wanted or sought by the Police for various reasons.
3 Persons missing or found.
4 Disqualified drivers.

As soon as the police receive details about any person who falls into one of more of the above categories, they can obtain the information from the PNC. Once they have this, they can then decide whether they need more information. These indexes also tell the user where to obtain further, more detailed, information.

The computer can assist the police greatly by informing them if a suspected person is likely to be armed or dangerous. It is also possible for the computer to search all the files simultaneously to find out anything known about a particular person.

Broadcast system

Other than the indexes, the PNC is also used to help the police in other ways. The **Broadcast system** allows one Police Force to send urgent information to other Police Forces. The clever thing about this system is that the PNC can choose the particular Forces which should be told the information. If a car is stolen and used in a serious crime, then all the Police Forces along, say, a certain stretch of motorway can be alerted. Ports and airports can also be alerted using this system to stop criminals escaping to another country.

Crossreference system

The PNC can also help to find information which is not on its files by telling the user, by a reference number, how he or she can obtain the details from a particular Police Station.

Other computers used by the police

Most of the Police Forces now have their own computers in their Police Headquarters. These computers are used for administrative work but some are used to help to solve crimes.

MIRIAM

Figure 18.10 *How MIRIAM sorts out all the information from a large-scale enquiry, so that the senior officers can make decisions about how to solve the crime*

Recently, the Essex Police have been trying out a £600 000 system called **MIRIAM (Major Incident Room Index and Action Management)**. This computer will

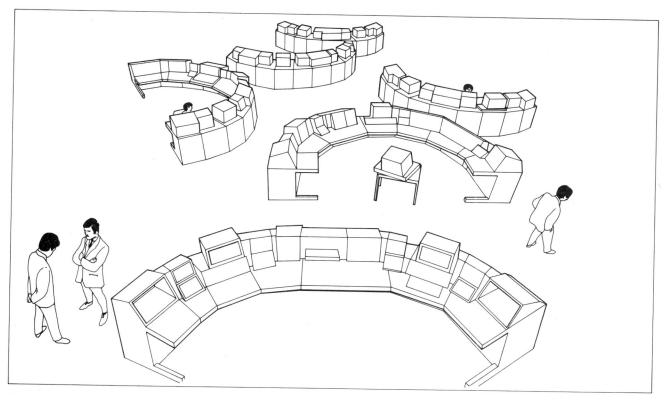

Figure 18.11 *A Command and Control system used by one of Britain's Police Forces*

be used to contain information from enquiries about serious crimes, so that senior officers can decide how to go about their investigations (Figure 18.10). It is hoped that MIRIAM will enable criminals to be caught much sooner (remember the Yorkshire Ripper, who evaded capture for five years!)

If the Essex Police find MIRIAM effective, then the Home Office will look into the possibility of every Police Force having one. Figure 18.11 shows a Command Control System used by one of Britain's Police Forces.

Computers and traffic control

Computers are also used by the police for the control of traffic. Junctions which have major problems with traffic jams, often have computer-controlled traffic light systems. The computer can control which lights should be given priority due to the build up of traffic. By quickly analysing the numbers of cars that are approaching the lights, it can decide how long the lights should stay red or green. This method can prevent traffic building up at trouble spots.

In case accidents happen at these spots, it is possible for the computerized system to be overriden using a manual system. You have probably seen television cameras at some of the large road junctions. The police use these cameras to watch the position of the traffic so that, if an accident happens, the lights can be altered manually. (Figure 18.12).

Figure 18.12 *The police use cameras to monitor the traffic at large road junctions*

Computers in Libraries _____

You may be lucky to have a computer in your local library. If your library ticket looks like that in Figure 18.13 then your library uses a computerized system for recording the details of when books are loaned or returned.

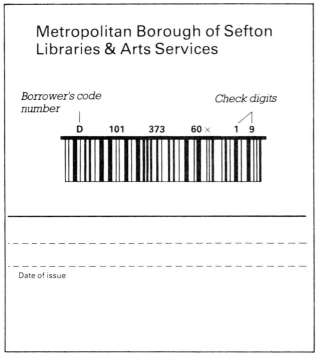

Figure 18.13 *The bar code on a library ticket. The last two digits of the borrower's code number are used as check digits*

Recording details when books are loaned and returned _____

Most libraries use a **bar code** system. This involves having a bar code on the borrower's library ticket and another bar code on the fly-leaf of the book. The librarian uses a **bar code reader**, usually a wand, to input the information contained on the borrower's ticket and on the book.

If you look at Figure 18.13 you will notice that a code number can be seen above the bars. If the bar code gets damaged, then this code can be typed in by the librarian using a keyboard. The last two digits in this code are check digits that are used to check that the details of the borrower can be linked with the details of the book using the bar codes. (Figure 18.14).

When a book is returned, the borrower doesn't need his library ticket because the computer already knows who has borrowed the book. The bar code reader is passed across the bar code in the library book and this lets the computer know that the book has been returned. A light flashes if the book is reserved by another reader, and the book can be placed on one side.

Figure 18.14 *Recording the details when a book is borrowed*

Reserving books _____

Reserving books is easy. The book code is typed into the terminal and, when a borrower returns the reserved book, the librarian is alerted so that she won't lend the book to someone else.

Recording details about new members _____

Libraries keep library cards with bar codes on them. Each new member is given one of these after his name and address has been filled in on the card.

Before joining a library you will be asked to fill in a form. This form is used as a **source document** for input to the computer. Normally the form will have these **fields**:
Name
Address
Some indication as to whether the borrower is a child.
The borrower's library code (this is above the bar code).

All the details about members are held on the **Members Master File**. Information about new members is added to a **Members Transaction File** which is sorted into order and then used to update the Members Master File at the end of the week. Some computers give details about members who have not used their tickets for a few years, so that they can be deleted so as not to take up valuable computer space.

Cataloguing of books

All libraries have catalogues of their books. Sometimes the catalogue consists of cards with information about each book and these cards are kept in sets of drawers. Computers can make cataloguing a lot easier. New book are constantly coming in, and these have to be recorded. Also, old and damaged books will need to be taken out of service. When each new book arrives, it is given a bar code. These bar codes are prepared in advance, just like borrower's bar codes. Additions and deletions of books are recorded by the librarian onto a **Book Transaction File** (Figure 18.15). At the end of each week the Book Transaction File is sorted into book code number order and used to update the Book Master File. This is shown in Figure 18.16. Notice in the diagram that after the information about the book is entered via the keyboard and VDU that it is validated to make sure that it is correct. All the files are sorted into book number order. The reason for this is that in this system magnetic tape is used. If the details are not in order then the tape will have to be continually rewound when the file is being updated.

Microfilm and microfiche

Catalogues of all the books a library has are usually contained on microfilm or microfiche. This is because, using these, large quantities of information can be kept in a very small space. The film or fiche is updated regularly, and so new additions and deletions of books are made.

Figure 18.15 *Recording details of a new book into the computer via a terminal*

Privacy

Libraries could keep records of which books a particular person reads. This would be very time-consuming, but the information could be interesting to, perhaps, a potential employer. Borrower's names and addresses are on the **Borrowers Master File**. This could be sold to an outside organization e.g. a book club, which might send unwanted mail.

It is also possible to sort borrowers into groups according to which sorts of books they borrow. So it would be possible for this information to be passed on to, say, a manufacturer. This could mean, for example, that a manufacturer of greenhouses could send out information to every who borrowed gardening books. It is very unlikely that this sort of invasion of privacy could actually happen, but it is, nevertheless possible. The councils who control the libraries need to make sure that it doesn't happen.

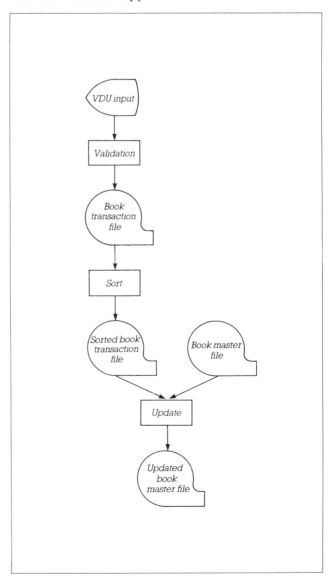

Figure 18.16 *Systems flowchart for updating the Book Master File*

Information technology and education

A few hundred years ago, life was relatively simple. Any person could be taught to live in society by his or her parents. Children in an agricultural society can begin work at quite a young age. It is common in Africa for eight-year-olds to be given the task of looking after the cattle. Our technological society is now so complex that it takes many more years to learn how to cope with it. Nowadays, the effective school leaving age is eighteen, since very few sixteen-year-olds are now in full-time employment. Requiring individuals to spend the first twenty years of their lives in education is becoming more and more common.

At the same time, few people can be trained to do just one job during their lifetimes. They will probably need retraining every four of five years. The result is that education and training will become lifelong experiences (spending the rest of your life at school!).

However, the new technology is itself contributing to this process. Instead of an instructor telling students everything they need to know, the class room of tomorrow will contain microcomputers, linked to a mainframe. This will instruct the students, test their understanding and give help where it is needed. Of course, there will still be a human teacher at hand to explain certain points to students who do not understand. It would not be possible to program a computer to cope with every problem that a student might have.

As well as this change in **how** students are taught, computers will affect **what** is taught, too. Schools in the past tended to favour children with good memories. The examination system tested what facts children could remember, it did not examine what they could **do** with their knowledge. This will not be good enough in the future. The computers will have far better memories than any humans, so the skills of the future will be those of finding information and using it.

Education toys and games

Nowadays, most children will have come into contact with microprocessor-controlled toys and games. A look through a toy catalogue reveals the multitude of computer based toys and games. Such popular toys include: 'Speak & Spell'; 'Speak & Maths'; and 'Maths Marvel'.

'Speak & Spell' was the first popular use of speech synthesis. The game consists of a keyboard, speech synthesizer and an LED (light emitting display) used to display letters. The 'brains' of the machine is a microprocessor.

In the game, a word is 'spoken' (with an American accent) and you type in the word using the keyboard. If your spelling of the word is correct, then the game tells you you are right. The game provides an ideal introduction to English as well as teaching some simple keyboard skills (Figure 18.17).

Both 'Speak & Maths' and 'Maths Marvel' are like 'Speak & Spell', except that they ask questions on maths to test the user on addition, subtraction, multiplication and division.

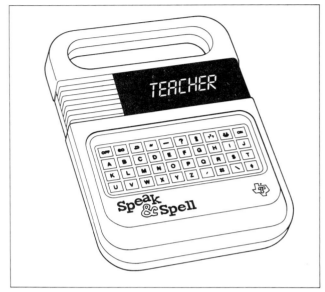

Figure 18.17   'Speak & Spell' game

The BBC Domesday Project

The **BBC Domesday Project** was begun in 1986 to commemorate the 900th anniversary of the Domesday Book. You may remember from your history lessons that the Domesday Book was set up by William the Conqueror to survey his recently acquired kingdom. The idea of the modern day Domesday Project is to provide a unique picture of the United Kingdom in the eighties, using the latest computer and video technology.

The modern-day Domesday Book is the equivalent of more than 300 mighty volumes contained on two **Laser Vision ROM** videodiscs. These discs are made of plastic and look rather like compact discs, except they are larger (12 inches). They are able to hold both digital and analogue data and so video pictures, computer text and graphics are held, all on the same disc. Of the two videodiscs, the **national** disc consists of official data, maps and photographic records. The other disc, called the **community** disc is a more personal view of the country, and has been compiled by more than one million adults and children.

The discs can hold a huge amount of information. In fact, each disc holds the equivalent of one million pages of text.

In addition to the two Domesday Project discs, another two discs are planned; one entitled 'Our Rural Heritage' and the other, 'Art Galleries'.

Home computer games

Figure 18.18 *Many computer games are educational!*

Figure 18.19 *Computer games should not be allowed to get out of hand!*

Many computer games are educational to a greater or a lesser extent (Figure 18.18). For many young children, computer games are their first introduction to computers. Any such game is educational to some extent because it teaches the user to set up the computer, how to load software and some simple keyboard skills. Games, however, should not be allowed to get out of hand (Figure 18.19).

Many of the popular games such as 'Monopoly', 'Chess', 'Blockbusters', 'Scrabble', 'Trivial Pursuits' etc., can be played on your home computer. Some have the added advantage that you don't need anyone else to play with.

After playing games, many people start to look around for more serious uses for their computer. Many successful computer experts started off playing computer games.

Computer Assisted Learning (CAL)

(CAL) is a way of using the computer to act as a teacher. The good thing about CAL is that the computer has an infinite amount of patience and time. If you get an answer wrong the computer won't mind.

Most secondary schools now have computer networks. A **network** consists of computers acting as terminals which are all connected together and to a central computer that controls the running of the system. The central computer is called the **supervisor** because it supervises the running of the network. The disk drive, printer and other peripheral services can be shared by all the terminals, so cutting out a lot of the hardware costs. Only one program is needed, since all the terminals can access a single disk drive.

Medicine

Using the words in the list below, copy out and complete sentences A to F. Underline the words you have inserted. The words may be used once, more than once, or not at all.

disk   code   lists   monitor   diagnosis
office   tape

A Computers are good at looking at and comparing_____and this makes them very useful in finding suitable recipients of hearts, kidneys and other organs that have been donated.

B Computers are used to help determine certain illnesses. This is called computer_____.

C Computers can be used to_____instruments in intensive care units.

D Hospitals use computers to keep information about patients. Inpatient records are held on magnetic_____whereas outpatients records can be held on magnetic_____because the records are only needed now and again.

E So that only certain people can look at confidential patient files, a_____has to be keyed in before the computer can be used.

F Computer terminals in the supplies_____are used to reorder important medical supplies.

Teleshopping

Using the words in the list below, copy out and complete sentences A to F. Underline the words you have inserted. The words may be used once, more than once, or not at all.

teleshopping   terminal   disabled   Videotex
catalogue   welfare

A Computers are being used by some local authorities to help socially-disadvantaged people, such as the elderly or_____.

B The computer enables these people to shop from home or at a local centre. This is called_____.

C Teleshopping uses a_____system.

D The shoppers use a_____to key in their orders and the information is fed into the store's computer.

E The customers know what to order because the store supplies them with a_____beforehand.

F The service also provides an information service with details about_____benefits and local events.

The Police

Using the words in the list below, copy out and complete sentences A to F. Underline the words you have inserted. The words may be used once, more than once, or not at all.

owner   indexes   PNC   traffic   MIRIAM
modems   fingerprints   DVLC

A The Police National Computer or_____for short, is situated at Hendon and is connected to terminals in police stations throughout the British Isles via telephone lines using_____.

B The PNC is separated into_____.

C The vehicle_____index comes from the_____at Swansea.

D A new police system called_____is used by Essex police to help solve serious crimes.

E Computers can also be used to control_____in large cities.

F The national_____collection is also held on computer at New Scotland Yard.

Libraries

Using the words in the list below, copy out and complete sentences A to G. Underline the words you have inserted. The words may be used once, more than once, or not at all.

bar code   terminals   code   check
keyboard   book   microfilm

A The most up-to-date library system for recording the details when books are borrowed or returned uses a_____system.

B A series of black and white lines represent a_____.

C If the bar code gets damaged, then the code can be input via a_____.

D The last two numbers in the code are_____digits.

E The computer links the_____code with the borrower's code.

F _____are used for enquiries about books as well as reserving books.

G Catalogues of the books are often kept on_____or microfiche.

Education

Using the words in the list below, copy out and complete sentences A to H. Underline the words you have inserted. The words may be used once, more than once, or not at all.

microprocessor   information   Maths Marvel
Speak & Maths   Speak & Spell
Computer Assisted Learning   computer games
network   peripheral   supervisor   central

A In the past the skills needed to start work were fairly simple, but nowadays they are very complex. The skills of the future will be those of finding _____ and using it.

B Young children soon come into contact with _____ controlled toys and games.

C Many children use a microprocessor-controlled speech synthesizer called _____, to learn how to spell certain words.

D Similar devices asks maths questions. Two such devices are _____ and _____.

E Home _____ have some educational value.

F A computer is often used as a substitute for a teacher. CAL or _____ can be used to teach students about a variety of subjects.

G Many schools now have a _____ of computers. Each computers is connected via wires to a _____ computer called the _____.

H Each terminal in the network has access to _____ devices such as line printers, graph plotters and disk drives.

≫ Things to do

Medicine

1 Computer systems are now being used extensively in hospitals. Computers form part of life-support systems and medical records are kept in computer files.

  a Blood pressure is a human physical response suitable for monitoring by computer. Suggest **two** others.

  b Give **three** reasons why computers are used in life-support systems.

  c Give **three** tasks for which human medical staff are more suitable than computers.

  d Give **three** of the benefits gained by both hospital staff and patients, in having medical records held in a computer file.

  e It has been suggested that, when personal data is held on file, people should have the right to see the contents of records which refer to them. Argue the case for and against the right of a patient to see his or her own records.

2 Small computers now find more frequent application in places such as medical centres.

  a Why should such a place find it helpful to use a computer?

  b What type of backing storage would be used, and why should this type be chosen?

  c What changes would there be to the job of the receptionist?

  d Write a list of the sort of information about the patients, that the centre would keep on file.

3 Explain briefly, giving **one** example in each case, how a computer-based information retrieval system could help each of the following:

  a A doctor in his surgery

  b A nurse in a hospital

  c A hospital administrator

The Police

1 a Explain what PNC stands for and how it is used by the police to help solve crimes.

  b The PNC is divided into indexes. Each index deals with a different subject.
Name **three** of the indexes and write a short paragraph about each index describing how it is used.

  c Many people commit crimes in areas hundreds of miles away from where they live. Catching these criminals can involve several Police Forces liaising. Explain how the Broadcast system is used.

2 The records shown in the illustration were held in manual files before computers. Now, with the use of computers, much more information can be held.

  a Give **three** things which can now be done which would have been much more difficult with manual files.

  b What is likely to have happened to the people who used to be employed in keeping the manual files up to date?

	Number of Individual files
General computers	
DHSS	51 000 000
Vehicle owners	32 800 000
TV licences	18 600 000
Blood groups	11 000
Immigration computers	
Landing and embarkation	1 500 000
Refugee index	15 000
Police computers	
Criminal names	4 800 000
Fingerprints	3 300 000
Probation records	400 000
Disqualified drivers	290 000
Prison records	300 000
Wanted or missing persons	107 000
MI5 suspect list	18 000
Total 113 141 000 individual files	

3 Computers are often used to control traffic. Explain how this is done.

4 It has been suggested that all persons over the age of 16 should be fingerprinted and the records kept on computer files. Whilst this would be very helpful to the police, it is felt by some people that this is not a good idea.
  a Give **one** way in which this would help the police.
  b Do you consider it a good idea? Give **two** reasons for your answer.

Libraries

1 A library uses a computerized system to record which books have been loaned. When books are loaned the following data is recorded on computer files:
The borrower's code number.
The code numbers of the books which have been borrowed.
  a Suggest, with a reason, a suitable method of data capture.
  b State **two** reasons why code numbers are used rather than the book titles.
  c State **one** way in which a computerized library system might affect the privacy of a borrower.

2 a How can you tell by looking at your library ticket whether the library uses a computerized system?
  b Give **two** advantages that a computerized library system would have over a manual system.
  c When a borrower returns his books he does not need to have his library ticket with him. Explain why this is so.
  d Libraries often make use of computer output on microfilm (COM). Explain how COM is used in a library.

3 Here is a passage about a computerized library system. Read it carefully.
A lending library uses a computer to hold details of its books and of its users. It keeps two files, the book file and the user file. The book file has details of every book in the library, and the user file has details of every user. The system:
Allows users to reserve library books which are on loan to someone else.
Check when books are returned, to see if they have been reserved by someone else.
Sends out reminders on overdue books.
Checks that a borrower is not trying to take more books than he is allowed.

Answer the following questions.
  a What kind of backing store would be most suitable for this application?
  b Name **two** other peripherals which would be needed.

  c Apart from the name of each book and its author and publisher, give **four** other items of information which would be kept in each record of the book file.
  d Apart from the name and address and other personal details, give **two** other items of information which would be kept in each record of the user file.
  e How would each file be updated when a user borrowed a book?
  f How would each file be updated when a user returned a book?
  g What would happen when a user wanted to reserve a book?
  h How would reminders about overdue books be prepared?

Education

1 a Many children encounter computer or microprocessor toys or games at a very early age.
Name **two** such games or toys you have seen or heard about and describe what they do.
  b Computers can be found in almost every school. The picture was completely different ten or so years ago. Only certain schools then had computers.
What developments have led to the widespread use of computers in schools?

2 Find out how your school makes use of computers for teaching certain subjects and for administration. Give **two** ways in which each of the following might make use of a microcomputer in school.
  a The school office
  b Administration of school examinations
  c One of the following department in the school:
Science
Art
Geography

3 The head of a school decides to use a microcomputer to help her in the running of the school. The head would like to store information about each pupil in the school.
  a What details about each pupil would probably be held on the computer?
  b What benefits would the head get from the use of the computer?
  c What possible dangers could there be in storing pupil records on a computer, rather than keeping them in a filing cabinet?
  d What precautions and rules would be needed to reduce these dangers?

4 *The BBC Domesday Project was set up in 1986 to commemorate the 900th anniversary of the Domesday Book.*
Explain what the Domesday Project is and how you think it could be used by schools.

5 *A file holds records of pupils. Two details which are kept are the name and year of birth of each pupil. Describe **two** checks which could be used to validate a record.*

6 *The computer can be used as a 'teacher' in the classroom. This type of learning is called CAL (Computer Assisted Learning). Describe any program that you have used yourself, or have heard or read about, which uses CAL.*

7 *Many schools now use a computer network. Explain what advantages a network has over buying individual computers.*

19

The people who work with computers

Figure 19.1 *A large computer system*

Only the large organizations, with large computer systems, have a full-time staff concerned with the computer system (Figure 19.1). Many of the smaller computer installations don't employ specialist staff. Instead they retrain their existing staff and use the computer as a piece of office equipment in the same way that they would use a telephone or photocopier.

A typical medium-sized installation might employ some three or four staff, whereas a large installation might need twenty to thirty staff. A very large installation, such as found in a bank or an insurance company, might employ several hundred people. For this type of installation it will be necessary for the staff to work shifts in order that the computer is kept working 24 hours per day, 7 days per week.

Many computers, called **personal computers** are used by individuals to help them in the running of their businesses. These individuals have to be versatile and have to be able to cope with all the likely problems as they crop up.

People directly involved with running a large computer department

We shall now look at the work of personnel who would be involved in the running of a large computer department, where they are employed in clearly defined jobs (Figure 19.2).

The computer (or data processing) manager

This is the person who is in overall charge of the whole computer department. Robert reports directly to the directors of the company. As well as being responsible for the technical side of things, he also needs to be able to organize staff and appoint new staff.

As the data processing manager, he will have had experience in the three branches below him i.e. systems analysis, programming and operations.

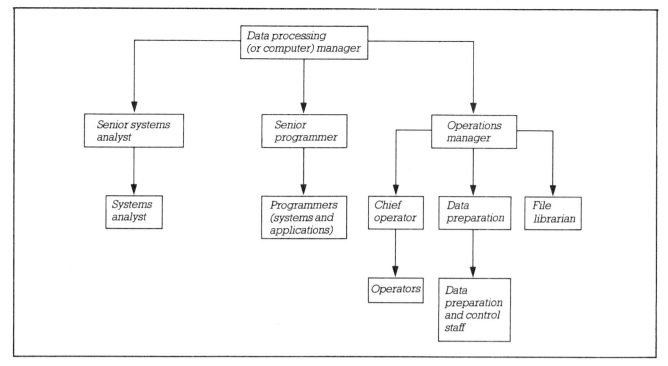

Figure 19.2 *How the jobs in a large computer department are organized*

The senior systems analyst _____

Susan is the senior systems analyst and is responsible to the data processing manager. She is responsible for all the systems analysts under her.

Systems analysts _____

Figure 19.3 *Jane, a systems analyst*

Figure 19.3 shows Jane who is a systems analyst. Jane's job is to look at the way the information is passed and processed by the existing computer system and to see if it could be better done by new hardware or software or by altering the existing system. If the company hasn't used a computer system before, then the systems analyst will look at the manual system to see how best it could be done with a computer.

Jane also has to decide which particular hardware and software is best for the job and should be bought. She has to look ahead at the next computer system. It is common to find one computer being dismantled while another is being used and yet another, newer, computer is being connected up! (Figure 19.4).

Jane's job is an extremely skilled one. She needs to have an extensive knowledge of computers and their capabilities.

A lot of her time is spent talking to the people who use the computer, called **users**, to find out what it is that they want the computer to do.

The senior programmer _____

Keith is the senior programmer and he is responsible for the organization of the programming department. He is in charge of both types of programmers: systems and applications.

Programmers

There are two types of programmers: the **systems programmer** and the **applications programmer**. The applications programmer writes programs to do various tasks or applications. The systems programmer writes the programs to control the computer system.

117

Figure 19.4 *It is common to find one computer being dismantled, another being used, and yet another, newer, computer being connected up!*

John is an applications computer programmer and it is his job to produce or amend computer programs. Before writing a new program, the programmer will receive specific instructions from the systems analyst to tell him what exactly the program must do.

John will spend some of his time amending programs. As an example, in a payroll program (a program for working out wages) the tax rates or National Insurance contributions might change after a budget and need to be re-programmed. Very few programs work first time, so John spends a lot of his time correcting mistakes in **(debugging)** his programs. So that other programmers can use and where necessary alter the program, John writes down an outline of the way the program works, called **documentation**.

The operations manager

David is the operations manager. He has a lot more staff than the other members of junior management (i.e. the senior systems analyst and senior programmer).

A lot of his time is spent in the day-to-day management of staff. Generally, the operations manager will be working with less qualified staff and a lot of his time will be spent in training them.

Shift leader/chief operator

Stephen is a shift leader and is responsible for the work of his computer operators. His boss is David, the operations manager.

Computer operators

Suzanne is a computer operator. She sits at a desk called an **operator's console**. A computer operator is responsible for the setting up of the computer system (starting it up) and running various programs. Suzanne's job also involves making sure that the computer has everything necessary, and correctly set up, to perform its task, e.g. paper in the line printer, disks or tapes in their drives etc. A computer **log** is kept by the operator which monitors the jobs that are done by the computer. In some systems a log is also kept by the computer itself. Any malfunctions in the equipment are reported by Suzanne to the engineers.

The data preparation supervisor

Norma is a data preparation supervisor and is responsible for the work of the data preparation/keyboard operators. She allocates the work and provides training for new staff. She is reponsible to the operations manager.

Data preparation operators/keyboard operators

Paula is a keyboard operator who sits at a VDU and keyboard and types into the computer, information from a specially prepared form called a **source document**. When she types or keys in the information it is stored on magnetic disk for future processing by the computer. This type of data capture is called **key-to-disk**. Paula is a bit worried, at the moment, about the future of her job, because a lot of other staff are now keying in their own information at their own terminals instead of sending the work for her to do.

File librarian

John is a file librarian and is responsible for programs and data files when they are not being used by the computer (Figure 19.5). John has to make sure that there is no unauthorized use of the software and he keeps a record of the use of the software. He is also responsible for maintaining catalogues and indexes of all the files kept so that they may be found quickly. He arranges the repairs of any damaged tapes or disks and ensure that duplicates are kept for file security.

Figure 19.5 *The file librarian keeps tapes and disks in a certain order so that they can be found quickly*

Engineers and technicians

The word 'engineer' has no exact meaning in English. In, for example, Germany, an engineer is a highly trained person, equivalent to a lawyer or doctor. Many people believe that Britain's poor economy is because we do not give engineers enough importance.

The people who design computers are **professional** engineers. They usually have a university degree in physics or engineering. They have to be good at science (to understand the new devices that are invented), at mathematics and at economics and marketing. They are also experts at electronics.

Because they need so many skills, professional engineers can rarely be expert at everything. They may, for example, not know very much about how to make particular circuits or how a particular chip works. Therefore they rely greatly on **technician** engineers. These are the people who really make computers work. When a professional engineer wants to try out a new idea, he or she will usually consult the technician engineer about a **prototype** – a hand-built working version.

Service engineers and technicians

To operate or program a computer it is not necessary to know anything about the complex electronic components contained in it. However, the service engineer or technician needs this technical knowledge in order to service or repair them.

Computers today are extremely reliable but, when one does go wrong, it is essential that the computer is repaired as quickly as possible. Because the computer is sometimes used 24 hours a day, the service engineers and technicians may work shifts or be available for 'call out'. Nowadays, the computers are designed so that they have various test points which the technicians attach to meters (Figure 19.6). This will tell them on which circuit board the fault lies, so that the complete circuit board can be replaced. It is much quicker and cheaper to replace the whole circuit board rather than try to locate the faulty component on a board containing thousands of them.

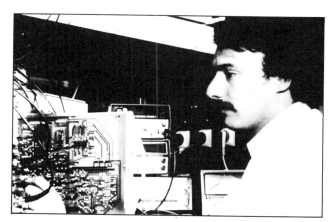

Figure 19.6 *This computer engineer is testing the slot in the circuit boards inside the CPU*

People who work in computer production

Research

Researchers are constantly seeking to improve computers by trying to make them faster, smaller, more efficient and less costly.

Computer design

Once the ideas have come from the research team, the next step is to sit down and design the actual computer. The computers are designed by **computer designers** (sometimes called computer architects).

Computer construction

As do motor cars, computers consist of many individual components. These components are often manufactured separately and then brought together for the final assembly.

Construction of computers is highly automated and doesn't employ many people.

Computer sales and marketing

Computer salespeople have the job of selling the computer hardward and software to the customers.

Test yourself

Using the words in the list below copy out and complete sentences A to K. Underline the words you have inserted. The words may be used once, more than once, or not at all.

computer programmer computer operator
user documents file librarian debugging
repair personal computer line printer
systems analyst computer manager technician

A *A lot of individuals use a_____ to help them run their business.*

B *When a company thinks of installing a computer system for the first time, a_____ looks at the manual systems to see if they could be performed more efficiently by a_____.*

C *He will consult the_____ to see what his or her requirements are.*

D *The person who instructs the computer what to do and how to do it is the_____.*

E *Before writing the program, the programmer obtains specifications from the_____.*

F *A lot of time is spent by the programmer finding and correcting errors in the program. This process is called_____.*

G *When correct, the programmer fully_____ the program.*

H *The_____ is the person whose job it is to make sure that the right programs are being used and that there is paper in the_____.*

I *The_____ is responsible for the running of the whole computer department.*

J *The_____ keeps all the software catalogued and indexed. He also arranges the_____ of damaged tapes.*

K *The computer_____ maintains and repairs the computer and its peripheral equipment.*

Things to do

1 *The person with the responsibility for the day-to-day efficiency of the computer and the operating staff is which of these?*
   a *Computer operator*
   b *Chief programmer*
   c *Systems analyst*
   d *Operations manager*
   e *Engineer*

2 *Which of these people has the job of changing magnetic tapes and disks?*
   a *A computer engineer*
   b *A data preparation operator*
   c *A computer operator*
   d *A systems analyst*
   e *An operations manager*

3 *Which of these jobs does a computer programmer do?*
   a *Investigates problems that may be eased by using a computer.*
   b *Writes instructions in a language a computer will accept.*
   c *Organizes the efficient use of computer personnel.*
   d *Prepares data on to punched cards or tape.*
   e *Runs computer programs and inputs data when required.*

4 a *What is a file librarian's job?*
   b *Name two items in a program user manual that would be of special interest to the file librarian.*
   c *Who would do the file librarian's job in a small computer installation?*

5 *The data processing department in a large company is to be split into two sections: those who prepare the programs and those who run them.*
   a *Name three different job titles from the running section.*
   b *Briefly describe the job of a systems analyst.*

6 *Use the information contained in this chapter to decide who would do the following tasks.*
   a *Establish how a job could be done better using a computer.*
   b *Maintain and keep records of all the available software.*
   c *Persuade someone that a computer could do his or her job more efficiently and cheaply.*
   d *Load input and output peripherals and backing store devices.*
   e *Store files and arrange regular maintenance of tapes and disks.*
   f *Look into new ways of storing information and making computers faster, smaller and cheaper.*
   g *Use the key-to-disk method to input information straight into the computer.*

Glossary

A

Abacus A computing device consisting of a frame with movable beads, used for counting and simple arithmetic.

Access Obtain **data** from some storage device.

Access time The average time to retrieve **data** from some storage device.

Accumulator The most important **register** in a computer or **microprocessor**, where the results of calculations are stored.

Address The unique number given to each memory location to identify it.

Algorithm The step-by-step solution to a problem.

ALU (Arithmetic and Logic Unit) The part of a computer or **microprocessor** that carries out calculations.

Analogue-to-digital converter A device that changes continuously changing quantities (such as temperature) into **digital** quanities.

Ancestral file system A system whereby some of the older **files** are kept so that, if a more recent version of a file is lost, it may be recreated from the older files.

Artificial intelligence The science of developing computers that 'think' like humans.

ASCII (American Standard Code for Information Interchange) A code for representing **characters** in **binary** form.

Assembly language A low-level programming language which represents binary codes by easy-to-remember **mnemonics**. Such programs are converted into **machine code** by an assembler.

ATMS (Automated Teller Machine System) Commonly called a cash dispenser, but also used for obtaining bank statements or depositing funds.

Automation The automatic control of a process or system without requiring a human operator.

B

Backing storage A system for storing data outside the main computer memory.

Back-up copies Copies kept in case things go wrong and **records** are destroyed.

BACS (Bankers' Automated Clearing Services Ltd) The service provided by the larger banks for the clearing of bank cheques and the paying of standing orders and direct debits.

Bar-code reader An optical **input device** that reads the data from a set of parallel lines on a commodity being sold (see **POS**).

BASIC (Beginners All-purpose Symbolic Instruction Code) A high-level language specially developed for those learning computer programming.

Baud rate A data transmission rate, the number of **bits** per second.

BBC Domesday Project A project to collect information about life in the United Kingdom in the 1980s and display it on a special computer system.

Binary A counting system with a base of 2, which only uses the two symbols 1 and 0 and can therefore be represented by the ON and OFF states of electronic switches.

Bit (BInary digiT) The **data** stored by a single electronic 'switch' which may be ON or OFF.

Bottom-up A term used to describe problem-solving by starting with the programming language and working to a solution by gradual modification. This method leads to **fragile** programs, and is only used when the programmer wishes to experiment with some new ideas.

Buffer A set of temporary memory locations used to hold data which is being moved into or out of the computer.

Bug A mistake in a computer program.

Byte A set of eight bits, used to store single **characters** or parts of a **binary** number.

C

CAD (Computer Aided Design) An applications program that allows a designer to draw and edit on a computer screen before transferring to paper.

CAL (Computer Assisted Learning) The process of using computers for the instruction, training or testing of learners.

Calculator An electronic or mechanical device used for performing arithmetic.

Capacity The number of **bytes** of data that can be stored in a system.

Card punch Equipment that allows the storage of data on a special card by punching holes in it according to a special code.

Card reader An **input device** that reads data from the holes in a punched card.

Ceefax The **teletext** service of the BBC.

Character Any symbol, letter or digit stored in or entered into a computer.

Check digit An extra digit added to the end of a number to check if it has been transmitted correctly.

Chip A slice of **semiconductor** material, containing electronic memory or logic circuits encapsulated in plastic or ceramic.

CMI (Computer Managed Instruction) The use of computers to record the progress of students through a course of instruction, particularly if the computer does not actually present the instruction itself (see **CAL**).

COBOL (COmmon Business Oriented Language) A high-level programming language used mainly by business and commerce.

Code The meaning given to **bit** pattern; for example, the **binary** code.

COM (Computer Output on Microfilm) The output from a computer screen is photographed and put on **microfilm**. This allows a large amount of information to be held in a small space.

COMAL A high-level programming language made by combining the simplicity of **BASIC** with the power of **PASCAL**. Used mainly for teaching purposes.

Command An instruction, usually in a high-level language, that is performed directly; for example, LOAD, SAVE and RUN in Basic.

Compatibility The ability of one computer to run the programs, or access the data, of another.

Compiler A low-level program that translates the whole of a **source code** into **machine code** before running it (see also **Interpreter**).

Computer A machine that collects, stores, processes and outputs data.

Computerate A newly invented word to describe a person who understands computers and knows what they are used for (by analogy with 'literate').

Computer operator The person who operates a computer (usually only applied to **mainframe** computers).

Copper-clad board Insulated plastic board with a surface coating of copper. Used for making **printed circuit boards**.

CPU (Central Processing Unit) The part of a computer that controls all its procsses and is responsible for collecting and executing the instructions in the **program**.

Crash The unexpected stop of a program when it meets a particular condition. Usually caused by a **bug** in the software.

CRT (Cathode Ray Tube) A display screen, rather like that of a television set.

Cursor The marker (usually flashing) on the computer screen, that shows where the next typed character will be displayed.

D

Daisy-wheel A particular type of printer, where each character is formed by a different print head. These print heads are stored on a wheel that looks rather like a daisy.

Data Information in a form that the computer can understand.

Database A series of files that allow access to data in convenient forms.

Data capture How the computer gets information for processing.

Data processing The collection, **verification**, storage, processing and presentation of information, usually by electronic means.

Debugging The process of removing **bugs** from a program.

Digital Similar in meaning to **binary**.

Disk (or disc) A magnetic storage device for external **data**.

Disk drive An **input/output device** that reads data from, or writes data to, the disk.

DMA (Direct Memory Access) The ability of an external device to access the memory of a computer without going through its **microprocessor** or **CPU**.

Documentation Information, usually on paper, that explains how equipment or programs are used. Program documentation may also explain how the program is constructed, and this allows alterations to be made to it at a later date.

Document reader A device that can turn specially written print into **binary** code, automatically.

DOS (Disk Operating System) A program which controls the operation of a **disk drive**.

Dot-matrix printer A type of printer where the characters are formed by a set of needles each of which produces a single dot.

Download To take data from a large computer (usually **mainframe**) to a smaller one **(microcomputer)**, usually using a telephone, radio or television link between the two computers.

E

Edit To alter **wordprocessed** documents or computer programs.

Editor, line Part of an **operating system** that allows a programmer to change the lines of a program, for instance during **debugging**.

Editor, screen A program that allows any part of a document to be altered while being displayed on a screen.

EDP Electronic **Data Processing**.

EFT (Electronic Fund Transfer) A system that allows 'money' to be transferred from one account to another by electronic means, usually without any paper money or cheques being involved.

EPROM (Erasable Programmable Read Only Memory) A type of **ROM,** where type data can be changed, provided it is all changed at once (i.e. **NOT RAM**).

Etching A technique of removing the unwanted copper from a **copper-clad board** prior to its being drilled to make a **printed circuit board**

Execute Run a computer program, or carry out a single instruction.

F

Fax (facsimile) This involves the scanning of a document and conversion into signals that can be transmitted via wires or radio waves. The signals are converted back to a copy of the original at the receiving end. A Fax machine is a little like a long-distance photocopier.

Feedback Returning part of the output back to the input to give more accurate control.

Fibre optics Transmission of data along a transparent tube by means of **modulated** light.

Field One part of a **record** containing data about a particular aspect, such as the surname or date of birth of a person.

File A collection of **records** about a particular subject. Also used to describe a program or set of data stored on a **disk**.

Firmware Mid-way between **software** and **hardware**. Usually refers to programs held in **ROM** that are plugged into a microcomputer to run them.

Floppy disk A **disk** made of flexible plastic coated with magnetic material, usually with 8 inch, 5¼ inch or 3½ inch diameters.

Flowchart A diagram of different-shaped boxes showing the logical sequence of actions occurring in a computer program.

Format Organizing the way that data, usually numbered, is printed on the screen or on paper.

Format a disk Set up a **floppy disk** so that the **disk drive** can use it.

FORTH A fast **interpreted** language, used mainly for computer control.

FORTRAN (FORmula TRANslation) An early high-level programming language specially developed for scientific and mathematical processing and still the most commonly used programming language.

Fragile A term used to describe a program that is likely to **crash** under certain conditions.

G

Garbage A term meaning rubbish or meaningless data.

GIGO (Garbage In, Garbage Out) The results produced by a computer are only as good as the program it is running and the information it is given to work on.

Graphics tablet A board on which a special pen can draw pictures which are transmitted directly to the screen. Used in **CAD**.

H

Hard copy A print-out on paper.

Hard disk A magnetic disk for data storage. Used as a **backing store**.

Hardware Physical equipment, such as the computer, printer, disk drive etc.

Hexadecimal A way of counting to base 16 which allows the binary code to be used more easily by humans. It uses the digits 0 through 9, and A, B, C, D, E and F, to count up to 1111 in binary.

High-level language A programming language that is as easy to understand as possible. Usually designed to be run on several different computer systems.

I

Information retrieval The process of obtaining specific information from a computer **database**.

Input device Equipment that allows data to be entered into a computer, for example **card reader** or keyboard.

Input/Output device Equipment that allows data to be entered into or output from a computer, for example a **disk drive**.

I/O The **chips**, or electronic circuits within a chip, used to enable data from an external device to enter or leave.

Integrated circuit A combination of **transistors** on a single chip.

Interactive A program that allows the user to respond to questions from the computer (and vice versa) during **run-time**.

Interpreter A low-level program that takes each line of **source code** and turns it into **machine code** before executing it (see also **Compiler**).

K

Key-to-disk A way of inputting data directly into the computer and on to **disk** using the keyboard.

Keyword The words used in a high-level language that have a special meaning for that language. For example, PRINT, INPUT and REPEAT, in Basic.

Kimball tag A piece of card with holes punched in it which represent a code. When something is bought, the card is removed from the goods and can be input into a computer.

L

LAN (Local Area Network) A **network** of computers able to exchange data via a telephone line.

Laser printer A type of printer that uses a laser beam to form the printed characters.

Light pen An **input device** which can be pointed at the screen and used for drawing etc.

Line printer Printer which can print an entire line in one go.

LOAD A **keyword** used in many programming languages to transfer a program or data from an external store into the computer's memory.

Logic gate, electronic A circuit that processes digital data.

LOGO An **interpreted** high-level, programming language, specially developed to be easy to use and yet still powerful.

Logo The picture or title used to show the name of the person or company that developed a program or piece of equipment.

Loop A sequence of steps in a program which is repeated more than once.

Low-level language A programming language that depends on the computer being used. Each instruction can easily be converted into a **machine code** instruction. Low-level languages are faster in use than **high-level languages**.

M

Machine code or **machine language** The **binary** codes used to give a **microprocessor** or **CPU** instructions to be executed. Machine code is the lowest possible low-level language.

Mainframe A computer with a large **capacity** and usually many **terminals**, capable of **multi-tasking**.

Magnetic encoder A machine used to read the information contained in a magnetic stripe such as on a credit or cash card.

Master file This is the main **file** containing all the records about a particular subject.

Memory The place where a computer stores data internally.

Menu The list at the start of a program that gives the user a choice of options. One of these items might be chosen by pressing an appropriate key.

MICR (Magnetic Ink Character Recognition) A way of coding digits so that they can be read automatically by an MICR reader.

Microcomputer A self-contained computer, usually with one keyboard and one **VDU**, which normally runs one program at a time. Some microcomputers are nearly as powerful as **minicomputers**.

Microelectronics The science and technology of **integrated circuits**.

Microfiche A piece of film, about the size of a postcard, that can hold about 250 A4 pages of information.

Microfilm A piece of film, rather like a transparency, which can contain a large amount of information. It has to be magnified to be read.

Microprocessor A **VLSI** chip that combines **registers**, an **ALU** and control circuits, all on one single **chip**.

Microsecond One millionth of a second.

Minicomputer A small version of a **mainframe** computer, capable of **multi-tasking** and having several **terminals**.

MIPS (Micro-Instructions Per Second) A measure of how fast a **microprocessor** or **CPU** works.

MIRIAM (Major Incident Room Index and Action Management) A computer system used by police officers to help in the solving of major crimes.

Mnemonics Easily remembered words that represent instruction codes. Used in **assembly language**.

Modem A device that allows a computer to send data to, or receive data from, a telephone line. Modem is derived from MODulator/DEModulator.

Modulation Altering a carrier (such as light waves or radio waves) so that it transmits data.

Module Often, software is written in short sections called modules, with each module performing a specific task.

Mouse A hand-held device that moves around a flat surface and transmits details of its position to the computer. Used for **CAD** and other applications.

Multi-tasking The ability of a computer to run several different programs at the same time.

N

Network A system of connecting several **microcomputers** so that they can share common facilities such as a **printer** and **hard disk**.

O

Object code The **binary** instructions produced by a **compiler** from **source code**. Object code is usually directly in **machine language**.

Online/Offline Terms used to describe when a **peripheral device** is, or is not, able to communicate with the computer.

Operating System A program that controls the computer from when it is first switched on, and which organizes the way that the keyboard is read, the inputs and outputs, and the way that the **VDU** displays information. It is usually stored in **ROM**.

Oracle The ITV version of **teletext**.

Output device Equipment that allows data from a computer to be made available externally, for example **VDU** or printer.

P

PASCAL A high-level language developed especially for **top-down** programming. Increasingly used for applications programs.

Peripheral device A device attached to, but outside of, the **CPU** and controlled by it.

Personal computer A computer, usually a **microcomputer**, that is used on its own without any connection to a mainframe computer.

PIN (Personal Identification Number) To use an **ATMS** (cash dispenser) you have to type in a secret number called your **PIN**.

PNC (Police National Computer) The main police computer which is used by terminals situated in police stations throughout England, Scotland, and Wales.

POS (Point-Of-Sale marketing) A technique of entering data into a computer system at the moment the article is sold. Usually requires a **bar-code reader** or **magnetic stripe reader**.

Prestel British Telecom's **viewdata** system.

Printed circuit board A **copper-clad board** with the circuit **etched** into it, into which electronic components are placed before being soldered.

Printer A device or **peripheral** used to obtain a **hard copy** of the output from a computer.

Privacy The rights of individuals to decide what information about them should be known by others.

Procedure Part of a program that is a self-contained unit.

Program The set of instructions that makes the computer carry out the desired processes. It is unusual to spell this word 'programme', even in the UK.

Program, application A program that carries out a particular task.

Programmer The person who designs and writes computer programs.

Programmer, business The person who investigates and performs the overall design of a business computer system.

Programmer, systems The person who writes the **operating system** of a computer system.

Programming language A means of organizing a set of instructions that can then be **interpreted** or **compiled** to produce **object code** to be executed by the computer.

Punched card A special card that holds data as punched holes according to a special code. These cards can be read automatically into a computer.

R

RAM A **random access** electronic memory device, to which data can be written or from which it can be read. Nowadays, the word RAM is taken to mean 'Readily Alterable Memory'.

Random access Any computer storage system where the data it contains can be accessed in any order.

Real-time A real-time system accepts **data** and processes it immediately, reading back its results immediately. The results have a direct effect on the next set of available **data**.

Record A single unit of data in a **file**, containing information about a single object (such as a person). Records are subdivided into **fields**.

Recursion A programming term used to describe the process whereby a **procedure** calls itself.

Register Any memory device capable of storing a single character etc., usually internal to a **microprocessor** or **CPU**, used for temporary storage of data, which allows it to be processed more rapidly.

Remote device One that is usually connected indirectly to a computer, for example, by a **network**.

Robot A machine or device that has been programmed to carry out some (usually mechanical) process automatically.

ROM (Read-Only Memory) Computer memory that cannot be changed by a program. Used to store the **operating system** of the computer.

Run-time When the computer is running an application program.

S

SAVE A **keyword** used in many programming languages to transfer a program or data from the computer's memory to an external store.

Semiconductor The material from which modern electronic devices are made.

Serial (sequential) access Accessing data in sequence. The time it takes to locate an item depends on its position.

Simulation The imitation with a computer program of some system (usually mechanical, for example, an aircraft flight simulator) or some phenomenon that can be described mathematically (for example, how the economy of a country works).

Softstrip This is software on a strip of paper that may be photocopied or sent through the post.

Software The programs used in a computer.

Software house A company that specializes in writing computer programs.

Sort To arrange in an ordered sequence.

Source documents The original documents from which the **data** is taken.

Speech recognition The ability of a computer to 'understand' spoken words by comparing them with stored data.

Speech synthesis The production of speech by electronic means.

Spreadsheet A program used to manipulate tables consisting of rows and columns of numbers. It is used for accounts or any other application where large numbers of calculations need to be performed on rows and columns of numbers.

Systems analyst A person who studies the overall organization and implementation of a business computer system.

T

Tabulation Automatically arranging data in ordered columns.

Telecommunications The transmission of data by electronic means, usually by radio or microwaves.

Telesoftware This is **software** sent from one computer to another using **telecommunications**.

Teletext The transmission of pictures and text by television.

Terminal A **keyboard** and/or **VDU** used to communicate with a computer.

Time sharing A term describing **multi-tasking**, when one computer is running several different programs at once.

Top-down A term used to describe the solution of a problem, where the programmer starts from the problem and gradually breaks it down into small self-contained **procedures**, which can then be turned into source code (see **Bottom-up**).

Transaction file This is a **file** on which all the transactions over a certain period of time are kept. It is used to update a **master file**.

Transistor The device on a **chip**, which is the basic building block. One chip may contain many thousands of transistors.

Truth table A table showing the logical relationships between the inputs and outputs of a **logic gate**.

V

Variable A quantity stored in a computer that can be changed while the program is being run.

VDU (Visual or Video Display Unit) The **CRT** on which data is displayed and on which it can be **edited**.

Verification checks These are pre-input checks on **data**, that is before it is accepted into the computer.

Videodisc A plastic disk that looks like a compact disk and is used to hold large amounts of information. A laser beam is used to read the information off the disk.

Videotex An information service that can display text on a **VDU**.

Viewdata The transmission and display of information in coded form (see **Teletext**).

VLSI (Very Large Scale Integration) A term describing the building of electronic circuits on a single **chip** containing many thousands of **transistors**.

W

Winchester drive A small type of **hard disk**.

Word The smallest unit of memory that can be separately **addressed**, usually two bytes long.

Wordprocessor A wordprocessor program allows text to be typed and displayed on a **VDU** and to be **edited** before being printed out.

Write-protect notch A notch found on a **floppy disk**. When the notch is covered with a piece of tape, it is impossible to write information on to the disk.

A

VERY

Disney

CHRISTMAS

First published in the UK in 2021 by Studio Press Books,
an imprint of Bonnier Books UK,
4th Floor, Victoria House, Bloomsbury Square, London WC1B 4DA
Owned by Bonnier Books,
Sveavägen 56, Stockholm, Sweden

bonnierbooks.co.uk

Printed in Italy
2 4 6 8 10 9 7 5 3 1

ISBN 978-1-80078-113-9

Edited by Ellie Rose
Designed by Rob Ward
Production by Emma Kidd

A VERY  CHRISTMAS

CONTENTS

1
DECEMBER

CHRISTMAS LAUGHS

Mike Wazowski, the green one-eyed monster, was on the Monsters, Inc. Laugh Floor. He couldn't stop looking at the Laugh Meter. It showed all of the laughs the monsters had collected by telling kids jokes. The laughs were turned into energy for the city of Monstropolis.

Monsters, Inc. had always been able to collect enough laughs to make sure the monsters never had to worry about losing power. But with Christmas around the corner, it seemed as if more and more kids were on holiday. That made it harder to collect laughs.

Mike worried there wouldn't be enough power to light the Christmas tree in the city. It was a Monstropolis tradition that everyone looked forward to.

'Come on, monsters,' he called out. 'Think funny!' Mike watched one monster go through a child's wardrobe door. When he came back onto the Laugh Floor, Mike looked at the canister that collected laughs. It wasn't even half full.

Just then, Sulley showed up. The big, furry blue monster was the president of Monsters, Inc. He was also Mike's best friend.

'How's it going, Mike?' asked Sulley.

'Fine, fine,' Mike answered nervously. He didn't want his boss to know they were running short on laughs. 'That Christmas tree will be lit up in no time.'

Mike saw Sulley peek over at the Laugh Meter. 'I bet there are a lot of kids who are—' Sulley started.

'No time to talk, buddy,' Mike cut him off. He guided Sulley towards the door. 'Got to get back to work and collect those laughs.'

'Okay,' said Sulley. 'See you later.'

As soon as Sulley left, Mike called out again, 'Let's go, let's go! Collect those laughs! Christmas is just around the corner!'

The monsters worked even harder at being funny and entertaining. One monster even juggled seven plates and spun another plate on his head. The kid watching him broke into giggles and clapped wildly. The laugh canister quickly filled up.

George, a big, furry orange monster, went through another child's door. He sat on a stool next to the little girl's bed, holding a microphone in one hand.

'Hey, is this thing on? Hello?' George said, tapping the microphone. 'Ready to have some laughs? Good. Why did the monster eat a lightbulb?'

'Why?' the child asked.

'He needed a light snack!' George exclaimed, and the little girl roared with laughter. 'Wait, wait! I have more.' He told another joke that sent the child into giggles. On the Laugh Floor, Mike watched the canister outside the door fill up.

'Nice work,' Mike said when George had finished.

'Thanks,' George said. He and Mike looked up at the Laugh Meter on the wall. It was growing steadily, much to everyone's delight.

'We actually might make our goal,' Mike said with a hopeful smile.

All of a sudden, Mike and the other monsters watched in horror as the Laugh Meter began to go down instead of up!

'What's going on? What's happening?' Mike said, his voice growing louder.

The laugh wranglers, Smitty and Needleman, weren't sure.

'This has never happened before,' said Smitty, the head wrangler.

'Well, don't just stand there,' Mike cried. 'Fix it!'

The wranglers sprang into action. After a while, they discovered a leak in the laugh tank, where all the laughs were stored.

The monsters on the Laugh Floor were worried. They wondered if all of their hard work had been for nothing.

'Ho, ho, ho!' came a cheerful voice.

Mike looked up and saw Santa Claus walking onto the floor. Then he realised it was Sulley dressed in a Santa suit.

'I'm just getting into the Christmas spirit,' Sulley explained. Then he looked around. 'It looks like I'm the only one. What's going on?'

Mike explained. 'But I've got everything under control, Santa, er, Sulley.'

7

'I'm sure you do,' Sulley replied. 'I'm just going to see if there's anything I can do to help.'

Sulley followed Mike into the basement of Monsters, Inc., where the laugh wranglers were hard at work. Everyone wanted to get the laugh tank fixed as soon as possible and time was running out. The tree-lighting ceremony was only a few hours away!

But the wranglers couldn't agree on how to fix the problem.

'Anything I can do?' Sulley asked.

'One of the pipes that leads into the laugh tank has burst,' explained Smitty. 'We need to tie it off but none of our tools are strong enough to turn the pipe.'

'Hmm...' said Sulley, scratching his head. Then Mike had a great idea. 'Why not actually tie it off?' Since Sulley was so strong, he could bend that pipe right into a pretzel shape!

Sulley was willing to give it a try. Mike stood by his side and coached him.

It worked! The pipe stopped leaking!

Mike and Sulley headed back up to the Laugh Floor. All the monsters congratulated Sulley!

Mike wondered why no one was thanking him. It had been his idea, after all. But there was no time to think about that now. 'We're back up and running!' Mike announced. 'Let's make some laughs!'

All the monsters got to work. They knew they'd have to work extra hard to make up for all of the lost laughs.

Sulley decided to jump in and help. 'Hey, we've only got a couple of hours to get the tree lit,' he said to Mike.

Still dressed as Santa, Sulley went through a child's wardrobe door.

When he came back onto the Laugh Floor, he looked up at the Laugh Meter on the wall. It was increasing, but slowly.

'We've got to make it,' Sulley whispered to Mike.

Finally, the Laugh Meter was back up to the level it had reached before the leak. Sulley looked at the clock on the wall and frowned. It was only thirty minutes until the tree-lighting ceremony.

Suddenly, Sulley had an idea. 'The only way we're going to make our laugh quota is to get some really over-the-top laughs.'

Mike nodded in agreement.

'We need a big one,' continued Sulley. 'We need a special kind of monster. One with perfect timing, star quality, a natural at comedy, a one-eyed sensation.'

Mike realised what Sulley was trying to do. He crossed his arms and shook his head. 'No, Sulley. Absolutely not.'

'The Christmas tree lighting is only half an hour away,' Sulley told him. 'Come on, Mike. The whole city is depending on you.'

That was all Mike needed to hear. 'You're right. Let's do it!' he said. 'But you're coming with me!'

Sulley and Mike went through a door together. Sulley was still dressed as Santa and Mike had dressed up as an elf. To their delight, a little girls' sleepover was going on!

Mike started with some of his best jokes. 'Hey, Sulley, I've got to walk twenty-five miles to get home.'

'Why don't you take a train?' Sulley asked, playing along.

'I did once, but my mother made me give it back!' Mike said. The kids in the room laughed but not as hard as the monsters had hoped. After a few more jokes, Mike realised he'd have to try something else. He picked up the sack of toys Sulley had brought in, but it was far too heavy for him.

'Whoa!' he exclaimed as he tripped. He landed upside down and the sack of toys spilled out around him. He sat up with a doll draped over his head and a toy race car stuck to his foot.

The kids roared with laughter. They begged for more and Mike happily tumbled and tripped for them again.

Mike and Sulley made it back onto the Laugh Floor in time to watch the Laugh Meter hit its limit!

At the tree-lighting ceremony, Mike and Sulley stood proudly in the front of the crowd.

Sulley whispered in Mike's ear, 'You did a great job. Thank you.'

Mike smiled. 'You know what I always say: funny doesn't grow on trees. When you got it, you got it. And I got it.'

Sulley laughed. He was happy Mike had it and shared it. It was going to be a bright Christmas, after all.

Make an
Advent Calendar

Get creative and make your own activity advent calendar!

You Will Need

- coloured card
  or wrapping paper
- coloured pens or pencils

- scissors
- coloured ribbon
- string

ASK AN ADULT FOR HELP

1. Cut out 25 shapes from the coloured card or wrapping paper. You could cut Christmas trees, wreaths, presents, snowmen, stockings or baubles.

2. On the front, write a number from 1 to 25. On the back, write a fun activity to do every day leading up to Christmas Day.

3. Add extra decoration to each card – try adding glitter, stickers or even fresh holly!

4. Ask an adult to hang up the ribbon – you could hang it on a wall or along a bannister.

5. Make a small hole in the corner of each card and thread through string. Hang up the cards, in order, ready to open each day!

ACTIVITY IDEAS

- Make a hot chocolate with marshmallows
- Watch a Christmas film
- Decorate the Christmas tree
- Make a gingerbread house
- Put on a festive play

2

DECEMBER

THE BEST PRESENT EVER

'Hey, Lightning, look at me! Wooooeeeee!' Mater sledged past his best buddy, Lightning McQueen.

It was winter in Radiator Springs. Christmas was just a few days away and fresh snow blanketed the ground. The two friends were taking turns sliding down a snow-covered hill using Mater's one-of-a-kind junkyard sledge.

'I'm tellin' you, this here's the best sledge in Radiator Springs!' Mater exclaimed.

'I know, you have told me,' Lightning laughed. 'Several times. It has its own headlights, superfast gliders—'

'And built-in bumper tyres!' the friends said together.

'Well, hold your horsepower,' said Mater. 'Because it's gonna be even funner when we take it sledging at Kersploosh Mountain!'

Kersploosh Mountain was a water park near Radiator Springs. For just one day a year, on Christmas, the waterslides were frozen over so that cars could go sledging down the chutes.

'Uh, Mater, there's something I need to tell you.' Lightning looked worried. 'Remember that Russian Ice Racers Cup I told you I'm competing in?'

'Well, sure,' said Mater. 'The one in a few weeks.'

'That's just it,' Lightning said. 'They moved it up to this week. I'm not going to be here for Christmas after all.'

Mater stopped dead in his tracks. 'You're not?'

Lightning shook his head. 'I'm really sorry, buddy. I know I'll miss Christmas at Kersploosh Mountain. But maybe we can do something else when I get back?'

'Yeah... sure thing,' Mater said.

Later that afternoon, Mater pulled into Flo's V8 Cafe.

'Hey there, Mater,' Flo called. 'Want to try a sip of my new eggnog oil? It's guaranteed to fill you up with Christmas cheer.'

'I could use some,' said Mater. 'I'm plumb out of Christmas cheer.'

'Something got you down, honey?' Flo asked.

Mater sighed. 'Lightning won't be home for Christmas. He's in some Rushin' Rice Cup.'

'That's too bad,' Flo said. 'I guess you'll have to celebrate the holiday early.'

'Yeah, celebrate early! That's a good idea!' said Mater. Then he thought for a moment. 'Oh, shoot, I forgot about presents. I've gotta get Lightning something! But what?'

Flo looked thoughtful. 'Hmmm. Well, you're going to miss him while he's away, right?'

'Yeah,' Mater nodded eagerly.

'So how about getting him something for the race, so he knows you'll be thinking of him? Like ear mufflers? Or a snow scraper?'

Mater smiled. 'Or snow tyres! That's a great idea, Flo. I know just where to go!' With that, Mater dashed off.

'Luigi!' Mater yelled as he skidded up to Casa Della Tires. 'I need your help!'

Luigi smiled. 'For you, Mater, anything!'

'Those snow tyres,' said Mater. 'The ones that used to be in your front window. Where'd they go? I need to buy them for Lightning for his Crushin' Dice Cup!'

Luigi's smile faded. 'Ah... I can do anything but that. I'm afraid someone's already bought them. They just left a moment ago.'

Sure enough, outside a big truck was driving away from the shop.

Mater raced after the truck, finally catching up with him at the intersection. Mater explained the situation then pleaded with the truck. 'I need those tyres for my best buddy's Christmas gift. I'll give you anything.'

The truck sighed. 'Sorry, but I've been dreaming of speeding through the snow with these superfast tyres.'

Mater raised an eyebrow. 'Fast, huh? What if I told you I had something that goes even faster than those tyres?'

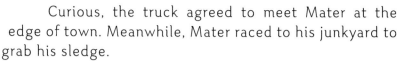

Curious, the truck agreed to meet Mater at the edge of town. Meanwhile, Mater raced to his junkyard to grab his sledge.

'All right,' Mater said when the two trucks met again. 'I'll bet my sledge is faster going down that hill than you in those tyres. If I'm right, we'll trade. Deal?'

The truck agreed and soon they were zipping down the snowy slope. Mater zoomed past the truck – and won!

The truck happily traded the tyres for Mater's sledge.

Meanwhile, Lightning was helping Sally decorate the Cozy Cone Motel.

'I feel awful,' he said. 'Mater looked so sad when I told him.'

'Well,' said Sally. 'Do you need to do the race?'

'Huh?' asked Lightning.

'It's not part of your normal circuit,' Sally pointed out. 'I'm sure they'd understand if you didn't go.'

Lightning's eyes lit up. 'You're right. Mater is my best friend. And a trophy is just another trophy. I'm going to withdraw from the race and stay here for Christmas!'

Lightning raced home to call Vitaly Petrov, who was hosting the Russian Ice Racers Cup. Vitaly told Lightning not to worry, he could reschedule the race for after the holiday.

'That works out great. Thanks, Vitaly!' said Lightning.

He couldn't wait to tell Mater the good news. On his way to see his best buddy, Lightning drove past a big sign for Kersploosh Mountain. He suddenly had an idea for the perfect gift...

The next day, Lightning and Mater exchanged gifts.

'Open yours, open yours, open yours!' Mater cried.

'Okay,' said Lightning. 'But, Mater, I have some good news that...' Lightning trailed off as he unwrapped the tyres.

'You got these for me?' he asked, looking up at his friend.

'Yeah!' Mater grinned from mirror to mirror. 'If my best buddy can't be here for Christmas, then he'd sure as heck better win his Blushin' Mice Cup! Do you like 'em?'

Lightning was touched. 'Mater, I love them. But...'

Mater was already ripping open his gift. When he saw the two tickets to Kersploosh Mountain, his eyes grew wide.

Lightning shrugged. 'My race was delayed, so now I can spend Christmas with you, buddy.'

'No way!' Mater exclaimed. 'This is awesome! I can't believe we're going to Kersploosh Mountain on Christmas Day! Now we can take my sledge and... uh oh.'

'Hey, where is your sledge?' Lightning asked, looking around. Mater shuffled nervously. 'Uh, I may have kind of, sort of, traded it to get you them there snow tyres.'

The two friends stared at each other. Then they started laughing. 'Can you believe this?' Lightning exclaimed. 'We thought we were getting each other the perfect Christmas presents but we ended up getting stuff we can't use!'

Mater nodded. 'Yeah, but I'll tell you one thing, buddy, spending Christmas together is still the best present ever.'

Lightning smiled. 'Same here, pal. I wouldn't change a thing.'

Mater looked at the gifts. 'Well, shoot. What are we going to do with four tyres and no race and two tickets with no sledge?'

A twinkle came to Lightning's eye. 'Well, we may not have a junkyard sledge but we do have a junkyard. Mater, didn't your old sledge have bumper tyres?'

Mater bounced up and down. 'Oh, oh! I see where you're going.' He started racing around his junkyard, collecting scraps. 'Dad gum, this is gonna be so cool!'

On Christmas Day, Mater and Lightning sat at the top of Kersploosh Mountain. Beneath them was a new junkyard sledge. Except this one was extra special – it had two seats, flashing Christmas lights, double gliders and extra-large bumper tyres.

'It's Mater's Junkyard Sledge 2.0, with double the sledding fun!' cried Mater.

'You ready for this?' Lightning asked as they teetered on the top of the slide.

'You bet,' said Mater. 'As long as I've got my good buddy with me, I'm as ready as I'll ever beeeeeeeeeeee!'

DESIGN A CHRISTMAS CARD

Use scraps of old wrapping paper to make this card for someone special!

YOU WILL NEED

- scraps of wrapping paper
- scissors
- glue

- brown card
- sheet of coloured card
- coloured ribbon

1. Cut roughly 14 pieces of wrapping paper around 1 cm wide. Each piece should be slightly shorter than the last – these will form your tree.

2. Roll each piece of wrapping paper into a tube and glue to hold together.

3. Cut a rectangle roughly 5 cm by 3 cm from the brown card. This will be the tree trunk.

4. Fold the coloured card in half – this is the base of your card.

5. Glue the tree trunk at the bottom of one side of the card.

6. Then glue each wrapping paper tube above the tree trunk, from the longest to the shortest.

7. Tie the ribbon into a bow and glue to the top of the tree.

8. Write your festive message inside the card!

December

Dumbo's Snowy Day

Dumbo was a very special elephant – with his huge ears, he could soar through the sky like a bird. Dumbo performed in a circus with his mother, Mrs. Jumbo. One chilly day, the circus animals were on their way to a new town. But their train, Casey Jr., was struggling to get through the falling snow. His wheels slid on the icy railroad tracks.

Finally, Casey Jr. decided it was too dangerous to keep going. The train came to a stop and everyone waited for the snow to pass.

Dumbo was happy that the train had stopped. He'd never played in the snow before! He thought it felt awfully strange as he tried to walk through it. The snow pressed against his feet like cold sand.

'You can do it!' said Mrs. Jumbo. She gave him a gentle nuzzle.

Soon Dumbo got the hang of walking through the snow. He liked the *crunch-crunch-crunch* sound he heard with every step.

All morning, Dumbo and his mother played in the snow. They gathered snowballs together with their trunks. They made snow elephants. They even played hide-and-seek! But as Dumbo and his mother explored, they got further and further away from the waiting train.

Suddenly, Dumbo slid down a steep

hill. He called after his mother to follow him. But when she reached the bottom of the hill, Mrs. Jumbo realised she couldn't climb back up!

Dumbo tried to push. He tried to pull. But nothing worked. Mrs. Jumbo slipped farther down the slope towards a steep cliff edge.

'You will have to fly off and get help,' Mrs. Jumbo told him.

So off Dumbo flew, as fast as his ears would take him.

As he soared towards the train, the wind began to blow. It pushed harder and harder against him. The snow stung his eyes and the cold nipped at his toes.

Finally, Dumbo's ears got so cold he couldn't fly. As he waited for the wind to pass, he worried about his mother.

Once the wind died down, Dumbo raced back to the train. Quickly, he gathered all the animals together so that they could help.

'What are we waiting for?' Timothy Mouse cried. 'I've got to save Mrs. Jumbo!'

Dumbo led his friends back to the cliff.

By the time they found Mrs. Jumbo, the windstorm had pushed her even closer to the cliff's edge. The animals knew they had to think of something fast!

'Oh, dear,' worried the giraffe. 'How can we get down there to help?'

Timothy snapped his fingers – he had an idea.

'Everybody line up!' he shouted. He ordered the animals to grab one another's tails. At the front of the line, the ostrich leaned over the cliff to take hold of Mrs. Jumbo's trunk.

'One, two, three, PULL!' Timothy yelled.

The animals worked together, huffing and puffing, pulling and stretching, until Mrs. Jumbo made it safely to the top of the cliff.

'Hooray!' everyone shouted. Suddenly, there was a loud CRACK!

The cliff side gave way and the animals all tumbled down!

'Watch out!' yelled the hippo.

'Yikes!' cried the monkeys.

'Uh-oh!' said the giraffe.

'Help!' hollered the bear.

All of the animals tumbled together and rolled down the hill. Before long, they had become a giant snowball!

'How do you stop this thing?' Timothy shouted as they zoomed along.

The snowball gathered speed until... *Crash! Bang! Boom! Oof!*

The animal snowball hit the bottom of the hill and broke apart!

'Is everyone okay?' Timothy asked as he straightened his hat. Luckily, everyone was fine, just a little dizzy from their unexpected snow ride. All the animals began walking back to the train. Walking wasn't nearly as fast as riding a snowball, but it was a lot less scary!

That night, Mrs. Jumbo gave Dumbo a warm bath.

'Thank you for flying to find help today,' Mrs. Jumbo said to her son. 'I'm so proud of you.'

Dumbo smiled and blew a trunkful of water over his head.

'Hey! Don't forget about me,' said Timothy from his teacup bath. 'I helped, too!'

Mrs. Jumbo nodded 'You certainly did. Thank you.'

'Aw, gee,' said Timothy. 'It was nothing. Nothing at all.'

Then it was time for bed. Dumbo snuggled up against his mother, and Timothy nestled underneath Dumbo's ear. 'Good night, my darling,' Mrs. Jumbo said softly.

'Sleep tight!' said Timothy.

Dumbo fell asleep right away. Tomorrow he and the circus animals would perform for hundreds of happy children in the new town. But for now, Dumbo was glad to be warm and safe with his mother as the snow fell gently outside.

LEARN TO DRAW DUMBO

Dumbo may be the smallest elephant under the Big Top but he has a very special talent – he can use his ears to fly! Follow the steps to draw the little elephant.

1. Start by drawing two large circles and a smaller circle.

2. Add the guidelines to show where Dumbo's face will go.

3. Remember that Dumbo is a baby, so make sure to give him a rounded body and chubby legs.

4. Add details to your drawing, such as the ruffles on Dumbo's collar and the wrinkles on his knees!

5. Dumbo's skin is a light grey with a hint of blue.

4 DECEMBER

THE SWEETEST CHRISTMAS

One snowy Christmas Eve, Winnie the Pooh looked up and down, in and out and all around his house. He had a tree set up in his living room. It was decorated with some candles in honey pots. Pooh looked at the tree and tapped his head. 'Something seems to be missing,' he said.

He walked over to the window and peered outside. Then he walked back to the tree and thought some more.

Suddenly, a knocking sound startled Pooh. *Rap-a-tap-tap!* He turned towards his front door.

'Maybe whatever it is I can't remember I'm missing is outside my door,' Pooh said.

When Pooh opened the door, he found a small snowman on his front step.

'H-h-he-l-l-l-o, P-Pooh B-Bear,' the snowman said as he shivered.

Pooh thought the voice sounded very familiar. He invited the snowman inside.

After standing beside the fire for a few minutes, the snowman began to melt. The more he melted, the more he started to look like Piglet!

'Oh, my,' said Pooh. He was happy to see his friend where there used to be a snowman.

'Oh, my,' said Piglet. Now that the snow had melted off him, he could see Pooh's glowing Christmas tree.

'Are you going to string popcorn for your tree?' Piglet asked.

'There was popcorn and string,' Pooh admitted. 'But now there is only string.'

Pooh thought some more, wondering if popcorn was what he'd forgotten. But that wasn't it, either.

'Then we can use the string to wrap the presents you're giving,' Piglet said.

Something began to tickle at Pooh's brain. It was the something missing that he hadn't been able to remember.

'I forgot to get presents!' Pooh exclaimed.

'Don't worry, Pooh,' Piglet said. 'I'm sure you'll think of something.'

Soon it was time for Piglet to go home and wrap his own presents. He said goodbye to his friend and went back out into the cold, snowy night.

Pooh stood beside his tree and tapped his head while he thought. Where could he find presents for his friends? It was already Christmas Eve. Was it too late?

He thought some more. He sat down in his cosy chair. Then he got up and had a small snack of honey. He peered out the window and watched the snow fall.

Then he had an idea.

He still didn't know what to do about the presents he'd forgotten. But he knew where to find help.

'Hello!' Pooh called as he knocked on Christopher Robin's door.

Christopher Robin opened the door and smiled when he saw the visitor.

'Come in, Pooh Bear,' he said. 'Merry Christmas! Why do you look so sad on the most wonderful night of the year?'

Pooh was just about to explain about the forgotten presents when something caught his eye. He pointed at the stockings over the fireplace. 'What are those for?' he asked.

'Those are stockings to hold Christmas presents,' explained Christopher Robin.

'But Christopher Robin,' Pooh said, 'what if someone forgot to find presents for his friends? And what if that same someone doesn't have stockings to hang because he doesn't wear any?'

Pooh looked down at his bare feet, then

back up at Christopher Robin.

'Silly old bear,' Christopher Robin said. He took Pooh up to his room. They dug through his drawers until Pooh found seven stockings.

'Thank you, Christopher Robin,' Pooh said. He smiled. He'd picked a stocking for each of his friends to put their presents in: purple for Piglet, red-and-white striped for Tigger, orange for Rabbit, yellow for Eeyore, maroon for Gopher and blue for Owl. And one for him to hang over his fireplace.

He hurried off to deliver the stockings to his friends. As he walked through the Hundred-Acre Wood, he thought about the presents he still needed for the stockings.

'I will get the presents later,' Pooh said to himself. 'The stockings come first.'

Pooh stopped at each of his friends' houses. Everyone was asleep. He quietly hung the stockings where his friends would find them. Each one had a tag that read: FROM POOH.

When Pooh got back to his house, he climbed into his cosy chair in front of a roaring fire.

'Now I must think about presents for my friends,' he said.

But Pooh was tired from finding the stockings and delivering them to his friends' houses. Before he knew it, his thinking turned into dreaming. He was fast asleep.

The next morning, Pooh awoke to a loud thumping noise. *Thump-a-bump-bump!*

'I wonder who that could be,' he said. He climbed out of his chair and opened the door.

'Merry Christmas, Pooh!' his friends cried.

There on Pooh's doorstep stood Tigger, Rabbit, Piglet, Owl, Eeyore and Gopher. They were each carrying a stocking from Pooh.

Pooh scratched his head. All of a sudden he remembered what had happened the night before. He had fallen asleep before giving presents to his friends!

'Oh, bother,' he said. Then he realised that his

friends were all talking at once. They were thanking him for their gifts!

'No more cold ears in the winter with my new cap,' Piglet said.

'My stripedy sleeping bag is tiggerific!' exclaimed Tigger.

'So is my new carrot cover,' Rabbit said.

'This rock-collecting bag will sure make work go faster,' Gopher said.

Eeyore swished his tail to show Pooh his new tail-warmer. 'No one's ever given me such a useful gift before,' he said.

Owl told Pooh his new wind sock would help him with the day's weather report.

Pooh looked at his friends. They were very happy with their stockings, even though there weren't any presents in them!

'Something very nice is going on,' Pooh said.

'It is very nice, Pooh Bear,' Piglet said.

'It's called Christmas, buddy bear,' Tigger said. He patted Pooh on the back.

Then Pooh watched in surprise as each of his friends put a honey pot in Pooh's own stocking.

'I don't know what to say,' Pooh told his friends. He was thrilled by their gifts. Honey was his favourite treat!

'Christmas is a wonderful holiday,' Rabbit said. 'Especially when you have good friends to share it with.'

'Yep!' Tigger agreed. 'But I know how we could make the day even sweeter.'

He looked at the honey pot in Pooh's hands. An idea tickled at Pooh's brain.

'Let's all have lunch together,' Pooh said. He passed out the honey pots his friends had just brought him. 'Christmas... what a sweet day, indeed.'

BAKE CHRISTMAS
BISCUITS

These biscuits might not be made with Pooh's favourite honey but they still make pretty and delicious decorations!

YOU WILL NEED

- 100g unsalted butter, softened
- 100g caster sugar
- 1 egg
- 1 tsp vanilla extract
- 275g plain flour
- sprinkles
- baking tray

- greaseproof paper
- mixing bowl
- wooden spoon
- rolling pin
- cookie cutters
- knife
- wire rack
- ribbon

ASK AN ADULT FOR HELP

1. Preheat the oven to 190°C. Line the baking tray with greaseproof paper.

2. Cream the butter and sugar together into a bowl until pale and fluffy.

3. Beat in the egg and vanilla extract a little at a time until combined.

4. Add the flour and mix to form a dough.

5. Roll out the dough on a lightly floured surface until it is about 1 cm thick.

6. Use cookie cutters to cut biscuits out of the dough. Re-roll any leftover dough until it has all been used.

7. Carefully use a knife to cut a hole in each biscuit. You can cut a larger shape in the middle or a small hole at the top of the biscuit.

8. Add sprinkles to the top of each biscuit.

9. Put the biscuits on a baking tray and bake for 8-10 minutes, or until pale golden brown. Leave to cool on a wire rack.

10. Once completely cooled, carefully thread the ribbon through the hole in each biscuit.

 TOP TIP! You could make a simple icing by mixing icing sugar, water and food colouring to add more decoration to each biscuit!

5
DECEMBER

OLAF'S FROZEN ADVENTURE

Olaf burst out of a kransekake, with pieces of the cake falling every which way.

'Surprise!' He shouted.

'Olaf, not yet!' said Anna.

Elsa smiled. 'The surpise holiday party starts *after* the Yule Bell rings.'

It was Arendelle's first holiday season in forever, and the two sisters would be spending it together with their kingdom.

The castle courtyard was filled with festive townspeople. Everyone had been excited as Kristoff and Sven brought in the Yule Bell.

'The Yule Bell signals the start of the holidays in Arendelle!' Elsa told Olaf.

'Okay, now,' Anna whispered.

Bong! Bong! Bong! The bell rang out, and all the villagers cheered!

'Surprise!' Shouted Olaf to the crowd.

And with that, Elsa and Anna flung open the doors to the castle to invite everyone in. But instead of staying for the surprise party, the townspeople started to leave!

'Wait!' Anna said. 'Going so soon?'

One woman replied, 'The Yule Bell rang, so I must get home for my family's tradition: rolling the *lefse*!'

A couple added, 'Our tradition is putting out porridge for the *tomte*.'

Two sisters explained, 'We're baking traditional *bordstabelbakkels*!'

Elsa invited Mr. And Mrs. Olsen to the castle, but they shook their heads.

'Thank you, but Olga and I need to get home to knit socks for our grandchildren.' Old Roy smiled. 'We wouldn't want to intrude on your family traditions.'

With the villagers gone, the sisters needed cheering up. Kristoff serenaded them with his holiday tradition from the trolls, The Ballad of Flemingrad. But the song took a strange turn when Kristof started singing about nostrils.

Then Kristoff revealed another troll tradition: Flemmy the Fungus Troll!

'Woah, gross,' said Anna.

'Now you lick his forehead and make a wish!' Kristoff said. Everyone laughed.

Olaf folllowed the sisters into the bathroom. He couldn't wait to hear what Anna and Elsa's holiday tradition was. 'Do we have any traditions, Elsa?' asked Anna. 'Do you remember?'

'After the gates were closed, we were never together,' Elsa replied. 'I'm sorry, Anna. It's my fault that we don't have a tradition.'

Over the past few months, Olaf had learned a little about why certain events and items were important to different people. And now he understood something new – everyone in Arendelle had a holiday tradition. Everyone except Anna and Elsa.

Olaf ran to the stable.

'Sven! Anna and Elsa don't have a holiday tradition.' Then he had an idea. 'Let's go and find the best tradition Anna and Elsa have ever seen, and we'll bring it back to the castle!'

Olaf hooked Sven to Kristoff's sleigh, and the two immediately set out.

Olaf knocked on the door of the first house they came to.

'What is your holiday tradition?' Olaf asked a young boy and his mother.

'We make candy canes together.' The boy handed

one to Olaf.

Olaf pulled out his carrot nose and popped in the candy cane. His eyes whirled. 'Ohhhhh, sugar rush!'

The boy stared at Olaf. 'You're supposed to eat it.'

'Eat my new nose? Why would I do that?' asked Olaf.

'Because it's that time of year!' the boy said.

Olaf and Sven stopped at home after home to learn about different holiday traditions.

They loaded all the traditions onto Sven's sleigh, so they could take them back to Anna and Elsa.

At their last stop, Olaf found the entire Oaken family celebrating in the sauna. Olaf thought that was a great tradition... and added a portable sauna to the pile!

But hot coals from the sauna caused problems. The sleigh caught fire and the traditions began to burn! When the sleigh went over a cliff, Sven and Olaf landed on opposite sides of a ravine and the holiday traditions were gone!

Olaf was still hopeful because he had one last tradition, a fruitcake, that he could give Anna and Elsa.

But Sven was worried. He could hear wolves howling in the dark forest.

Back at the castle, Elsa found Anna in the attic.

'What are you doing up here?' asked Elsa.

'Looking for traditions,' said Anna. She had been pulling items out of a trunk filled with her childhood belongings.

'What's in your trunk?' asked Anna.

'Mostly gloves,' said Elsa.

But as Elsa reached inside her trunk, they heard a little bell ring. Elsa lifted out a small box and handed it to Anna. When Anna opened it, she couldn't believe her eyes.

Suddenly, the two sisters heard a kerfuffle outside.

They ran down to the stables, where Sven was trying to tell Kristoff something.

'Olaf is lost in the forest!' said Anna.

'And being chased by hungry wolves!' said Elsa.

The sisters knew they needed to gather everyone and search for Olaf right away.

Anna and Elsa headed into the forest, calling out Olaf's name. Kristoff and Sven were close behind, with a search party of villagers.

'Olaf, where are you?' wondered a worried Anna.

Just when they thought they might never find him, the sisters spotted a carrot sticking out of a snowdrift – Olaf!

Olaf explained how he had lost all the traditions he'd collected for his friends. Even the fruitcake, which had been grabbed by a bird!

'I'm sorry you still don't have a tradition,' the little snowman said.

'Olaf, we do. Look,' said Anna.

She opened the mystery box and showed Olaf what was inside.

The box was filled with sketches Anna had made of Olaf when she was a little girl!

'You're the one who first brought us together,' said Anna.

'And kept us connected when we were apart,' added Elsa.

'Every Christmas, I made Elsa a gift,' Anna continued.

Elsa nodded. 'All those long years alone, we had you to remind us of our childhood.'

'And of how much we still loved each other,' Anna agreed.

'It's you, Olaf. You are our holiday tradition,' said Anna. 'SURPRISE!'

Glowing lanterns emerged from the dark forest. The townspeople were relieved to see that Olaf was safe.

That's when Elsa had a brilliant idea...

Because this was Anna and Elsa's first winter holiday in forever, the celebration needed to be special. With a little help from the villagers, they hosted their big party after all, right there in the forest!

Best of all, Anna and Elsa rediscovered their holiday tradition and a new one was created for Arendelle. All thanks to Olaf.

MAKE AN
OLAF DECORATION

Olaf loves learning about different holiday traditions! Include Olaf in your celebrations by making this fun centrepiece for your dinner table.

YOU WILL NEED

- a compass
- a pencil
- white card
- piece of white paper

- glue
- three sticks or straws
- coloured ribbon
- black and orange felt pens

1. Using the compass, draw three circles of different sizes on the white card.

2. Cut out two strips of paper roughly 2 cm by 15 cm and fold them up like an accordion.

3. Glue the sticks or straws to the side of the largest circle and glue one of the folded paper strips in the centre of the circle.

4. Glue the medium-sized circle on top of the folded paper strip.

5. Glue the ribbon onto the medium-sized circle to look like a scarf.

6. Glue three pieces of stick or straw to the top of the medium circle to look like Olaf's hair.

7. Glue the second folded paper strip to the centre of the circle and glue the smallest circle on top.

8. Use the black felt pen to draw Olaf's eyes, carrot nose and mouth. Colour in his nose using the orange felt pen.

TOP TIP! Try adding glitter or spraying fake snow around Olaf for an extra festive look!

6
DECEMBER

THE PERFECT GIFT

Christmas was just a few days away. Geppetto, the old woodcarver, was busy making toy soldiers and pretty dolls for the boys and girls in the village. There seemed to be more toys than usual to make this year. Geppetto was afraid that he wouldn't get all the work done in time.

Geppetto's son, Pinocchio, was eager to help his father. He knew Geppetto worked harder during the Christmas season than at any other time of the year.

While Geppetto worked day and night to make all the toys, Pinocchio, with the help of Jiminy Cricket, decorated the house for the holidays. Then they put up a tree and strung popcorn on its branches and hung garlands of holly.

This would be Pinocchio's first Christmas as a real boy. He wanted it to be very special.

'Jiminy,' Pinocchio said, 'I want to find the perfect gift for Geppetto. He should have something special. Will you help me?'

'Hmm,' Jiminy said. 'Well, if you ask me—'

'Maybe he would like a new knife to carve with?' Pinocchio said. Then he realised he probably didn't have enough money for that. 'Oh, what about some warm gloves? He could use them when he goes out on cold nights to deliver toys.'

'You know, Pinocchio, I wonder if a better gift would be—' Jiminy began.

'Socks!' Pinocchio cried. 'Or a new hat! Come on, Jiminy, let's go to the shops and see what we can find.' Pinocchio hurried out the door. Jiminy had to run to keep up.

In the shops, Pinocchio looked at socks, warm hats, gloves, scarves and even a warm woollen coat. But everything was too small, too expensive or too ordinary. Pinocchio wanted to find something special.

By Christmas Eve, Pinocchio still hadn't found the perfect gift for Geppetto. He felt sad.

'What am I going to do?' he asked Jiminy.

'Well, I do have this idea,' the cricket said.

'Really?' Pinocchio asked. 'Please tell me!'

Jiminy sat him at the table and handed him a quill pen. 'You want to give your father something he really needs?'

'I sure do.' Pinocchio beamed.

'Write this,' Jiminy said. 'Dear Geppetto, my gift to you is an extra pair of hands and an extra-willing heart. Love, Pinocchio.'

When Pinocchio finished writing, he looked up at Jiminy. 'Now what?' he asked.

'Now you put the note in here.' Jiminy held out a box. Pinocchio dropped the note in. Then Jiminy wrapped the package with bright paper and a big bow.

'Geppetto will be very happy with this gift,' Jiminy said.

'But it's just a scrap of paper,' Pinocchio said. 'What sort of gift is that?'

Jiminy smiled. 'You might be surprised.'

Geppetto took a break from his work to share Christmas Eve dinner with his son. After the meal, Pinocchio gave Geppetto his gift.

'What's this?' he asked.

'Your Christmas present,' Pinocchio replied. 'I hope you like it.'

Geppetto untied the bow and tore the wrapping paper away. 'Why... this is the perfect present!' he exclaimed. 'I could use an extra pair of hands in my workshop. How did you know, Pinocchio?'

Pinocchio just smiled. Jiminy had been right, he was surprised at how much joy his gift brought to his father.

'I'm glad to help,' Pinocchio said. 'I can start right now if you want.'

Pinocchio cleared the dinner dishes from the table. He washed them and put them away. Then he went to Geppetto's workshop. He swept up the wood shavings and boxed and wrapped the new toys. He made labels for each box so Geppetto would know who each gift was for.

When Geppetto set out to deliver the last of the gifts, Pinocchio went up to bed. He was tired after helping his father all night. But he was also very pleased that he made his father so happy. As he drifted off to sleep, he promised himself that he would help out more often.

That night, the Blue Fairy appeared. 'Because you have been so thoughtful this year, I came to grant you one very special Christmas wish,' she said. 'Think carefully about what you want.'

Pinocchio thought about the many things he could ask for. But he still only wanted one thing. 'I want to give Geppetto the perfect Christmas gift,' he told the Blue Fairy. 'Something that he will love forever.'

The Blue Fairy smiled. She knew just what that present should be. 'You are a very kind and loving boy, Pinocchio,' she said. 'I'm sure Geppetto will treasure this gift for years to come.'

The next morning, Geppetto woke up early. He quietly went downstairs to light the fire and make breakfast. He was so happy that Pinocchio had helped him the night before that he wanted to surprise his son. He wanted Pinocchio's first Christmas to be special.

Geppetto went to place his gifts for Pinocchio under the Christmas tree. He had carved a beautiful toy rocking horse and had crafted a playful jack-in-the-box. When he looked at the tree, he paused. Then he gasped.

A puppet that looked exactly like his son hung from the branches. 'My dear Pinocchio!' Geppetto said with a smile.

He examined the puppet. It looked just like a puppet he had made a long time ago. One lonely night, he had made a wish on the Wishing Star that the puppet would turn into a real boy. The Blue Fairy had granted his wish, and that was when Pinocchio the puppet had become his son.

When Pinocchio heard his father, he and Jiminy ran downstairs. 'Merry Christmas!' he shouted.

Geppetto sat in his favourite chair, holding the puppet. 'My gift! How did you make it?'

Pinocchio stared at the copy of the puppet he used to be. He smiled. The Blue Fairy had chosen the

perfect present for his father.

'Puppet Pinocchio was my favourite creation,' Geppetto said. 'Oh, how I've missed him.'

A frown appeared on Pinocchio's face. 'You have?' he asked. 'Have I disappointed you?'

Geppetto laughed. 'Not at all, son. You've been perfect in every way. This toy reminds me how very much I wanted a real son. He reminds me of how happy I am to have you.'

Pinocchio smiled. He went over to the puppet and looked at it closely. He felt as if he were looking in a mirror – the puppet had the same dark hair and blue eyes he did.

Geppetto stood up and started dancing with the puppet and singing. Pinocchio clapped along. He was thrilled that his father was so happy.

Stopping to catch his breath, Geppetto looked at his son and said, 'No one has ever thought to give me a toy of my own to play with because I'm a toy maker. But you understand how much I love toys, Pinocchio. Thank you, son.'

'See,' Jiminy whispered to Pinocchio, 'I told you that you would be surprised. And now you've been surprised twice!'

Pinocchio nodded as he watched his father dance with the puppet some more. Then he went over and danced beside the puppet that looked so much like him.

Geppetto held out the strings for Pinocchio so he could try to make the puppet dance himself. It was difficult because the puppet was the same size as Pinocchio. But he didn't care. He was happy to share this moment with his father.

A little later, Pinocchio opened the gifts Geppetto had placed under the tree for him. He laughed as the jack-in-the-box popped up, and he rocked the small wooden horse across the floor. But the best present he'd gotten had come from the Blue Fairy. He would never forget the smile on his father's face. He hoped they would share many more holidays just like this one.

MAKE A CHRISTMAS

TREE DECORATION

Geppetto makes beautiful toys for children at Christmas. Use your creative skills to make a decoration for your tree.

ASK AN ADULT FOR HELP

YOU WILL NEED

- a compass
- a pencil
- green felt
- brown felt

- scissors
- a needle and thread
- a bead

1. Using the compass, draw circles onto the green felt. Make sure to draw lots of circles of different sizes – these will make your Christmas tree.

2. Draw six or seven circles of the same size on the brown felt. These will make your tree trunk.

3. Cut out all of the felt circles.

4. Thread the needle and tie a knot in the end of the thread.

5. Stack the brown felt circles on top of one another and thread the needle through the middle.

6. Carefully thread the needle through the largest green circle so it sits on top of your trunk.

7. Now add the rest of your green circles, working from largest to smallest. The more you add, the taller your tree will be!

8. When you get to the top of your tree, thread on the bead. Remember to leave a small loop of thread so you can hang up your decoration.

9. Carefully thread the needle back down through all of the circles and out through the trunk. Tie a knot at the bottom to secure.

TOP TIP!

Use different shades of green felt to make your tree even more special!

DECEMBER

GHOSTS OF CHRISTMAS PAST

It should have been a joyous time. Christmas was coming – Rapunzel's very first Christmas since returning home to the castle. She had spent every Christmas locked away in Mother Gothel's tower since she was a baby.

The castle halls were decked with boughs of holly. The butlers had just chosen the royal Christmas tree. Everyone did their best to spread holiday cheer. Even the crankiest townsfolk were merry.

But in the royal family, one person was not ready for a happy holiday. 'No way. Uh-uh,' said Rapunzel. 'I refuse to celebrate Christmas!'

'What?' cried Flynn. 'Why don't you want to celebrate the most wonderful holiday of the year?'

Rapunzel looked shocked. Flynn was confused until Rapunzel shared her memories of Christmases spent in Mother Gothel's tower.

'You know how it is,' Rapunzel said. 'There's all of that eerie Christmas music. Mother Gothel sang it nonstop at Christmastime. I hate chanting and growling.'

That didn't sound like any Christmas music Flynn had ever heard. But he let Rapunzel continue, 'Mother Gothel also told us the tale of Nicholas, the ghostly Christmas elf – how he creeps into children's rooms on Christmas Eve and steals them away. It kept me up at bedtime!'

Rapunzel sighed and shrugged.

'But I guess that's why all kids have trouble sleeping on Christmas Eve.'

'Actually, no!' Flynn said. 'That's not what Christmas is like at all!'

It was clear to Flynn that Mother Gothel had made Christmas sound frightening on purpose. It was just another way she had tried to make Rapunzel afraid of the world outside her tower.

He smiled, taking Rapunzel by the hand. 'You know what?' he said. 'I'll show you what Christmas is really like. Come on!'

Flynn took Rapunzel outside the castle. She seemed unsure and a little skittish, but Flynn reassured her. 'Just look around and listen,' he said. 'Does this seem like a spooky holiday to you?'

They passed a group of children singing Christmas carols. The sound was sweet and soothing. The words were all about hope and joy. It was like no Christmas music Rapunzel had ever heard before.

Just then, a small boy ran up to Rapunzel. He held out a package wrapped with a bow. 'Merry Christmas, Princess Rapunzel!' he said. 'I made this for you!'

But Rapunzel didn't take the gift. Her eyes widened in alarm. 'Trick package! Duck!' she cried, diving for cover behind a low stone wall.

She peeked out warily from her hiding place. Flynn and the children stared at her in disbelief.

'It's not a trick,' Flynn said. 'Just a gift.' He opened the box. Inside was a handwoven crown of evergreens.

Slowly, Rapunzel walked over to him and took the crown. She placed it on her head. 'A real Christmas gift?' she said as if she hadn't heard of such a thing. 'Not an exploding trick package?' She knelt by the little boy and took his hands in hers. 'Thank you so much!'

Next, Flynn and Rapunzel came across a tree-decorating party. Together, the townsfolk were decorating an enormous Christmas tree in the centre of the town square.

Rapunzel pointed towards the top of the tree. 'You need a lot more charms up there,' she advised, 'if you want to scare off the ghostly Christmas elf.'

She picked up one of the ornaments. 'And I'm not sure these charms are anywhere near scary enough.'

Flynn took her aside. 'They're not charms,' he explained. 'They're ornaments. For decoration.'

Rapunzel looked confused. 'Oh. Well, then how do you keep the Christmas elf away?'

Flynn couldn't help laughing. 'Okay, next lesson...'

They went back inside the castle, where Flynn read to Rapunzel from several books about St. Nicholas.

'Oh! We had this one at the orphanage,' Flynn said, holding up a red-and-green book. 'See, St. Nicholas isn't a ghostly Christmas elf. He's a jolly old fellow who travels far and wide on Christmas Eve, bringing gifts to all the boys and girls.'

Flynn showed Rapunzel drawings of a smiling bearded man carrying a sack full of presents. 'Definitely no kidnapping.'

Rapunzel and Pascal looked at each other, marvelling at the idea. And to think of all those Christmas Eves they'd spent huddled together by the fire, too afraid to sleep! 'You mean, children have trouble sleeping on Christmas Eve because they are excited?' she asked.

Flynn nodded. 'That's right,' he said. 'So, now that you know what Christmas is really like, do you think you might be interested in celebrating it this year? For real? For the first time?'

Rapunzel's face lit up. 'Yes!' she replied, and she sprang into action.

For weeks, Rapunzel lived and breathed Christmas, enjoying everything that the holiday season had to offer – everything she had missed out on while living in the tower.

In the castle kitchen, she helped bake dozens and dozens of Christmas cookies.

She learned every word of every Christmas carol she had never heard before.

She decked every undecked inch of hall with garlands and ribbon and, for the first time, she made beautiful, not spooky, Christmas ornaments.

Finally, she wrapped handmade gifts for each member of her family. She could hardly wait until Christmas to see them opened.

By the time Christmas Eve arrived, Rapunzel was exhausted, but very, very happy. Her family gathered to celebrate around their Christmas tree.

Rapunzel's father, the King, proposed a toast. 'For years, our hearts have not felt whole at this time of year, because an important part of them was missing.' He smiled at Rapunzel.

The Queen raised her glass and added, 'But now, for the first time since you were born, Rapunzel, this holiday is a joyful one – for all of us.'

Rapunzel couldn't agree more. Surrounded by her warm, loving family, in front of the crackling fire, she could not imagine a better Christmas.

Rapunzel sighed happily and flopped down next to Flynn on a cosy settee. 'Thank you. For all of this,' she said.

'I should really be thanking you,' Flynn admitted. 'You know, this is my first Christmas with a real family. All those years in the orphanage, I knew what Christmas was supposed to be like, but it somehow never felt that merry. Until now.'

Flynn and Rapunzel sat together in front of the fire, waiting for Christmas to come. But before long, Rapunzel fell asleep.

Flynn smiled. After all those spooky, sleepless Christmas Eves in the tower, Rapunzel had certainly earned a peaceful holiday.

It had been a wonderful Christmas Eve. And there would be many more like it for years to come.

WRITE A LETTER TO
FATHER CHRISTMAS

Rapunzel only learned about St. Nicholas when she returned to her family. Write a letter to St. Nicholas, who also goes by the name Father Christmas!

Father Christmas
Santa's Grotto
Reindeerland
The North Pole

Dear Father Christmas,

Thank you for my presents last year, I love my scooter and ride it every day!

YOU WILL NEED

- paper
- pens or pencils
- stickers

- glitter
- an envelope
- a stamp

1. Start your letter with 'Dear Father Christmas'.

2. You could begin by introducing yourself and telling Father Christmas your name and age.

3. You could say thank you for any presents you received last year and maybe tell him a fun story from your year.

4. Then you can ask Father Christmas for any gifts you'd like this year – remember to say please!

5. Don't forget to say hello to the elves and reindeer!

6. Decorate your letter with lots of doodles, stickers and glitter.

7. Fold your letter up and put it in the envelope. On the front of the envelope, write Father Christmas's address:
    Father Christmas
    Santa's Grotto
    Reindeerland
    The North Pole

9. Finally, stick on the stamp and post your letter!

MICKEY AND MINNIE'S GIFT OF THE MAGI

It was the day before Christmas. The bright morning sun was sparkling on the freshly fallen snow. There was a chill in the air as Mickey and Pluto strolled down the street.

Mickey's coat was old and tattered. His Christmas tree was small. And his pockets were as empty as the stockings hanging in homes all over town, waiting to be filled. But Mickey was happy.

Suddenly, Pluto started to bark. He pulled Mickey over to a shop window. Inside was a beautiful golden chain that twinkled in the morning sunlight.

'That's it, Pluto,' Mickey sighed. 'The perfect gift to go with Minnie's watch.'

Mickey reached into his pockets. 'I'm a little short of money right now,' he told Pluto. 'But we're going to make lots of tips today, aren't we?'

Pluto looked doubtfully at Mickey.

'Come on,' Mickey said. 'Let's get this tree to Minnie's. We'll come back for the chain later.'

Meanwhile, at home, Minnie was worrying over a pile of unpaid bills. 'Oh, Figaro,' she sighed, 'how am I ever going to afford to buy Mickey a present?'

Just then, Minnie heard a knock at the door. She quickly shoved the bills in a drawer and raced into the living room.

Minnie opened the front door to find Mickey carrying a tree and playing a happy song on his harmonica.

Minnie giggled. 'Oh, Mickey, when you play the harmonica, my heart sings.'

Mickey brought the tree inside. Then he wrapped his harmonica in an old rag.

'You know, an instrument like that deserves a special case,' Minnie told him.

'I suppose it does,' Mickey said. 'Maybe someday it will have one.'

Mickey asked Minnie what time it was.

'Let's see,' Minnie replied, pulling a string out of her pocket. On the end hung a lovely old watch.

'I bet that would look real nice on a gold chain,' Mickey said.

Minnie took another look at her watch.

'Oh, my goodness! I'm late for work!' she exclaimed.

Minnie quickly put her watch away and headed for the door. But Mickey beat her outside. He and Pluto wanted to drop her off.

Pluto pulled up in front of Mortimer's Department Store. Minnie had made it to work just in time!

Minnie gave Mickey a quick kiss and then dashed inside.

Mickey turned to Pluto. 'Come on, fella, we have work to do!' Together, the pair hurried off.

Unfortunately, dropping Minnie off had made Mickey late for his own job at Crazy Pete's Christmas Tree Farm.

'Merry Christmas, Mr. Pete,' Mickey said when he arrived.

'I'll be merry when I've sold all those ten-footers!' Pete barked. 'Now get to work!'

The day was busier than Mickey had expected. It seemed that many people had waited till the last minute to buy their trees. Even better, the customers were so impressed with Mickey's help that he earned a lot of extra money.

'Hot dog!' Mickey exclaimed. 'Looks like we'll be able to get Minnie that chain for her watch after all!'

Nearby, Pete was trying to convince a poor family to buy an expensive Christmas tree.

'That's all I've got left,' Pete lied. 'You don't want these kids going without a tree now, do ya?'

Over on his side of the lot, Mickey heard Pete. He didn't think his boss was being fair. 'How about this smaller tree?' Mickey called out. 'I found it in the back!'

The children were delighted. 'It's perfect!'

'We'll take it.' their father said. 'Thank you! And Merry Christmas!'

After the family left, Pete was furious. 'I had them on the hook for a ten-foot tree!' he growled at Mickey. 'I'm taking what I would have made off that tree out of your pay!'

And with that, Pete snatched Mickey's money right out of his hand.

'Now get out of my sight!' Pete roared, tossing Mickey and Pluto headfirst into the snow. 'You're fired!'

Across town at Mortimer's, Minnie was busy wrapping Christmas gifts.

'I really want to get Mickey something special this year,' Minnie told her friend Daisy. 'But I can't do it without that Christmas bonus!'

Just then, the phone rang. It was Minnie's boss. He wanted to see her in his office. Minnie put down the gift she was wrapping and raced upstairs.

Minnie was sure she was about to get her Christmas bonus. But when she reached her boss's office, Mr. Mortimer handed her a gift instead.

'A fruitcake?' Minnie said, surprised. She tried to hide her disappointment. 'Thank you, sir.'

'No need to thank me,' Mr. Mortimer replied.

Minnie left his office. 'How am I ever going to get Mickey a present now?' she sighed sadly.

Meanwhile, Mickey sat in the park playing his harmonica. He had lost his job and his money. How could he pay for Minnie's present now?

Then the fire chief heard Mickey playing. The local firemen were putting on a concert to collect Christmas toys for orphans and they needed a harmonica player!

Mickey happily agreed to play for them.

Soon his music was delighting everyone. The listeners were so moved that they donated lots of toys!

'You and that harmonica make a great team,' the fire chief told Mickey when the concert was over.

'She's worth her weight in gold,' Mickey agreed.

His eyes lit up. 'That's it!' he shouted. 'Come on, Pluto! We still have time to get to the shop before it closes.'

The pair borrowed a snowboard and flew through the streets. They made it to the shop just as the shopkeeper was locking the door.

Mickey begged the shopkeeper to reopen the store but the owner just shook his head. He needed to get home to his family.

Mickey sat on the curb and played his harmonica sadly. Touched by Mickey's beautiful Christmas song, the shopkeeper changed his mind about closing his shop. He unlocked the door and let Mickey trade his harmonica for the gold chain in the window.

Later that night, Mickey and Minnie sat in front of the fire with Pluto and Figaro, preparing to exchange gifts. Mickey handed Minnie a beautifully wrapped box.

'I hope you like it!' he told her.

Minnie unwrapped her gift first. 'A chain for my watch!' she exclaimed. 'Oh Mickey, it's beautiful. I love it! But I traded in my watch to buy your gift...'

Mickey slowly unwrapped his gift.

'A case for my harmonica,' he said.

Mickey looked at Minnie. 'I traded my harmonica to get the chain for your watch,' he confessed.

'Oh, Mickey, I can't believe you gave up what means the most to you for me!' Minnie exclaimed.

'Minnie, don't you know you're all the music I'll ever need?' Mickey asked.

'Merry Christmas, Mickey!' Minnie said happily.

Mickey took her hand. 'Merry Christmas, Minnie.'

The couple smiled at each other. It was a Christmas they'd never forget!

MAKE A
SNOW GLOBE

Making your own wintry snow globe is easier than you think!

YOU WILL NEED

- jar with screw top lid
- glitter

- small toy or Christmas decoration
- non-water-soluble glue

1. Fill your jar with water, screw on the lid and shake it to make sure it doesn't leak.

2. Remove the lid and dry it thoroughly.

3. Glue your toy or decorations to the inside of the lid and leave to dry completely.

4. Sprinkle glitter into the water and stir it around.

5. Screw the lid back on – make sure it's on tightly!

6. Shake your snow globe and watch the glitter snow fall!

TOP TIP!

If you can find glycerine in the baking aisle of a supermarket, it will help your glitter fall more slowly. Mix two parts water with one part glycerine before adding your glitter.

DECEMBER

BELLE TO THE RESCUE

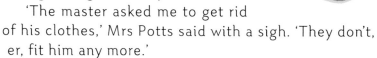

'Mrs Potts!' Belle called, as she walked into the kitchen. 'I found this bag of clothing sitting in the foyer.'

'The master asked me to get rid of his clothes,' Mrs Potts said with a sigh. 'They don't, er, fit him any more.'

'I'll say,' said Lumiere. 'Not to mention that none of the trousers have a hole for his tail!'

'Luckily, the peddler is coming today,' said Mrs Potts. 'He'll be happy to take them off our hands.'

Belle returned the bag to the foyer, then came back to the kitchen.

Just then, Chip appeared. 'Hi Belle!' he said. 'Would you like to play hide-and-seek with me?'

'I would love to,' said Belle. 'Why don't I count while you hide?'

'... ninety-eight, ninety-nine, one hundred. Ready or not, here I come!' called Belle.

Rat-a-tat-tat. She was interrupted by a knock on the door.

A peddler stood at the door, proudly displaying his goods. Belle looked at the shiny ice skates. 'You have so many lovely items,' she said. 'But we don't need anything today. However I do have this bag of clothing for you,' she told him.

The peddler's eyes lit up. 'You are too kind!' he exclaimed. 'You must take these in return.' He gave Belle the ice skates.

'Now what was I doing?' said Belle, as she watched the peddler leave. 'Oh, my goodness – I was looking for Chip!'

She searched among the books in the library.

She even peered inside the suits of armour in the great hall.

'Come out, come out, wherever you are!' Belle shouted in the ballroom. But her voice just echoed back at her. Chip was nowhere to be found.

'You win, Chip,' Belle called. 'Chip...?'

'May I be of assistance, Mademoiselle?' asked Lumiere.

'I can't find Chip anywhere,' Belle told him. 'I haven't seen him since the peddler – oh, no! He must have been hiding in the bag of clothes I gave away!'

'Come on, Lumiere,' she said. 'We have to find Chip before he's lost forever!'

Belle quickly pulled on her cape and boots. Then, she grabbed her new ice skates and put them over her arm, just in case.

Outside, Lumiere pointed to the tracks the peddler's wagon had left in the snow. 'It looks like he took a wrong turn.'

'That means he's on the castle grounds!' Belle cried. 'There's still time to catch up with him.'

Belle and Lumiere galloped through the snow on Belle's horse, Philippe.

Awooooo! Belle and Lumiere gasped. They knew that sound. It was a wolf!

Spooked, Philippe reared up and stumbled off the road into a huge snowbank. Belle and Lumiere went flying!

Once Belle had caught her breath, she grabbed a nearby branch and hoisted herself out of the snow. Next, she rescued Lumiere. Belle pulled and pulled but couldn't budge Philippe. Then, she had an idea! Using her skates like spades, Belle dug out Philippe!

Belle walked up to the tree, grabbed a branch and began to climb, higher and higher. 'I see him up ahead by the lake!' Belle called out triumphantly.

They walked to the lake's edge. 'He's so far away!' Lumiere wailed.

Belle smiled. 'Or is he?' she said.

Belle led them all onto the frozen lake, hoping to go

straight across. But as soon as Philippe stepped onto the ice, there was a sharp crack!

'Philippe is too heavy!' cried Lumiere.

What were they going to do? Belle looked down and saw the answer.

She quickly strapped on her new skates and stepped onto the ice.

'Whoa!' Belle cried, as she tried to keep her balance. But after a moment, she was skating smoothly.

Belle's skates glided over the gleaming ice. The wind whipped through her hair as she sped across the lake, faster and faster.

With her eyes fixed on the peddler, Belle didn't notice a fallen tree until it was almost too late. Luckily, she swerved out of the way just in time!

Finally, Belle reached the other side. 'Monsieur!' she cried, out of breath. 'You took a wrong turn. But first, I think something very dear to me fell into the bag of clothes I gave you. A small teacup with a chip on its rim.'

'All that trouble for a teacup with a chip in it,' said the peddler, shaking his head.

'It's my favourite one!' said Belle. She opened the bag and there was Chip, cosy as could be.

'Great hiding spot, huh, Belle?' he whispered.

'The very best,' said Belle with a grin.

CHRISTMAS TRADITIONS

Christmas is a time for traditions with friends and family. Why not try something new this festive season that you can enjoy year after year?

1 Make a special hot chocolate and watch a Christmas film with your family. A different person could choose the film each year.

2 Choose two old toys you no longer play with and donate them to charity.

3 Decorate a gingerbread house to display in the lead up to Christmas Day.

4 Put on a Christmas concert for friends and family.

5 Start a Christmas scrapbook you can add to every year. You could include:
- photos of you and your family
- stories about fun things that happened over the festive period
- your favourite meal
- the presents you received
- what the weather was like

DECEMBER

A BIG, BLUE CHRISTMAS

'Dad, wake up!' Nemo shouted early one morning as he swam back and forth across their anemone home.

'What is it, Nemo?' asked Marlin, waking in a hurry. 'Are you hurt? Is something wrong?'

'No, Dad,' the little clownfish answered. 'It's just that I have a terrific idea! It's almost Christmas. Could we have a holiday party?'

'Sounds like fun, Nemo,' Marlin said with a yawn. 'But let's wait until after breakfast to start planning.'

Right after breakfast, Nemo and Marlin made a list of friends to invite. It was a long list because they had friends all over the ocean. Marlin wondered how they'd let everyone know in time.

'I can ask Bruce, Chum and Anchor to help spread the word,' Nemo offered. 'No one can say no to those guys.'

Marlin thought it over. Nemo was right. No fish he knew wanted to get on a shark's bad side. 'Well, all right, son,' he said. 'But be careful.'

'I know, Dad,' Nemo said. 'See you later!' he called as he swam off.

Nemo swam as fast as he could to the old shipwreck where his shark friends hung out. 'Hey, Bruce! Guys!' Nemo said when he arrived.

'Check out what the tide washed in,' said Anchor.

'Why it's our little food, I mean, friend, Nemo,' Chum said.

'What brings you out this way, Nemo?' asked Bruce.

The little clownfish told them all about the Christmas party. The sharks were thrilled. They hadn't been invited to many parties. Then Nemo asked them to help tell everyone about it. 'You can count on us,' Bruce said proudly.

'Thanks,' said Nemo. 'And, guys, we will be counting our guests, too, so remember...'

'Fish are friends, not food,' the four of them said together.

Nemo swam home as fast as he could. His father was swimming back and forth across their anemone nervously.

'We need to plan the menu,' Marlin muttered. 'And then there's cleaning and decorating and—'

'Stop right there, Dad,' said Nemo. 'We're going to need help. I'll be back later with more fins!'

Nemo had made some great friends when he had been captured and put in a tank in a dentist's office.

The whole Tank Gang had eventually escaped and were now living in the ocean. Nemo went to find them and ask for their help with the party.

When Nemo returned home that afternoon, two of his old pals from the Tank Gang were with him.

Deb was a blue-and-white humbug fish. She got to work on the food. But she insisted on keeping the dessert a surprise.

Jacques was a cleaner shrimp. He started to work doing what he did best – cleaning. Soon the anemone was so clean it sparkled.

'It's too bad Flo couldn't be here,' said Deb sadly. 'She does like a party.'

Nemo and Marlin winked at each other. They knew that Flo was really only Deb's reflection in the tank glass.

Next Nemo swam off to find their friend Dory, the regal blue tang fish.

'Do I know you?' Dory asked when Nemo finally found her. Nemo smiled. Dory was the most forgetful fish he knew. All of a sudden, Dory hugged him and said, 'Nemo! I've missed you!'

'Would you like to help us decorate for a party?' said Nemo.

'I love parties,' said Dory. 'At least I think I love parties. I can't really remember if I've ever been to one.'

That afternoon, Dory, Marlin and Nemo worked hard putting up all the decorations. They hung streamers and wreaths and decorated a conch shell Christmas tree.

Meanwhile, the sharks were busy inviting all the guests. Finally, just the sea turtles were left. The three sharks took a ride on the East Australian Current to catch up with them.

Make a Bauble

These pretty baubles would make a great present, as well as looking pretty on your Christmas tree!

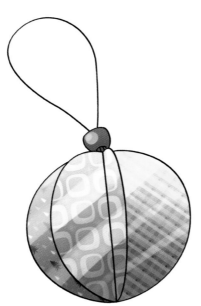

You Will Need

- thin coloured card or wrapping paper
- compass
- pencil
- scissors
- glue
- thread
- coloured sequins or beads

1. Use a compass to draw eight circles all the same size on different coloured card or wrapping paper. If you use wrapping paper, you might want to stick it to some thin card first so your bauble is more sturdy.

2. Fold each circle in half.

3. Glue a long piece of thread to the back of one of the circles, close to the fold. You'll use this to hang up your bauble.

4. Glue two circles together so two halves are back-to-back, covering the thread.

5. Continue gluing the circles together by their halves until you have a complete bauble.

6. Thread a couple of sequins or beads onto the thread and tie a knot to keep them in place.

7. Make a loop with the thread and tie in place. Your bauble is ready to hang!

TOP TIP!

Cut star shapes from card to make a star bauble!

THE WONDERFUL WINTER TREE

Bambi awoke one morning to find the whole world covered in a soft white blanket.

'What is it, Mother?' Bambi asked as he gazed around in wonder.

'This is snow,' replied his mother. 'It means winter is upon us.'

'Snow!' said Bambi. He took a cautious step... and then another... and another. He felt the icy crystals crunch under his hooves. He looked back at the tiny tracks he had made. 'I like snow!'

'Snow is pretty to look at,' his mother told him, 'but it makes winter hard for all the animals.'

Bambi was about to ask her why winter was harder than other seasons. But just then, his friend Thumper came hopping over.

'Hiya, Bambi!' said the bunny. 'Come on! Let's go sliding!' He led Bambi to the pond, which was frozen solid.

Thumper slapped at the ice with his foot. 'Come on! It's all right,' he told Bambi. 'See? The water's stiff!'

Bambi saw his friend, Flower the skunk. 'You want to come sliding?' Bambi called, running over. 'Thumper says the water's stiff.'

But Flower shook his head. 'No, thanks. I'm off to my den. I'm going to sleep through the winter.' He yawned.

'Goodbye, Bambi,' he said.

'Bye, Flower,' said Bambi. Then he spied another friend, a squirrel, scurrying up an oak tree.

'The pond is stiff, Squirrel,' called Bambi. 'Want to come sliding with me?'

'Thanks,' replied the squirrel as he ducked into a hollow in the tree, 'but I have to store nuts for the long winter.' He showed Bambi the pile he had already collected. 'No sliding for me today.'

So Bambi headed back to Thumper and the ice-covered pond by himself.

By that time, Thumper was sliding across the ice with some of his sisters. They made it look so easy. But when Bambi stepped on the ice, he lost his balance right away. His hooves went sliding in four different directions!

'Kind of wobbly, aren't ya,' said Thumper. He laughed. 'Come on, Bambi. You can do it!'

But Bambi wasn't so sure. Sliding across the stiff water wasn't quite as much fun for deer, it seemed, as it was for rabbits. And it also made him hungry. He said goodbye to the bunnies and went back to find his mother.

'Mother, I'm hungry,' Bambi told her.

In the spring, summer and autumn they had been able to find food almost anywhere they looked. But now that it was winter, Bambi could see that finding food wasn't so easy.

There were no leaves on the trees and the grass was covered with snow and ice. The snow was so cold that when he poked through it, Bambi thought his nose might freeze. At last Bambi's mother uncovered a small patch of grass. Bambi nibbled it eagerly.

Then Bambi curled up with his mother for a nap. The ground was hard and cold and the wind was chilly. Bambi was grateful to have his mother there to keep him warm.

'Is this why the birds fly south and why our other friends sleep through the winter?' Bambi asked her.

His mother nodded and snuggled even closer. 'But don't worry, Bambi,' she told him. 'Winter doesn't last forever.'

By the end of December, it seemed like there was nothing left in the forest but bitter bark for Bambi to eat. The days grew short and the nights grew long, and throughout them Bambi's stomach rumbled. And then one day, something truly amazing happened.

Thumper was the first to see it. 'Hey, Bambi!' he hollered. 'Would you look at that tree!'

Bambi followed Thumper's paw. He couldn't believe his eyes.

There before them was a tall pine tree unlike Bambi had ever seen. It was draped with strings of bright berries and yummy popcorn and from each branch hung a ripe, juicy apple. But the most wonderful thing to Bambi was the gold star at the very top.

'Mother!' exclaimed Bambi. 'Look what Thumper found!'

Cautiously, his mother drew closer. 'It can't be...' she whispered. 'It seems almost too good to be true.'

'What is it, Mother?' Bambi asked her.

'The most beautiful tree in the world,' she answered. She smiled down at Bambi. 'What a special gift to have on your first Christmas.'

'Who left it, Mother?' Bambi asked.

'I don't know, ' she replied.

'Maybe someone who loves animals,' Thumper said, hopping up and down. 'This is the best gift ever.' He sniffed one of the apples hanging low to the ground.

'Can we share this food with every one of our friends, Mother?' Bambi asked.

'Yeah and with my sisters, too?' Thumper chimed in.

'I don't see why not,' Bambi's mother said. 'Christmas is a time to share what we have with those we love.'

Bambi and Thumper danced happily around the tree. 'Look at all the popcorn and berries!' Thumper cried. 'And look at that star at the tippy top, too!'

Bambi stopped prancing. He looked up at the golden star at the top of the tree. Then he looked up at the sky above him. The sun was just beginning to go down. He knew that very soon, there would be a star twinkling in the sky just like the one at the top of the tree. A gentle hush fell over the clearing.

He danced back over to his mother and took a big bite out of one of the juicy green apples. *Mmm!* he thought. Nothing had ever tasted so good!

Gazing up at the star and at the wonderful winter tree, Bambi could feel a happy, warm glow swelling inside him. There was enough food on the tree to feed all the animals who were hungry. *What a magical gift*, thought Bambi.

Winter was long and hard... and yet wonderful, after all.

Design your own
Wrapping Paper

Making your own wrapping paper is easy and fun! It's a great way to add a lovely personal touch to presents for family and friends.

You Will Need

- old sheet
- coloured paper
- christmas-shaped cookie cutters

- pencil
- coloured paints
- paintbrush
- felt-tip pens

1. Cover a table with an old sheet as this could get a little messy!

2. Lay out your coloured paper in front of you.

3. Place a cookie cutter onto the paper and carefully trace around it with your pencil.

4. Repeat the pattern all over your paper – or you could use lots of different shapes!

5. Once you are happy with the design, use your paints to colour in each shape.

6. Leave the paint to dry completely and then you can add extra detail with felt-tip pens.

7. When you are happy with your paper, you can use it to wrap up all your Christmas presents!

DESIGN IDEAS

- A Christmas tree covered in lots of colourful baubles
- A frosty snowman with a carrot nose
- Festive holly with bright red berries
- Presents wrapped in ribbon
- Glittery snowflakes

LADY'S CHRISTMAS SURPRISE

It was the week before Christmas. Tramp and the puppies gathered beneath Jim and Darling's brightly decorated tree.

'You all know what holiday is coming up, right?' Tramp asked, his eyes twinkling.

'Of course, Dad,' Scamp said. He was excited. Christmas was the puppies' favourite holiday. Lots of guests stopped by to wish Jim and Darling a happy holiday.

But the best part was the presents. The puppies got to help choose a special gift for each of their parents. They loved being trusted with two such important surprises.

'Do any of you kids know what your mother would like for Christmas?' Tramp asked.

'How about a steak from Tony's Restaurant?' Annette said.

Tramp shook his head. 'We can do better than that.'

'We need to give her something special,' said Colette, 'to show how much we love her.'

'Why don't you ask her what she'd like?' said Scamp, his voice muffled. He was chewing on a bow.

'We want to surprise her,' Tramp reminded his son. He nudged him away from the presents. 'That's the fun of Christmas.'

'Maybe we'll find something on our walk today,' Annette said. Tramp thought that was a good idea. While Lady was taking a nap, he took the kids into town to look for the perfect present.

The village bustled with shoppers, their carriage wheels carving deep ruts in the snowy road.

The dogs rambled up and down the avenue, looking in all the shop windows. They saw jumpers, cushions, brush and comb sets, bowls and collars. But Tramp knew that none of these things was the perfect gift for Lady. He wanted to find her something special. Something that she would enjoy and that no other dog would have.

Tramp and the puppies kept looking into shop windows and they peeked at the packages people carried. All they needed was one really good idea.

When the sun started to sink in the sky, Tramp turned to the puppies and said, 'We'd better head home now. Maybe we'll find something tomorrow.'

As they crossed the road, Tramp noticed something sparkling in the snow. It was much brighter than an icicle. He turned it over with his paw.

'Holy hambones!' he cried. It was a gold and emerald necklace!

'What a bunch of rocks!' exclaimed Scamp.

'What a good stroke of luck!' remarked Annette.

'Just the right size for Mother!' added Colette.

Tramp smiled and then scooped up the necklace with his mouth. It seemed they'd found the perfect gift. He knew it would look beautiful on Lady.

Suddenly, Tramp dropped the necklace into the snow. It sparkled in the icy crystals. He frowned.

'What's the matter?' Scamp asked.

'This isn't right,' Tramp muttered. Then he looked at his children. 'Sorry, kids, but we have to return the necklace. It's not ours to take.'

'But where would we go to return it?' Colette asked.

'Yeah, it was just here in the snow,' Annette said. 'How would we even find the owner?'

'I say finders keepers!' Scamp cried.

'Come on now, kids,' Tramp said. 'We can take it to the police. They'll know who to return it to.'

With the puppies following, he bounded down the block to the station.

Inside, officers hurried around taking phone calls and writing reports.

'Stay close, kids,' Tramp whispered to the puppies. 'I don't want to lose you in the crowd.'

Tramp trotted up to the front desk, the puppies following behind. He dropped the necklace in front of the policeman in charge.

'What's this?' the officer said as he looked at the dog and then back to the necklace on the desk. He picked up the necklace and looked at the sparkling jewels.

Tramp panted and wagged his tail. The puppies stood eagerly beside him. *Yip! Yip!*

'You found it?' the officer asked.

Tramp nodded.

'Good dog! ' he exclaimed.

The policeman took the necklace and began filling out his report while Tramp and the puppies watched.

At that moment, a woman rushed into the station. 'Help!' she cried. 'My necklace is gone! I'm offering a reward for its return.'

The policeman smiled at the woman. Then he held out the necklace. 'Is this yours?' he asked. He pointed to Tramp. 'This dog found it on the street and brought it here.'

The woman gasped. 'Thank you,' she said. She scratched Tramp behind his ear. 'How can I repay you?'

Woof! Tramp looked at the necklace. 'A new collar,' she said. 'That's it!'

She took Tramp and the puppies to the shop next door. Tramp walked up to the counter and picked up a gold collar with green stones that looked just like the woman's necklace.

'I'll take that one,' the woman told the shopkeeper.

On Christmas morning Lady tore open the gift. 'You shouldn't have!' Her eyes sparkled like the green stones.

When Darling fastened the collar around Lady's neck, she pranced around the room as if she were a show dog.

'I love my new collar,' Lady said. 'What a wonderful Christmas surprise! But I love my family even more.' She nuzzled Tramp and each of the puppies.

'Merry Christmas, Mother,' said the puppies. And it was a very merry Christmas, indeed.

MAKE A POMPOM

Make colourful fluffy pompoms of all shapes and sizes!
You could use extra wool and hang them on your Christmas tree.

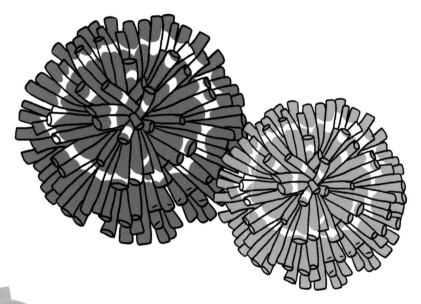

ASK AN ADULT FOR HELP

YOU WILL NEED

- cardboard
- pencil
- scissors
- wool

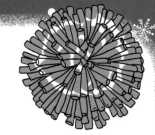

1. Draw two identical circles on to the cardboard – you could trace around a mug or a glass. Carefully cut out the circles.

2. Draw two smaller circles in the middle of each piece – you could trace around a coin or bottle lid. Carefully cut a slit from the outside and cut out the small circle to form two cardboard rings.

3. Holding the two rings together, start wrapping the wool around until the whole ring is covered. Wrap it as many times as you can, you want more than one layer of wool so your pompom is big and fluffy!

4. Carefully cut the wool all the way around the outer edge of the circle. You might want to use small sharp scissors for this.

5. Slightly separate the two pieces of card. Tie a piece of wool between the rings – knot it nice and tightly to hold your pompom together.

6. Pull off the two card rings and puff up the pompom. If you want, you can carefully trim the edges of the pompom to make it a little neater and help it to fluff up.

TOP TIP! Make pompoms in different sizes and colours and use them to decorate your wrapped presents.

THE PUPPIES' MESSY CHRISTMAS

One winter evening, Pongo and Perdita were watching TV with their puppies when a rustling noise in the hallway caught their attention. The puppies jumped off their chairs and ran to the doorway.

They all watched silently as Roger and Nanny hauled a huge tree into the parlour. It was fresh and green and made the room smell like a pine forest.

'What's going on?' Rolly asked, turning to look at his mother.

'Don't worry, dear,' said Perdita. 'It's Christmas Eve. This is just the beginning!'

'Chris-mess?' Lucky asked. 'It does look like a mess.' He wagged his tail.

The parlour floor was covered with pine needles, boxes of ornaments, tinsel garlands and strings of small lights.

Anita was waiting in the parlour to help Roger and Nanny. The puppies looked on in awe as their human pets began acting very strangely. Roger hung shiny coloured globes on the branches. Anita was winding a garland around the tree.

When the tree was finished and the room tidied, Roger flipped a switch. The lights and shiny ornaments cast a magical glow about the room. The puppies looked wide-eyed at the tree.

That night, when Pongo and Perdita tucked the puppies into their basket, they told them all about Christmas.

'It's a time when people show their families and friends how much they care for them,' Pongo said. He explained how humans sent cards, baked cookies and fruitcakes and sang festive carols.

'It may sound strange but you'll grow to love the holiday season,' Perdita said. She nuzzled Patch, who let out a yawn.

'Especially the beef bones left over from dinner,' Pongo added.

'Bones?' Patch said, perking up. His father smiled.

'And that's not all,' Perdita continued. 'On Christmas Eve, after everyone's in bed, people sneak presents under the tree.'

'Presents?' all the puppies said at once.

'What kind of presents?' Patch asked. 'Can you wish for them?'

'I'd wish for a new bed,' Lucky said as he climbed into the basket he shared with his brothers and sisters.

'Why do people put presents under the tree?' Pepper asked.

'Christmas is about giving,' Pongo told the puppies. 'People give presents to their friends and family to show how much they love them.'

'I wonder if we will get any presents?' said Rolly.

'Maybe,' Perdita replied. 'Anita gave me a new collar last year.'

'And I got a red ball,' said Pongo.

'I hope someone loves us,' said Penny.

'You are all loved, whether or not there are presents under the tree,' Perdita said. 'Now time for bed. Tomorrow is a big day.'

On Christmas morning, the puppies woke at dawn. They crept into the parlour. Sure enough, there were piles of brightly wrapped packages under the tree.

'We are loved!' Freckles cried.

The puppies dived into the pile of presents. They tossed the packages around and ripped and tore at the coloured paper.

'Christmas is fun!' Rolly exclaimed as he shook some wrapping paper out of his mouth.

Lucky pulled open a box. 'Perfume?' he said and wrinkled

his nose.

Penny dragged a spotted necktie out of some tissue paper. 'What do I need with more spots?'

Freckles held up a lace handkerchief. 'What is this for?' he asked.

Just then, they heard Roger's and Anita's voices in the hallway. The puppies looked at each other in alarm.

'Let's get out of here!' Rolly said. The puppies scampered around the room, hiding behind the sofa, under the chairs and in the folds of the curtains.

The puppies trembled when they heard Roger's footsteps. He stopped in the doorway. 'What on earth?' he said.

Anita walked up beside him. 'Oh, dear!' she cried.

'Perdita, Pongo,' Roger called out. 'Where are you?'

The puppies heard the click of their parents' claws on the wooden floor as they scurried toward the parlour.

When they came into the room, Pongo said, 'Woof!'

And Perdita repeated, 'Woof!'

The puppies looked at each other uncertainly. 'We're in for it now,' Lucky whispered.

Then they heard something very strange. Anita started to laugh.

Roger said, with a chuckle, 'Looks like we had some help opening our gifts.'

'Wasn't that kind of the puppies!' Nanny said as she walked into the room and saw the mess of paper and ribbon.

'I wonder where they've gone off to,' Roger said with a twinkle in his eye. 'Here, pups!'

'There are still so many boxes to unwrap,' Anita said, shaking her head. 'I do wish they'd come and help.'

The puppies slowly crept out from their hiding places and gathered around the tree.

Roger pointed to the packages. 'Go for it, boys and girls!'

Yip! Yip! The puppies attacked the presents, tearing

into the bright wrappings and the tangled ribbons.

When the puppies grew tired of rolling around in the wrapping paper, Anita brought out a large basket.

'Sorry we didn't have time to wrap these,' she said. 'But then,' she smiled, 'maybe you've done enough work for today.'

She handed each puppy a squeaky toy.

From the bottom of the basket she pulled out two Christmas sweaters for Pongo and Perdita.

'Anita knitted them herself,' said Roger with pride.

That evening, after Christmas dinner was over, the puppies were still full of energy. They weren't ready to go to bed.

'We like Christmas!' said Pepper.

'We like our toys!' said Rolly.

'We like wrapping paper!' said Patch.

'But remember what we told you about Christmas?' Perdita asked. She nudged her children towards their basket. 'It's a time for giving.'

'It's also about forgiving,' Pongo said gently. 'You were lucky that Roger and Anita weren't upset that you unwrapped their presents.'

The puppies heads drooped a little.

'We're lucky to have two wonderful humans,' Perdita said softly. 'That is the best present of all.'

The puppies raised their eyes to their mother hopefully.

'We are loved,' Penny said. She smiled.

'You are all, each and every one of you, loved,' Perdita assured her children.

'And that's what Christmas is really all about,' Pongo said as the puppies drifted off to sleep.

Make a
Christmas Wreath

Hang this wreath on your front door to welcome friends and family!

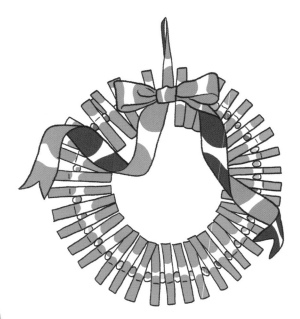

ASK AN ADULT FOR HELP

You Will Need

- clothes pegs
- cardboard box
- green paint
- paintbrush

- wire
- coloured beads
- coloured ribbon

1. Pin the clothes pegs around the edge of an old cardboard box.

2. Carefully paint each peg green and leave to dry.

3. Ask an adult to shape the wire into a circle but leave the ends open.

4. Thread a coloured bead onto the wire and then clip on a peg. Repeat this process until the wire is completely covered.

5. Ask an adult to twist together the ends of the wire to hold everything in place.

6. Tie the ribbon into a bow at the top of the wreath to cover the ends of the wire. Don't forget to add a loop to hang up your wreath!

TOP TIP!

Experiment with different paint colours to make a really unique wreath!

14
DECEMBER

DONALD'S CHRISTMAS TREE

It was the day before Christmas. Donald had baked cookies and wrapped gifts. Now all he needed was a Christmas tree.

Donald put on his coat and cap and grabbed his axe. 'Come on, Pluto,' he said. 'We're going to find our tree.'

Pluto and Donald went deep into the woods. Donald looked left. He looked right. Then he saw it – the perfect tree. Donald picked up his axe and went to work.

'TIMBER!' Donald cried as the tree toppled over and landed in the snow.

Inside the tree, two chipmunks named Chip and Dale held on for dear life. They lived in the tree Donald had chosen!

'Come on, Pluto,' called Donald. 'Let's take our tree home.'

Donald Duck went home through the woods, dragging the tree behind him. At home, he set up the tree. He hung ornaments on the branches and strung tinsel all over.

'There!' Donald said when the job was done. 'Doesn't that look fine! Now I just need the gifts. You stay here, Pluto. I'll be right back.'

As soon as Donald was out of sight, Chip and Dale left their hiding place. They danced on the branches until the needles quivered. They made faces at themselves in the shiny coloured balls, tugged on the tinsel, twisted the lights and laughed until their little sides shook.

'Grrr,' growled Pluto disapprovingly. But Chip and Dale did not care. Chip just picked off a shiny ball and threw it at Pluto!

Pluto jumped and barely caught it in his teeth.

At that moment, Donald came back into the room. 'Pluto!' he cried. 'Bad dog!' He thought Pluto had been snatching balls from the tree.

'Now be good,' said Donald, 'while I bring in the rest of the presents.'

No sooner was Donald out of sight than Chip and Dale appeared again. *Plunk!* Chip's head went through a coloured ball. Dale laughed and laughed at the funny sight. But Pluto did not think it was funny at all. They were going to spoil Donald's tree!

Pluto growled but the naughty chipmunks did not stop. He knew he had to do something. Pluto got ready to jump.

'Pluto!' cried Donald from the doorway. 'What is the matter with you? If you can't behave, you'll have to go out to your doghouse for the rest of Christmas Eve.'

Just then, up in the treetop, Chip grew tired of wearing his round golden mask. He pulled off the ball and let it drop.

Crash!

'What was that?' cried Donald, looking at the tree.

Dale began to play with the coloured lights, twisting them so they turned off and on. Donald peered among the branches until he spied Chip and Dale.

'Well, well,' he chuckled, lifting them down. 'So you're the mischief-makers. And to think I blamed poor Pluto. I'm sorry, Pluto.'

Pluto marched to the front door and held it open. He felt Chip and Dale should go out in the snow.

'Oh, Pluto!' cried Donald. 'It's Christmas Eve. We must be kind to everyone. The spirit of Christmas is love, you know.'

So Pluto made friends with Chip and Dale.

And when Mickey and Minnie came to the house for caroling, they all agreed that this was by far the happiest Christmas Eve they had ever had.

MAKE A MINI CHRISTMAS TREE

This mini Christmas tree is perfect to display in your bedroom!

YOU WILL NEED

- a pencil
- thin cardboard
- scissors

- paint
- a paintbrush
- glue

- cotton wool
- sequins, buttons or beads

1. On the cardboard, draw a pyramid with a curved base. Draw a thin flap down one of the pyramid's straight sides and then cut out the shape.

2. Paint one side of the shape green and leave to dry completely.

3. Add glue onto the flap then roll up the cone and glue in place. You might need to hold the cone together for a couple of minutes so the glue can start to set.

4. Rip off small pieces of cotton wool and, starting from the top, glue a spiral of cotton wool around the tree to look like tinsel.

5. Glue on sequins, buttons or beads to add baubles to your tree!

TOP TIP! Use red, black and white paint to make a Father Christmas decoration!

15
DECEMBER

NIGHT
LIGHTS

'I see one! I see one! Pull over, Mr. Fredricksen!' Russell said.

Carl swerved the station wagon to the side of the road.

'Is it a squirrel?' asked Dug as he jumped out of the car.

'Even better!' said Russell. 'According to the *Wilderness Explorer Guide to Flora and Fauna*, it's a Japanese morning glory.'

'Well, I'll be,' said Carl.

They were headed to Sylvan State Park to earn Russell's Better Botanist Badge – his first as a Senior Wilderness Explorer. All he had to do was find and identify ten varieties of wildflower.

'Only nine more to go,' he said as he took a photo of the flower.

Carl looked up at the sky. 'We'd better get moving then. We've got a long drive ahead of us. The wilderness must be explored!'

'Cacaw! Cacaw!' Russell said.

'Ruff!' said Dug.

As they drove, Russell looked at the flowers in his field guide.

'Wow, this book has everything in it,' he said. 'It has sunflowers. It has butterfly milkweed. It has purple wisteria.'

'Does it have a ghost crocus?' asked Carl with a sly smile.

'A what?' asked Russell.

'A ghost crocus,' said Carl. 'It's a legendary flower that blooms only at night. Pale as the moon, glows in the dark, with six silver petals and stars on its stamens. Brave explorers have looked for it for centuries. Most people don't think it exists, but Ellie swore she saw one once at the very park we're going to.'

'Wow!' said Russell. Then he frowned. 'I don't see it in the field guide.'

'Like I said, most people don't think it exists,' said Carl.

The drive was a long one, so they played I spy to pass the time. 'I spy something big and blue!' said Russell.

'I spy something feathery and brown!' said Carl.

'I spy somethi—SQUIRREL!' said Dug.

When they reached the park, it was already mid-morning. It took a while to find their campsite and to set up their tents. By the time they were ready to hike, it was already midday.

'I spy something tall and yellow,' said Carl.

'I spy something small and orange!' said Russell.

'I spy something grey and dark grey and medium grey!' said Dug.

'I spy something... stinky!'

By the time the sun was setting, they had found ten varieties of wildflower! But Russell couldn't stop thinking about the ghost crocus.

'Please, Mr. Fredricksen,' said Russell as they walked back to the campsite, 'can we look for a ghost crocus?'

'Sorry,' said Carl. 'It's getting late. We have to get back to camp before dark.'

That night, they sang around the campfire, told ghost stories and looked at the constellations.

'All right, it's getting very late. It's time for bed,' Carl said.

Carl opened his tent. He had forgotten all about the ghost crocus.

But Russell hadn't. He couldn't sleep knowing there was another flower he could find and identify. Hiking at night might be dangerous for a Junior Wilderness Explorer, but Russell was a Senior Wilderness Explorer. He knew he could handle it!

'Let's go, Dug,' he whispered. 'We're gonna go fetch something.'

'I love fetching,' said Dug.

The woods were a lot darker than Russell had expected. Maybe Mr. Fredricksen was right. It was very late.

But then he spotted a soft glow. It seemed to be coming from the back of a cave.

'I spy something pale and glowing,' he said. What he didn't see was the steep drop – until it was too late! He tumbled down into the mouth of the cave.

'Oh, no! Are you okay?' said Dug. Dug didn't hear a response from the cave, so he ran back to the campsite.

Carl awoke to a wet tongue licking his face.

'Master! Master! We were out in the dark looking for the ghost flower and then Russell fell into the cave!'

'What?' cried Carl. 'Quick! Lead me to him!'

Down in the cave, everything was dark. At first, Russell felt alone and afraid.

But then he remembered: he was a Senior Wilderness Explorer. 'I can handle this!' he said to himself.

He stood up and saw a glimmer of light. It was coming from around the corner. It looked like moonlight. Was it a way out?

'Russell!' someone cried. It was Carl. He had tied a rope to a tree and was lowering himself down into the cave.

'Look!' cried Dug happily. 'I have fetched my master and brought him back!'

'I'm sorry, Russell,' said Carl. 'I shouldn't have told you that story about the ghost crocus. Honestly, I never believed it myself. Ellie always had a great imagination.'

'Well, I found something anyway,' said Russell with a sly smile.

'Well, I'll be,' said Carl.

Carl, Russell and Dug all looked at the ghost crocus with wonder.

The next morning, Russell, Dug and Carl packed up their things and headed back home.

'The Wilderness Explorers are going to be so excited I found all the wildflowers plus one!' Russell chattered away in the back seat.

'Thank you, Ellie,' Carl whispered with a smile.

Nature Explorer

Russell had to find and photograph ten wildflowers to achieve his Better Botanist Badge. How many of the below can you spot?

- Holly
- Mistletoe
- Poinsettia
- Ivy
- Robin

- Goldfinch
- Blackbird
- Nesting ducks
- Grey squirrel
- Fox

Once you've spotted them all you could make yourself a Nature Explorer badge!

 TOP TIP! Don't forget to check Christmas decorations to help spot the plants!

PLAY

CHRISTMAS BINGO

Make these bingo cards to play with your friends and family over Christmas!

Christmas tree	Christmas bow	Bauble	Elf
Christmas cookie	Christmas gift	Christmas cracker	Snowflake
Fairy lights	Candy cane	Reindeer	Star
Holly	Father Christmas	Snowman	Advent candle

Bell	Christmas gift	Snowflake	Holly
Father Christmas	Star	Fairy lights	Candy cane
Wreath	Yule log	Christmas cracker	Elf
Christmas bow	Bauble	Advent candle	Christmas tree

YOU WILL NEED

- paper
- pencil
- ruler

- felt-tip pens
- bowl or hat
- buttons or small sweets

1. Use a ruler to draw a grid on your paper four squares across and four squares down. Make as many grids as players.

2. On squares of paper, write down 24 Christmas-themed items that will fill your bingo cards. As well as objects, you could include Christmas films, festive songs, places special to you or festive activities.

3. Write one of your chosen items in each of the squares on your bingo cards – make sure no two cards are exactly the same!

4. Choose someone to be bingo caller. Put all the squares of paper into a bowl or hat and have the caller pull out one square at a time and read it out loud.

5. If you have that item on your bingo card, cover it with a button or small sweet.

6. Whoever covers four items in a row first – either horizontally, vertically or diagonally – shouts out, BINGO! and is the winner.

TOP TIP!

Instead of writing items on your card, you could draw Christmas objects for a more colourful bingo card!

16

DECEMBER

CHRISTMAS FOR
EVERYONE

On Christmas Eve, a brave fox named Robin Hood and his bear friend Little John were roasting a goose and some chestnuts over an open fire.

'A true feast!' said Friar Tuck, a badger, when he saw the goose.

'We did our best,' said Little John. 'It wasn't easy to get a bird on Christmas Eve. But good ol' Rob knows where to find things.'

Robin Hood laughed. 'Johnny, you give me too much credit. The goose was a Christmas gift from the Sheriff of Nottingham. He won't miss one little bird. You should see the spread he's got over there.'

Friar Tuck shook his head. 'Doesn't seem right. That old Sheriff gets greedier by the day. By the hour!'

Robin Hood thought about what Friar Tuck had said. When they sat down to dinner with Toby Turtle, Robin noticed everyone looked a little down.

'Something's not right,' said Toby Turtle. Robin Hood nodded. He knew Toby was right, but he couldn't figure out what the problem was either. 'The goose tastes great,' Toby said. 'It's just that...'

'I know what it is, Robin,' Little John said. He looked sad. 'We took the day off to get ready for Christmas. The only thing we stole was—'

'The goose!' Robin Hood cried. He couldn't believe he hadn't thought of all the poor people of Nottingham who didn't have anything to eat this Christmas.

'The poor people of Nottingham don't have anything to eat?' Friar Tuck asked. He felt terrible. All day, he'd gone around to the poorest families handing out small purses full of coins gathered from the collection plate. He hadn't thought to bring a Christmas feast to anyone. A single tear rolled down his cheek.

'A Christmas feast is an important part of the festive season,' said Robin. 'And I think I know where we can find one at this late hour.'

Little John smiled. 'Who deserves a feast the least?' he crowed. He knew exactly what Robin was thinking.

'The Sheriff of Nottingham!' Toby said.

The friends set off through the forest on their sleigh. They were on their way to the sheriff's house. They knew he would have plenty of food to spare.

When they reached the sheriff's home, they peered through the frosted window. Robin gasped at the sight before them.

A Yule log blazed on the hearth. The tree twinkled with candles and gifts were everywhere. Steam rose from the large dining table.

'Look at all those gifts, all that food. I can think of a dozen families who would be grateful for just one item from that pile,' Robin Hood said to Little John. 'I'll go to the front door and distract the sheriff. Johnny, you take the men inside, bring the feast and presents out through the kitchen. Then load up the sleigh.'

Robin disguised himself as a blind beggar and rapped on the sheriff's door. When the sheriff opened the door, Robin said, 'Alms for a poor blind man on this wintry eve?'

'Oh, you beggars! Can't you give it a rest?' the sheriff said. 'It's Christmas Eve and I am trying to eat my dinner in peace.'

The sheriff went to close the door but Robin held it open. 'All the more reason to spare something, kind sir,' Robin said.

'Now wait just a minute there,' the sheriff said. 'Haven't I seen that outfit somewhere before?'

Robin shook his head, but the sheriff lunged forward to grab the beggar and lifted his hat. Then he saw the smiling face of Robin Hood! 'I knew it!' said the sheriff. 'You can't fool the good Sheriff of Nottingham.'

Robin smiled. He had tricked the sheriff plenty of times before. He wriggled free of the sheriff's grips and ran off.

The sheriff chased Robin into Sherwood Forest. Robin laughed as he ran. He was so quick that the sheriff could hardly keep up!

When Robin had put enough distance between himself and the sheriff, he climbed high into a tree. He carefully crept out onto a thick branch to look out for the sheriff. He knew the evil man wouldn't give up easily.

Robin heard footsteps crunching through the snow. He peered down and watched the sheriff run through the woods calling after him. The sheriff searched for Robin, but he couldn't find even a footprint.

'I'll get you next time, Robin Hood!' the sheriff called as he ran.

Robin chuckled and slid to the ground. He'd outsmarted the sheriff once again.

Meanwhile, Little John and the rest of the men had taken the sheriff's gifts and feast. They loaded their sleigh with brightly wrapped packages, roast turkey and plum pudding. They even took a magnificent Christmas tree.

Little John took hold of the front of the sleigh and started to run. Robin Hood soon caught up with his friends. 'There's no time to waste,' he said. 'The sheriff is mad. We've got to get these gifts delivered before he takes them all back!'

Maid Marian, a kind young fox, and her lady-in-waiting, a cheerful hen named Lady Kluck, passed by the sleigh in their carriage. 'Why, Robin Hood, what a merry surprise!' Marian said, as the carriage pulled to a stop.

Robin bowed low to the ladies. 'Merry Christmas Eve to you, too, Maid Marian,' he said. 'What are you ladies doing out this evening?'

'I've been out delivering baskets to the poor,' Marian said.

'There are so many in need,' said Lady Kluck. 'We've just run out.'

Robin smiled wide. 'It just so happens that I was doing the same thing. Let us share these gifts with you.'

The sheriff's Christmas trimmings were safely tucked into the carriage. 'See you back in Sherwood Forest,' Robin called, as Little John pulled the sleigh off into the woods. He stayed to hand out the food and gifts with Maid Marian. When they finished, they headed for Sherwood Forest to join Little John and the others.

Robin Hood couldn't help but feel that this had been a perfect Christmas. He'd given plenty of food and good cheer to the people of Nottingham. And he had the best gift of all – spending Christmas with Maid Marian.

MAKE MINCE PIES

Impress your friends and family by making your own mince pies!

YOU WILL NEED

- 500 g ready-made shortcrust pastry
- plain flour
- cookie cutters
- 250 g mincemeat
- 1 egg
- icing sugar

- rolling pin
- cupcake baking tray
- teaspoon
- bowl
- fork
- wire rack

ASK AN ADULT FOR HELP

1. Preheat the oven to 220°C. Scatter a little flour onto your work surface – this is so the pastry doesn't stick as you roll it out.

2. Roll the pastry out until it is about 3 mm thick. Use the cookie cutter to cut out 12 circles and place them in the cupcake tray.

3. Spoon mincemeat into each base. Don't add too much filling or you won't be able to add a lid.

4. Roll out the leftover pastry and cut out 12 smaller circles to go on top of your mince pies.

5. Place a lid on top of each filled base and gently pinch the edges of the pastry together.

6. Crack the egg into a bowl and beat with a fork. Brush the beaten egg on to the top of each mince pie.

7. Bake the mince pies for 15-20 minutes, or until golden brown.

8. Leave the mince pies to cool on a wire rack and then sprinkle with icing sugar.

TOP TIP!

Have fun with the tops of the mince pies – try cutting star shapes in the pastry before baking!

17

DECEMBER

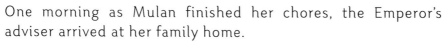

THE SHADOW
PUPPET SHOW

One morning as Mulan finished her chores, the Emperor's adviser arrived at her family home.

'Fa Mulan, I bring an official invitation from the Imperial City,' said Chi Fu, presenting a scroll with the Emperor's seal.

'I am humbled and excited to receive news from the palace,' said Mulan.

Chi Fu read the scroll aloud, 'His Excellency, the Emperor, summons you to the Imperial Palace to witness, in his presence, a shadow play performance.'

Mulan beamed at the idea of an Imperial City adventure. Though she had visited during the war, there was so much more of the palace she had yet to explore.

'It would be my pleasure to return to the palace for such an occasion. I can't wait to see the puppets,' exclaimed Mulan. 'Oh, and the Emperor, of course,' she added quickly, remembering her manners.

Fa Li took her daughter's hands in her own. 'I know you will bring honour to our family by being poised and punctual at court,' she said, pressing her favourite magnolia comb into Mulan's palm.

'Mulan will bring honour to us all by being true to herself,' said Fa Zhou. For he knew his free-spirited daughter flourished when she embraced what made her unique.

Grandmother Fa attached Cri-Kee's small cage to Mulan's sash.

'Can't have you going to the palace without a cricket for good luck,' she said with a laugh.

'Thank you, Grandmother,' Mulan said, nodding. Then she mounted her horse and set out on her journey.

When Mulan arrived at the Imperial Palace, she gasped with delight at the sight. 'It's even more breathtaking than I remember,' said Mulan.

Chi Fu frowned. 'Don't stand there and gape all afternoon. We are on a tight schedule. It would do you well to be prompt for tonight's performance.'

Chi Fu led Mulan through the maze of palace hallways before settling on a door. 'You may prepare for the evening's festivities here in the common room,' said Chi Fu. 'And please, Mulan, do not disrespect the Emperor with your tendency for tardiness and turmoil.'

'Tardiness! Turmoil! Ha!' exclaimed Mulan as the imperial attendants pinned up her hair. 'It's as if Chi Fu doesn't even know me. Tonight, I will bring honour to my family by being intelligent, elegant and graceful.'

But just as Mulan spoke, Cri-Kee sprang free from his cage! The lucky cricket scrambled up Mulan's arm, skittered across the room and scooted out the door.

'I'm pretty sure losing a lucky cricket is considered quite unlucky,' said Mulan. 'Which is why I plan to find him,' she announced to the attendants.

Mulan dashed down the hall and into the music room in search of her mischievous travel companion. Much to Mulan's delight, the playful notes of the pi-pa and the paixiao filled the chamber.

But her delight quickly turned into dismay.

'Oh, no,' cringed Mulan. Cri-Kee had climbed up the musician's sleeve and scaled the pi-pa strings. Now he sat on the musician's shoulder, rubbing his wings together and chirping to the beat.

'How can I catch that cricket without disturbing the music?' Mulan wondered, tapping her foot along to the song. The rhythm of the music sparked a solution. 'I could dance my way across the floor towards the cricket.'

Mulan swayed and spun to the music. But just as she reached Cri-Kee, he jumped from the pi-pa to the paixiao and then sped down the palace stairs.

Cri-Kee darted into the imperial study with Mulan close behind. The moment she stepped into the lovely room, Mulan felt its tranquility. It was here where the Emperor composed his official correspondence.

It will bring shame to the Fa name if my cricket disturbs

such peaceful surroundings, thought Mulan.

So she lunged for Cri-Kee as he hopped across the writing table, overturning brushes and upending inkstones in his wake. The clever cricket made a clean escape but Mulan's dress did not.

Mulan chased Cri-Kee into the war room and looked around in a moment of reverence. Having served in the Imperial Army, Mulan understood the importance of this place. This was where the Emperor and his generals strategised their battle plans.

Mulan panicked as Cri-Kee scampered across the hand-drawn maps and flitted about the Emperor's banners.

Then she noticed a suit of armour in the cabinet. Thinking fast, Mulan grabbed the battle helmet, knowing she could use it to catch the impish cricket. She followed Cri-Kee down the hall and swung open the doors to…

The Imperial Theatre!

The Emperor and his guests all turned to look at Mulan. 'So much for grace, punctuality and politeness,' sighed Mulan.

She had dishonoured her family in the presence of the Emperor. And to make matters worse, Cri-Kee had fled behind the screen set up for the shadow play.

But Mulan did not despair. 'I am who I am. I'm not perfect, sometimes clumsy but always determined,' she reflected.

Mulan bowed to the Emperor. Then she marched behind the screen, where she leapt, lunged and spun at Cri-Kee until she finally caught him. The audience laughed with pleasure at the comical performance.

Pleased by Mulan's impromptu show, the Emperor gave her an encouraging smile. 'The night star is most radiant when it is truest to itself,' he mused.

Mulan considered the Emperor's thoughtful words. She understood that her adventures with Cri-Kee had brought pride, not shame, to the Fa name.

As night fell on the palace, Mulan took a seat and marvelled as she watched the real shadow play unfold.

Cri-Kee, however, had other plans…

Design a Christmas Party Invitation

You Will Need

- coloured card
- pencil
- felt-tip pens
- scissors
- stickers (optional)
- glitter (optional)

1. Draw the outline of your invitations on the card. You could draw festive shapes like Santa's hat, snowmen, stockings or Christmas trees! Cut out your invites.

2. Write your invitation. Remember to include the name of the person you're inviting, where the party is, what time it starts and ends, and if there are any special dressing up instructions!

3. Sign your name at the bottom of the invitation.

To:
....

4. Add extra decoration to your invites by using stickers or glitter!

18
DECEMBER

OUR PERFECT
STORMY DAY

One morning, a storm passed over Motunui island. Most people didn't welcome the cold and wet weather. But Moana was not most people.

'We can't work today,' she said to Pua and Heihei. 'So instead, we're going to Gramma's!'

Ever since she was little, Moana had spent stormy days with her Gramma Tala.

After all, Gramma Tala was Moana's best friend – and a master storyteller.

Plus, Gramma Tala could always use an extra hand around the house and Moana loved to help. So she, Pua and Heihei hurried over.

Drenched by the rain, Moana, Pua and Heihei slid into Gramma Tala's fale with a crash!

'Now that was an entrance,' laughed Gramma Tala as she went in for a hug.

'Wait, we're soaked,' Moana warned.

But Gramma Tala didn't mind. 'Good thing rain is water and water dries,' she said. 'Now, get settled. I have a new story about a storm. I've been waiting for the perfect day to share it with you.'

Everyone settled in and Gramma began to speak. But Moana couldn't focus. She heard a *drip… drip… drip*. Moana looked up and spotted a small hole in the ceiling.

'Gramma, you have a leak,' interrupted Moana. 'Let me fix it for you.'

But Gramma Tala waved her off. 'Never mind that old leak. We learned to live together a long time ago.'

Moana tried her best but she couldn't ignore the puddle forming on the floor. *Gramma cannot patch this leak on her own*, Moana thought to herself.

But I can. If I'm quick, she might not even notice I was gone.
With that, Moana climbed up to the ceiling.

When Moana had finished, she slid back down and landed
– *plop* – right in front of Gramma.

Gramma Tala laughed. 'Thank you, Moana. No leak is safe from you,' she
said with a playful nudge. 'Now, can I get back to my story?'

Moana nodded in reply.

Gramma Tala was just gearing up, when *clap... crackle... BOOM!* Lightning
flashed and thunder roared.

The weather frightened Pua, who jumped sky-high and crashed into a pile
of Gramma Tala's prized storytelling tapa.

'Oh, Gramma. Your tapa!' cried Moana. She rushed to clean up the mess, but
Gramma Tala insisted Moana stop.

'The tapa can wait,' Gramma Tala said. 'Come and sit. I'm finally getting to
the good part!'

Moana took a seat and Gramma Tala continued.

Outside, the wind howled and the fale's woven curtains flapped wildly. Not
only that, Heihei had wandered outside and the wind was blowing him around
like a tumbleweed! Moana's eyes were locked on the swirling bird.

With a final whoosh, Heihei reentered the fale, somersaulted across Gramma
Tala's floor... and landed safely in Moana's lap.

Just then, Moana noticed that Gramma Tala had stopped talking.

In that moment, Moana's heart sank. 'I'm sorry, Gramma,' she said. 'I keep
getting distracted when all I really want is to spend time with you.'

Gramma Tala pressed her nose against Moana's and Moana took
Gramma Tala's hands in hers. 'One more time,' Moana said. 'And I promise, I am
listening.'

Then, once again, Gramma Tala began her story. And Moana
soaked up every word.

Outside, the storm continued. But inside, nothing could
dampen Moana and Gramma Tala's perfect stormy day.

WRITE A CHRISTMAS STORY

Gramma Tala loves telling Moana stories – get into the Christmas spirit by writing your own festive story. Use the story prompts to help you get started!

YOU WILL NEED

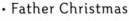

- paper
- colouring pens or pencils
- stickers
- glitter
- a pen or pencil

CHARACTERS

- Father Christmas
- A snowman
- A Christmas elf
- A magical reindeer
- A gingerbread man
- A Christmas fairy
- Enchanted animals

OBJECTS

- Presents
- Candy canes
- Mince pies
- Christmas tree
- Chimney
- Christmas list

SETTINGS

- Your home
- The North Pole
- Santa's workshop
- School
- A magical winter land

STORY STARTERS

Once upon a time, in an ordinary house on an ordinary street, there lived a young boy with a magical secret...

It was Christmas Eve and Santa's elves were worried – there was a problem with their present machine and it was almost midnight!

On a frosty winter night, a carrot-nosed snowman blinked. 'Where am I?' he wondered.

TOP TIP!

Once you've written your story, why not add some colourful illustrations?

A GIFT FOR
WALL·E

WALL·E and EVE peeked over the top of a pile of rubbish. The humans were acting very strangely. What were they up to now?

They saw two men stringing small coloured lights along a rusty iron fence. Another set up a plastic statue of a fat, white bearded man in a red suit, red hat and black boots. A woman propped up a fake silver tree and decorated it with shiny red and green glass balls. Now that people had returned to live on Earth along with robots, they were always doing something that surprised WALL·E and EVE. But even for humans they were acting very strangely.

Weirdest of all, the Captain from the *Axiom* was singing in a loud, joyful voice!

WALL·E and EVE listened to the words carefully. Confused, they looked at each other. Rudolph? A glowing nose? They thought Rudolph must be a kind of robot, like WALL·E and EVE. But neither of them had ever heard of a reindeer-bot before!

WALL·E and EVE snuck closer to where the humans were working. They called their bot friends over. While all the robots watched curiously, the humans hung a green circle with small red dots on a shopfront. More of the humans started singing. One small girl even shook a silver ball.

Some of the robots had seen behaviour

like this before, when they were living on the spaceship, *Axiom*. It seemed to happen every twelve months. They had never been able to figure it out.

WALL·E looked closely at the humans. He tried to figure out what made this so different. Then he put his little metal finger on it. The humans looked happy! Most of the time on the *Axiom* they had looked tired and bored. But there was something about what they were doing right now, here on Earth, that made them very happy.

If it made the humans so happy, WALL·E thought that maybe it would make the robots happy, too!

For hours, the robots studied the humans. They stored what they had seen in their computer brains. Next they set out to copy the humans.

Some of the bots picked up rubbish that the humans had used: bits of tinsel, fake holly and scraps of brightly coloured paper.

The light bots collected hundreds of strings of lights. WALL·E already had a couple in his trailer. He'd always thought they were pretty and EVE loved them.

The bots draped WALL·E's trailer with lights. When the electricity was turned on, the lights shined so brightly they looked like a supernova.

M-O hung up old socks on the other wall. He had no idea why anyone would want to put socks on the wall. But if the humans were doing it, so would he!

Vacuum-bot sucked up boxes and boxes of packing peanuts. Unfortunately, he also vacuumed up a nose full of dust. 'Ahhhh-chOOOO!' he sneezed. Little white peanuts floated down from the air, coating the floor like a blanket of snow.

WALL·E and EVE roamed the grounds outside the trailer looking for more things to use. WALL·E went one way, EVE went the other.

EVE picked up a piece of shiny metal. She found some scraps of wrapping paper. She stored them inside her chest cavity. Suddenly, she heard two humans talking. One of them was the Captain.

'I just love Christmas, don't you?' the other human said. 'The lights, the

decorations, the cookies, the presents. Christmas is my favourite time of year!'

Christmas! What a lovely word! EVE rolled it around in her mind. It sparked all her circuits. Was this the name for what the humans were doing?

She stopped to listen more closely to what they were saying.

'Yes,' said the Captain slowly. 'But don't forget, Christmas isn't about things. That's just what Buy-n-Large wants us to believe. It's about giving, not just getting presents. It's about showing your friends and family that you care.'

The Captain's words hummed inside EVE. Robots didn't have family but they did have friends. And she had one friend who meant more to her than any other – WALL·E. He had come to save her when she was on the ship. He had given her his spare parts. He had cared for her and watched over her. She needed to show him that she appreciated him.

But what kind of a present would do that?

EVE roamed far and wide. She searched and searched. She found many pieces of junk. None of them were quite right. Then, far from WALL·E's trailer, her gaze locked on the perfect present.

Two days later, it was Christmas Eve. The bots had prepared a celebration just like the humans. Some of the smaller bots were stirring with excitement. The umbrella bot wore a pointy red hat with a white pompom on top.

The robots beeped out the words to the songs they had heard. They didn't always understand the human words so they made up some of their own.

While all the bots were celebrating the holiday in their own high-tech way, EVE pulled WALL·E aside. She held out a present wrapped in pretty patterned paper.

WALL·E looked surprised. 'Ee-vah?' he asked.

EVE nodded.

WALL·E turned the present this way and that. He admired how the shiny paper shimmered in the coloured lights. He was so busy looking at the present that he almost missed EVE motioning to him.

Open it, EVE signalled.

WALL·E carefully unwrapped the present. He folded up each scrap of paper and laid it on the ground next to him. Finally, he pulled away the last piece.

WALL·E held a little evergreen tree in his hands, a miniature Christmas tree.

The longer version of EVE's name was Extra-terrestrial Vegetation Evaluator. She had been trained to find plants and was drawn to this little tree. She knew that WALL·E, with his kind ways and big heart, would take care of this present, this living thing, better than anyone.

WALL·E and EVE went outside. Together they dug a hole in the earth and planted the Christmas tree. WALL·E placed a shiny silver star on the top.

WALL·E and EVE looked at the tree. The star twinkled brightly. It reflected the light from the real stars shining in the night sky, far above.

EVE reached out her hand. WALL·E took it.

'Ee-vah,' he said. Now he understood why humans liked Christmas so much.

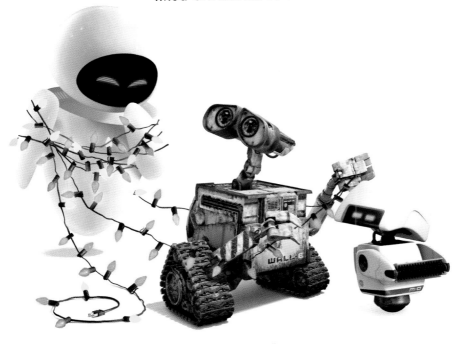

Make an

Orange Pomander

These pretty decorations are really easy to make and smell delicious!
Place them around the house in the lead up to Christmas.

You Will Need

- an orange
- cocktail stick or skewer
- cloves

- glue (optional)
- star anise (optional)
- coloured ribbon (optional)

ASK AN ADULT FOR HELP

1. Use a cocktail stick or skewer to carefully make holes in the skin of the orange. You can make holes randomly, or design a pattern for your pomander – spirals, lines or circles always look great.

2. Carefully push a clove into each hole to create your pattern.

3. If you like, add a little glue to the bottom of a star anise and stick to the top of your orange. This will add to the lovely smell of the pomander!

4. You could also wrap a coloured ribbon around the orange. If you create a loop, you can even hang the pomander from your Christmas tree.

5. Display your finished pomander on a shelf or as a centrepiece for your Christmas table.

A PERFECT PARTY

Cinderella and her prince sat before a roaring fire. Christmas was coming in a few days, and Cinderella was excited.

'Let's throw a party!' she suggested to the Prince.

'What a splendid idea!' he replied. 'How can I help?' Cinderella smiled. 'Just leave everything to me,' she said.

The next day, the princess began to decorate.

'May we help, Cinderelly?' Jaq and Gus asked.

'Of course!' she replied. 'Let's start with the grand staircase.' The mice were tying some bows when a spool of ribbon began to unwind and roll down the banister. Gus hopped aboard. It was just like a sleigh ride – without the sleigh!

When Cinderella and her friends finished the staircase, they moved on to the rest of the castle.

Jaq and Gus helped the princess put garlands over the windows in the ballroom.

They tied sprigs of holly over the doorways. They even hung stockings by the fireplaces.

Finally, Cinderella and her friends moved to the stone patio where Cinderella planned to hold her party.

'Won't our guests be chilly out here?' the Prince asked.

'I'm sure it will be fine,' Cinderella replied. 'Besides, what could be more magical than celebrating under the stars?'

'I like stars. They're twinkly,' Gus said as he nibbled on a popcorn garland.

'Gus!' Jaq scolded. 'You're supposed to be hanging decorations, not eating them!'

Later Cinderella went to the royal sewing room. When Prudence, the head of household staff, peeked in, she saw the princess sewing a handkerchief.

'Why don't you ask the royal seamstresses to do that?' Prudence suggested.

'I'm making presents for our guests,' Cinderella said. 'It's so much more personal if I do it myself.'

On Christmas Eve, the royal chef came to speak with Cinderella. He wanted to know what he should cook for the party.

'Not a thing,' Cinderella replied.

Later Prudence saw her in the storeroom filling baskets with fruit, ears of corn and different kinds of cheese. She was appalled.

Back on the patio, Cinderella laid out the food.

'Hmmm,' she said. 'Something's missing – but what?' Suddenly, Cinderella's fairy godmother appeared.

'My dear, you need a centrepiece,' she said. Waving her magic wand, she turned a water jug into an ice sculpture!

'Now everything is perfect for our holiday picnic!' Cinderella exclaimed.

When Cinderella left to change her gown, the Fairy Godmother slipped into the banquet room. 'Oh, no,' she said, looking at the decorations Cinderella and the mice had hung. 'This will never do for a royal ball.'

The Fairy Godmother waved her wand. Instantly, an elaborate feast appeared. She waved her wand twice more and the court musicians appeared, ready to play.

'Now, that's more like it,' the Fairy Godmother said.

When Cinderella and the Prince walked past the banquet room, the princess couldn't believe her eyes.

Just then, Prudence rushed in. 'Where are your guests?' she asked Cinderella.

'My party isn't being held in here,' Cinderella told her.

'Then what is?' Prudence asked.

Thinking quickly, the princess said, 'A Christmas party in honour of the royal staff. Would you please tell the others?'

'What a wonderful surprise!' the housekeeper exclaimed.

Cinderella opened the patio doors. 'Merry Christmas!'

A chorus of chirps, barks and whinnies answered her. All of Cinderella's animal friends had gathered for her party.

'Happy Christmas, Cinderelly!' Gus shouted.

'Merry Christmas,' Jaq said, correcting him.

Cinderella's animal friends loved the meal she had prepared.

Afterward, it was time for presents! There were new feed bags, cosy blankets and stylish mouse-sized outfits. Jaq loved his new jacket so much that he wouldn't stop looking at his reflection.

Later the Prince and Cinderella danced underneath the stars. When they stopped, they realised they were alone.

'Oh, my! Look!' Cinderella cried. Their animal friends had gone inside and were with the staff. Delighted that everyone was getting along, Cinderella and the Prince joined them.

It was the most unusual – and the merriest – Christmas celebration the kingdom had ever seen!

Make Paper Snowflakes

All you need is some paper and scissors to make beautiful snowflakes!

You Will Need

• squares of coloured paper

• scissors

1. Fold the paper in half diagonally to make a triangle.

2. Fold the paper in half again from one corner to the other to make a smaller triangle.

3. With the flat edge towards you, fold the corners in so they meet in the middle to make a kite shape.

4. Cut the point from the bottom of the paper so you have a triangle with three straight edges.

5. Cut shapes into each side of the triangle to create your snowflake pattern. Be careful not to cut all the way across.

6. Carefully unfold the triangle to reveal your unique snowflake! Repeat the process with different coloured squares to make more snowflakes.

TOP TIP! Carefully make a small hole in the top of your snowflake and thread through string so you can hang up your creation!

21
DECEMBER

THE CHRISTMAS FEAST

Princess Tiana and Prince Naveen were celebrating their first Christmas together. Tiana had invited their family and friends to her restaurant for a Christmas Eve feast. She wanted Naveen to share in the traditions she knew and loved.

'We might need to buy more ornaments,' Tiana said.

'As long as they're fit for a princess!' Naveen replied. That week he had helped Tiana decorate her restaurant, make centreprices and put up a tree – but there was still more work to be done.

Tiana needed to buy ingredients for Christmas Eve dinner. So she and Naveen headed to the market.

'I can't wait to taste the feast you're going to make,' Naveen said. 'With my help, of course!'

'Well, we need quite a few things,' Tiana said. 'Let's see. First we should get the vegetables.'

Tiana carefully looked through all the produce at the vegetable stall. She wanted to make sure she had all the freshest ingredients for their Christmas feast.

Next was the butcher shop and then they stopped for some eggs and cheese. Finally, all Tiana needed was some powdered sugar for her famous beignets.

'I think we'll have to make another trip,' said Naveen as he struggled with a tower of parcels. 'How many people are we cooking for?'

'My mother, Charlotte, Big Daddy, your parents and our friends from the town and the bayou. We'll be serving as many people as want to join us,' Tiana said happily. 'After all, the more the merrier!'

Tiana spent the next few days cooking and baking with Naveen by her side.

'For someone who didn't know how to chop a mushroom, you've become quite an expert,' Tiana told Naveen.

'You taught me everything I know,' Naveen reminded her.

When darkness fell on Christmas Eve, all the food for the banquet was finally ready.

'Before our guests arrive, I have a surprise for you,' Tiana announced, handing Naveen his coat.

'Where are we going?' he asked.

'You'll find out soon enough,' Tiana answered mysteriously.

'Just a hint?' Naveen pleaded. But Tiana simply smiled silently.

Tiana walked Naveen to the riverside and, together, they paddled a canoe into the bayou. As they turned a corner, Naveen's surprise came into view: there were huge bonfires burning alongside the river.

'The fires are for Papa Noël,' Tiana explained.

'So he can find his way in the sky?' asked Naveen.

Tiana laughed. 'Papa Noël doesn't use a sleigh. He travels in a pirogue. That's a flat-bottomed canoe, pulled by alligators.'

'I hope he leaves the gators outside when he delivers the presents!' Naveen exclaimed.

Fog rolled in, and Tiana and Naveen paddled towards home. The folks along the river pointed excitedly at the couple's canoe. Through the mist, all they could see was the couple's red blanket.

'Look!' the river folk shouted. 'It's him!' They thought Tiana and Naveen's canoe belonged to Papa Noël! All around them, people jumped into their boats and paddled behind the canoe, hoping to catch a glimpse of the mysterious visitor.

When the bayou folk paddled out of the fog, they found Tiana and Naveen standing on the dock.

'Have you seen Papa Noël?' someone asked.

'We haven't, but since you're in town, would you join us for dinner? There's plenty to share!' Tiana said.

'Thank you,' said one of the travellers. 'I guess we don't mind if we do!'

By the time Tiana and Naveen reached Tiana's Palace, guests were starting to arrive.

Tiana greeted Naveen's parents and her mother, Eudora. She welcomed her best friend, Charlotte, and her friend's father, Big Daddy La Bouff.

'Some of the guests are saying they saw Papa Noël on the river,' Charlotte said. 'Do you suppose that's him there?'

Tiana looked up and saw an elderly man in a red suit with the other guests.

She was curious, but she had to finish cooking and put on her party dress.

In the dining room, Tiana's alligator friend, Louis, handed out parcels of sugared fruits and candy. Each box was wrapped with shiny purple paper and topped with a beautiful golden bow.

One woman was especially excited to see Louis. 'It's one of Papa Noël's alligators!' the woman said. Louis gave her a wide, toothy smile. It was nice that none of the guests were afraid of him!

Soon, Tiana and Naveen brought out the food.

'Dinner is served!' Tiana announced. Everyone cheered when they saw the table full of food. There were pots of Tiana's delicious gumbo, turkey with chestnuts, roasted ham, grits, yams, vegetables and soufflés.

The guests heaped their plates high and dug in. Tiana smiled. There was nothing she liked better than friends enjoying her cooking. Some of the guests ate second, third and even fourth helpings!

After everyone had eaten, Naveen and Louis played jazzy versions of their favourite Christmas carols. Tiana invited her guests to dance to the music.

As the band finished off another toe-tapping tune, Tiana realised she had forgotten to serve dessert! Quickly, she ran to the kitchen and filled a cart with custards, cakes and beignets. The cart was so full that Tiana could barely open the kitchen door.

'Let me help you with that, my dear,' said a white-bearded gentleman. He helped Tiana push the cart into the dining room. As Tiana ducked back into the kitchen, she realised the man looked just like Papa Noël!

Tiana hurried back to the dining room but the man had already vanished.

Just then, Naveen walked up. 'What a wonderful dinner!' he exclaimed. 'The food! The music! The people! It's all so...'

'Wonderful? It is Christmastime in New Orleans.' Then Tiana spotted the man in the red suit. 'Do you think that's Papa Noël?'

Before Tiana could investigate, Naveen led her onto the dance floor. 'Stranger things have happened,' he said.

Tiana grinned. She was delighted that Naveen's first New Orleans Christmas was going so well – for her, that was magic enough.

CHRISTMAS TABLE
CENTREPIECE

This centrepiece is the perfect finishing touch for any Christmas table. Make it just before dinner so the holly doesn't get too wet!

YOU WILL NEED

- sprigs of holly
- glass vase
- water

- floating tea lights
- coloured ribbon

1. Choose some sprigs of fresh holly – try and pick ones that have lots of red berries.

ASK AN ADULT FOR HELP

2. Carefully place the holly in your vase.

3. Fill the container with water until it is about three-quarters full.

4. Gently place the tea light into the water so it floats on the surface.

5. Finish your centrepiece by wrapping a ribbon around the vase and tying into a bow.

6. Ask an adult to light the candle just before you're ready to eat!

22

DECEMBER

THE RILEY AND BING BONG BAND

Riley and her imaginary friend Bing Bong loved making music together. They would play and sing for hours. Riley was good at many instruments and nobody could play a nose like Bing Bong.

The Riley and Bing Bong Band was Joy's favourite! But the other Emotions weren't such big fans.

Anger thought the music was way too loud. He always covered his ears.

Fear kept a close eye on the instruments. One wrong move and Riley could poke her eye out with the drumstick or swallow the kazoo!

Sadness only liked the minor chords, of course.

And just the sight of Bing Bong playing his nose made Disgust cringe.

One day, after playing some new tunes, Riley and Bing Bong took a break.

'We should go on tour!' said Riley.

'Great idea! Where should we go?' asked Bing Bong.

'How about Australia?' said Riley. 'We can play for the kangaroos!'

'But how will we get there?' asked Bing Bong.

'We can take our rocket!' said Riley.

'Woohoo!' exclaimed Joy. 'A new adventure!'

'Australia is far away,' said Sadness. 'We'll get homesick.'

Fear gathered information on Australia. 'Koalas,

wallabies... goannas! Look at those claws! And what's a platypus? It has poison in its feet!'

'Ugh! Poisonous feet? I can't... I just can't,' said Disgust.

Anger brightened when he saw a picture of kangaroos boxing. 'Do they really box? I'm liking this!'

'We're going to Australia,' announced Riley to Mum and Dad.

'Be back for dinner,' said Mum. 'I'm making my famous mashed potatoes.'

'Don't forget there's a big ocean between Minnesota and Australia,' said Dad.

Riley whispered to Bing Bong, 'We'd better bring our armbands.'

'It's not a big ocean, it's a GIGANTIC ocean!' screamed Fear as he and the other Emotions looked at a map.

'Awesome!' sang Joy.

'Yeah, great. Salty air and humidity...' Disgust rolled her eyes. 'Frizz City.'

'Ohh,' groaned Sadness. 'What if we get lost out there?'

'We could always become pirates!' Anger said.

Riley and Bing Bong packed up everything they needed.

'It's going to be a long trip,' said Bing Bong.

'We'd better bring lots of snacks,' said Riley.

Then they climbed into the rocket and prepared for lift-off. Riley turned to Bing Bong. 'Okay, co-pilot. Ready to check all systems?'

'Check,' said Bing Bong, pointing at the controls. 'Check, check and... check!'

'Activating rocket booster,' said Riley. 'Mission Control, all systems are go!'

Riley and Bing Bong began the countdown. 'Ten, nine, eight, seven, six, five, four, three, two, one... BLAST OFF!' But nothing happened. Riley and Bing Bong were confused.

'Of course!' said Riley. 'The rocket can't fly without fuel!' Riley and Bing Bong smiled at each other.

Once again, they prepared for takeoff. But this time, they were really ready.

Riley and Bing Bong began to sing their special song. 'Who's your friend who likes to play?'

The rocket answered back, binging and bonging. Then it rumbled and roared as it flew out of the window!

Joy sang along as the rocket shot up into the sky.

Sadness watched Minnesota disappear into the distance. 'Goodbye, home,' she said.

'I feel sick,' said Fear, nervously clutching a paper bag.

Disgust wrinkled her nose. 'If you're going to barf, it'd better not be near me.'

'Aren't we there yet?' asked Anger.

As they soared over the ocean, Riley and Bing Bong saw a shark, a sea turtle, a walrus and penguins. So far, this was the best trip ever!

Excited, they started talking about all the things they would see in Australia.

'Dad said koala bears eat gum trees. Do you think they can blow bubbles?' said Riley.

Suddenly, Bing Bong noticed the water was getting closer.

'Are we landing?' he asked.

Riley and Bing Bong screamed as the rocket fell towards the big, blue ocean!

Riley grabbed the radio. 'Mission Control, we have a problem!'

'It's over!' shouted Fear, hiding his head inside the paper bag.

'I knew it,' said Sadness.

'The fuel,' said Joy. 'We were so busy being excited, we forgot to sing!' She plugged in an idea bulb.

'We have to sing!' shouted Riley.

'I'm so scared! I can't remember the words!' said Bing Bong.

'Sing the song! Sing the song!' shouted Anger.

'Sing, or we'll smell like seaweed!' yelled Disgust.

Riley shouted out the words as the rocket sputtered. Bing Bong joined her, and the two sang louder and faster than ever before.

'Who's your friend who likes to play?
Bing Bong, Bing Bong!
His rocket makes you yell "hooray!"
Bing Bong! Bing Bong!'

The rocket skimmed the surface of the ocean and then lifted back into the air! Riley and Bing Bong kept singing as the rocket soared. Soon they could see land.

'Australia!' shouted Riley.

The Emotions cheered.

'We made it?' Fear asked, stunned.

The creatures Down Under welcomed Riley and Bing Bong with big smiles.

'Play us a tune, mates,' said a koala.

Riley and Bing Bong played all of their songs and the crowd went wild.

Suddenly, a familiar smell drifted through the air.

'Mum's famous mashed potatoes,' Riley whispered to Bing Bong. 'It's time to go home.'

The two played one last song. Then they said goodbye to their new friends and rocketed back to Minnesota.

'It's nice to be home,' said Sadness.

'It would be nice not to have helmet hair,' Disgust said.

'And you wonder why I say hair is overrated?' said Anger.

'Sure, it's nice to be home, but travelling is so cool!' said Joy.

'I beg to differ,' said Fear. 'I like staying right here in good ol' Minnesota. No more trips for this guy.'

'So... how was playing in the band in Australia?' asked Dad.

'It was great!' said Riley. 'Tomorrow we're going on another trip – to play for the penguins in Antarctica.'

'Yes!' Joy shouted.

'Noooooooooooooo!' Fear screamed, as he fainted onto the floor.

MAKE A
RUDOLPH DECORATION

Rudolph lights the way for Father Christmas on Christmas Eve.
Make this decoration to welcome the reindeer to your home!

YOU WILL NEED

- one large paper plate
- one small paper plate
- brown paint
- paintbrush
- brown card
- pencil
- glue
- scissors
- red pompom
- two googly eyes
- dark brown or black felt-tip pen

1. Paint the underside of the two paper plates with brown paint and leave to dry completely.

2. Use a pencil to trace around your hand four times on the brown card and then cut them out.

3. Glue the small paper plate to the bottom of the large paper plate to make Rudolph's head.

4. Glue two of your cut out hand shapes on the left side of Rudolph's head and two on the right side to make antlers.

5. Glue the red pompom at the top of the small plate to make Rudolph's bright nose! You could make your own pompom – see pages 72-73.

6. Glue two googly eyes to the large plate and use a felt-tip pen to draw Rudolph's smiling mouth.

MIGUEL AND THE SECRET RECIPE

'The time has come, niños, to make Mamá Imelda's famous tamales. And this year, I'm going to teach you how,' Abuelita said to her grandchildren as they walked through Santa Cecilia.

'Is the secret recipe written down, Abuelita?' Miguel asked.

'I'm one hundred percent sure I remember it,' she said. 'Can you and your primos go to the carnicería to buy the meat?' Abuelita then turned to Abel. 'I need your help getting the masa and I will go home and soak the corn husks.'

In the Land of the Dead, Mamá Imelda clapped her hands. 'I always look forward to this time of year,' she said to her husband, Héctor, and her twin brothers, Felipe and Oscar. 'We get to see our family in the Land of the Living.'

'And we get tamales,' Tío Óscar added.

'But they aren't what they used to be,' Tío Felipe said. 'I wonder if the recipe was so secret that no one remembers it!'

'I know I wrote it down,' Imelda said. She looked at an image of Abuelita. 'Ay mijita, you can't go by memory alone. You must find the recipe.'

Héctor had an idea. 'Do you know where your mamá's tamale recipe is back in the Land of the Living?' he asked his daughter, Coco. 'I want to find it to make Día de Muertos as special as possible.'

'Yes,' Mamá Coco said. 'Elena and I memorised

the recipe and we followed it by heart. But I didn't want to lose the original. I put it inside the frame that holds Tío Felipe's photo for safekeeping, because tamales were always his favourite. It's on the ofrenda every year for Día de los Muertos.'

'Dante and Pepita, I need your help,' Héctor said to the two spirit guides. 'I have a very special mission and I only trust the two of you to get it done. Can you figure out a way to get Mamá Imelda's tamale recipe to Abuelita?'

When Dante and Pepita emerged in the Land of the Living, it was as a normal dog and cat. But even though they looked different, their mission was still the same.

Dante and Pepita ended up in the ofrenda room of the Rivera family. But when they looked at the photos, they couldn't tell the twins apart. Pepita knocked down one frame.

It broke open just enough that they could see there was no recipe inside. Dante tugged on the ofrenda cloth and the second frame tumbled towards the floor.

At that moment, Miguel came into the room. 'What happened?' he asked as he picked up the frames.

Pepita raised her paw and laid it on one. Miguel looked closely at the frame and saw a yellowed piece of paper inside.

Miguel, Dante and Pepita met Abuelita as they entered the courtyard.

'What have they done now?' Abuelita asked.

Miguel held out the piece of paper. 'They helped me find this!'

'Mamá Imelda's tamal recipe!' said Abuelita. 'Just like I remembered it.'

'Um, Abuelita?' Miguel said. 'Don't you use baking soda and not baking powder?'

His grandmother glanced at the paper. 'Oh. I guess there is a slight difference. Maybe we should try it the way it was written,' she said.

'I know we're all used to the tamales we've been eating for years,' Abuelita said to her family as they gathered together. 'But this year, we will make Mamá Imelda's real recipe.'

The Riveras chatted as they worked. Together, the adults and the children made the recipe that would continue on through the history of their family.

As the tamales were placed in the pot to steam, Miguel looked at Abuelita and smiled. 'It almost feels like Mamá Imelda is here with us.'

The next day, on Día de los Muertos, the Rivera family gathered at the cemetery to celebrate their ancestors. Among the items they brought were Mamá Imelda's famous tamales.

'I am so excited to leave all this food for our family,' Benny said as he and Manny set down the platter.

'I wonder if anyone will even notice the difference in the tamales,' Abuelita said.

The Dead Riveras were thrilled to see their living relatives and their favourite foods.

'Have you tried the tamales?' Tío Óscar asked. 'They seem... different.'

'They are perfecto! Just like Mamá Imelda's!' Tío Felipe said.

'Hmm,' said Mamá Imelda as she looked at Coco, Héctor and the two animals. 'I think I might know why.'

'These tamales are tantalising, Abuelita – the best we've ever had,' said Tía Carmen.

'I had more than one,' said Papá.

'You had more than two,' said Mamá.

'Don't worry Abuelita. Yours were delicious, too,' Miguel said.

'Gracias. I think the tamales turn out special every year because we always help one another make them,' Abuelita said.

'Ah, mijita,' Mamá Imelda said, overhearing Abuelita's words to Miguel, 'you've never forgotten that the love each person adds when they help one another is the most important ingredient. And that is the heart of every Rivera recipe.'

Make a
Popcorn Garland

You Will Need

- needle
- strong thread
- scissors
- plain popcorn

1. Pop your popcorn following the packet instructions and leave to cool. It's best to leave your popcorn out for 24 to 48 hours before stringing as fresh popcorn can break quite easily.

2. Pass a strong thread through your needle and tie a fat knot at one end.

3. Carefully push the needle through the centre of a piece of popcorn and move it to the end of the string.

4. Keep adding popcorn, one at a time, pushing to the end of the string.

5. Once you've reached a length you are happy with, tie another fat knot at the end of the string to keep the popcorn garland together. Your popcorn garland is ready to hang – try stringing it across a window or around your tree!

ASK AN ADULT FOR HELP

TOP TIP! If you use microwave popcorn, remember to buy the kind without butter and salt.

24
DECEMBER

A PRINCE'S DAY

It was early morning at Pride Rock. Simba and Nala couldn't wait to go out and play. 'Let's go down to the river!' Nala said loudly.

'Shhh,' Simba whispered. 'We have to be quiet or Zazu will hear us.' But it was too late. Zazu had been on the lookout for the young prince.

'Ahh! There you are, Simba,' Zazu said, landing in front of Simba. 'Come along. We have a busy day of training ahead of us.'

'But Nala and I were about to go down to the river!' Simba complained.

'Nonsense,' Zazu said. 'As a prince you have certain responsibilities, young sire. And we can't keep them waiting.'

'Bye, Simba!' Nala said. 'Have fun at prince school! Maybe we can go to the river tomorrow.'

'Not if Zazu has anything to say about it,' Simba grumbled, watching as Nala bounded away.

Zazu led Simba down to the watering hole, where the animals of the Pride Lands were taking turns drinking water.

'Part of a ruler's responsibilities is solving disputes between his subjects. A perfect example is the watering hole! Each animal needs to have a turn to drink,' Zazu explained. 'See that herd of antelopes? They have been here too long. It's the rhinos' turn!'

'You! You there!' the bird said, yelling at the antelopes.

Simba listened for what felt like hours as Zazu talked on and on to the antelopes.

Finally, the lion cub saw a chance to escape. A herd of giraffes was leaving the watering hole. If he could sneak out with them, he might still have time to play with Nala!

Just when Simba thought he had gotten away, Zazu landed in front of him. 'And where do you think you're going?' Zazu demanded.

'Come on, Zazu. We've been at the watering hole for hours. Can't I go play with Nala?' Simba asked.

But Zazu refused to let him go. 'A prince's job is never done!' he insisted. 'Onward to our next stop!'

Zazu led Simba back to Pride Rock, where Mufasa was listening to his subjects' concerns.

'A king must listen to all the other animals,' Zazu explained. 'You can learn a lot from your father.'

Simba tried to pay attention. He listened as Mufasa advised the elephants to find new grazing grounds. He listened as the zebras worried about the upcoming rainy season.

But soon the lion cub was just as bored as he had been at the watering hole. He started to fall asleep.

'Young sire!' Zazu yelled, angrily pecking Simba awake. 'Were you paying any attention at all?'

Simba yawned, shaking himself awake. He looked around. The other animals were gone. Mufasa must have finished for the day. 'Um, I heard some of it?' Simba replied.

Frustrated, Zazu flew up in the air. 'Come along, Simba. We aren't finished yet,' Zazu said.

Simba slowly followed as the bird led him away from Pride Rock. Soon they were walking past the river where Simba and Nala had planned to play that day.

Simba looked for his friend, but he didn't see her.

Suddenly, Simba heard a yell. 'Did you hear that, Zazu?' he asked.

'Hear what, Simba?' Zazu said.

There was another yell. 'That!' Simba said, running towards the river. Zazu flew after him.

It was Nala. She had fallen into the fast-moving river and couldn't get out!

'Hurry, go get my father!' Simba ordered Zazu.

The bird flew away in search of Mufasa but Simba knew there wasn't time to wait. Nala needed him now!

Simba looked everywhere for a way to get to his best friend. Finally, he saw a long tree branch on the shore of the river.

'Nala! Grab on!' Simba yelled. He grabbed the tree branch in his mouth and moved it over the river. Nala reached out and grabbed the branch just in time!

Simba pulled the branch back and dragged Nala out of the river. She was safe!

'Simba? Simba!' Mufasa called, running to the river.

'Here, Dad!' Simba said, panting. 'It's okay! I got Nala!' Relieved, Mufasa and Zazu gathered the cubs and started back to Pride Rock.

'Zazu, Nala, can you give me a moment with Simba?' Mufasa asked. Simba was worried. Was Mufasa angry at him for not paying attention to Zazu?

'Zazu told me about your day. I know that you want to play with your friend but Zazu was trying to teach you important lessons about what it means to be king,' Mufasa said.

'What did you learn at the watering hole?' Mufasa asked.

'That the rhinos follow the antelopes?' Simba replied.

Mufasa laughed. 'No, that you have to be fair as a ruler and make sure all your subjects are treated equally,' he said. 'And Zazu brought you to Pride Rock to show you that a leader must be wise as well. But the last lesson you taught yourself.'

'I did?' Simba said.

'Yes, my son. You rescued Nala and showed that a ruler must be brave. I am very proud of you, Simba.'

Simba smiled up at his father.

'Now,' Mufasa said, 'I think there may just be enough time for you and Nala to play before dinner.'

Simba smiled and bounded off to find Nala.

'He'll make a good king someday, sire,' Zazu said, landing on Mufasa's shoulder.

Mufasa smiled. 'Yes, he will.'

CHRISTMAS EVE
CHECKLIST

It's almost Christmas! Look at the list below
to make sure you're ready for the big day.

CHECKLIST FOR CHRISTMAS EVE

- Wrap your presents
- Read a Christmas story
- Watch a festive film

- Go for a walk and look at Christmas lights
- Put out your stocking

Before you go to bed on Christmas Eve don't forget to
leave out a treat for Father Christmas and his reindeer!

FOR FATHER CHRISTMAS

- mince pie or Christmas biscuit
- glass of milk

FOR RUDOLPH AND THE REINDEER

- bowl of water
- carrot sticks

25

DECEMBER

A TOY CHRISTMAS

'Take that!' Andy said in Woody's voice. 'You're spending Christmas in jail!' He put Hamm the piggy bank into an old shoebox with slits cut into the sides.

Andy was playing in his room with his toys. In one hand he held Woody the cowboy. In the other was Buzz Lightyear the space ranger.

'You'll be seeing bars for a long, long time,' Andy added in Buzz Lightyear's commanding tone.

Andy's mother came into the room and sat down on the bed. 'Andy, I have a surprise for you,' she said. 'You know Christmas is coming up. And this year for your big present... we're going to the Grand Canyon!'

Andy dropped Woody and Buzz on the floor. He jumped up and down. 'Hooray!' Andy said. 'That's the best present ever! Can I take Buzz and Woody?' He picked up his two favourite toys.

'I think it's better if you leave them here,' his mother said. 'You'll be so busy you won't have any time to play. Now come on. We have a lot to do to get ready.'

The moment the door shut behind Andy and his mother, the toys came to life. Buzz sat up. Woody straightened his cowboy hat.

'All right!' Rex the dinosaur said as he came out from under the bed. 'The trip is Andy's big present this year. That means no other toys to take our places!'

'I was worried Andy was going to get a video game,' Hamm added.

All the toys started talking at once.

'Hold on a minute,' Woody said. He walked to the centre of the room. 'Sure, it's great that there aren't going to be any new toys to replace us. But did you think about what else this means? It means Christmas without Andy.'

Everyone got quiet. Christmas without Andy? Why, Christmas without Andy wouldn't seem like Christmas at all! RC's fender drooped sadly. Slinky Dog hung his head. Even the Green Army Men looked glum.

Buzz Lightyear walked over to Woody. 'Andy will be gone, but that doesn't mean we can't have Christmas. We'll just make it a toy Christmas!'

Woody looked at the other toys around him. He forced a smile onto his face. 'Buzz is right,' he said. 'We'll have a great Christmas this year.'

But deep down, Woody knew it couldn't happen. It was true that they could have their own Christmas. But without the kid who loved them all, it wouldn't be much fun at all.

After Andy and his family left on their trip, the toys started getting ready for Christmas. They had a lot to do. They made decorations, practised singing songs and looked for presents for each other.

'Psst, Woody, over here,' Jessie hissed loudly. Woody found her hiding behind a stack of books. 'Look what I found,' she said proudly. She held up a red bandana.

'Jessie, Bullseye has been looking for his bandana for months!' Woody said.

'I know,' Jessie grinned. 'It's going to be a great present for him.'

'Come sing some Christmas carols,' Wheezy the penguin called to Woody.

'All right,' Woody said. He thought maybe the songs would put him in the Christmas spirit.

Wheezy grabbed Mike the tape recorder, and as the music began, his high squeaky voice dropped to a deep baritone. First he belted out a rocking rendition of *Santa Claus Is Coming to Town*. Then he glided into a jazzy *Frosty the Snowman*. But when Wheezy started crooning *Blue Christmas*, Woody had to move away. It made him think of how sad he'd be without Andy.

'Catch you later, Wheezy, Mike,' Woody said with a tip of his hat.

Wheezy and Mike continued to sing as Woody walked off. He was glad his friends were in the holiday spirit. But he couldn't stop thinking about how much he missed Andy. He went over to the other side of the room.

'Hey, Woody, want to help us decorate?' Slinky Dog asked. 'Watch this.' He gave Woody a poke in the ribs, then yelled, 'Hit it!'

In a flash, two Aliens bounced super high and draped a string of red and green buttons along the edge of the bookcase.

'Pretty neat, Slink,' Woody said with an approving nod.

'And nice job, Sarge,' he called to the army commander and his troops. They were hanging sparkly silver jacks that looked like 3D snowflakes around the room.

'We've got a Christmas tree, too,' Slinky Dog told him. He pointed to a tree made entirely of cotton balls. Red and green hair ribbons were wrapped around it and tied into a bow at the top. There already were presents under the tree. They were wrapped in shiny paper and topped with colourful bows.

'Looks like it's a white Christmas,' Sarge said.

Woody smiled a little bit. He was impressed that all the toys were working together to make Christmas a happy holiday.

Woody kept track of the days on the calendar in Andy's room. Finally, it was the big one, 24th December. Christmas Eve.

Hours passed with secrets and whispers and before long, it grew dark outside. The toys all gathered together to celebrate the holiday, but Woody held back. He was thinking of Andy.

'Hey there, Sheriff,' Buzz said. 'Why so down? It's a beautiful night out there and... it's Christmas Eve!'

'I don't know, Buzz,' Woody said. 'It's just not the same without Andy.'

'You're right,' Buzz said. 'It's not the same. But you have other friends besides Andy. Come on.' He put his arm around Woody's shoulders.

Woody and Buzz walked by Bo Peep. She was reading a Christmas story to the newest toys, the ones who had never had a Christmas before.

Bo winked at Woody. Lo and behold, Woody's heart felt a little lighter.

Then Buzz led Woody over to the Christmas tree. Etch A Sketch stood by the tree, a roaring fire drawn on his screen. Nearby, someone had set up the wooden blocks to spell out MERRY CHRISTMAS.

'Get the lights, Sarge!' Buzz shouted.

The sarge saluted and turned out the lights.

'Here's a little thing I like to call Christmas magic,' Buzz said.

He pressed the laser button on his right arm and a beam of light shot out onto the wall. He pressed the button again and again and again. It was so quick that his finger became a blur. He moved the lights around – to the right, the left, up, down, left, down, right, up. The light pulsed around the dark room, making a show of dancing snowflakes, sugarplums and lots and lots of toy dolls, trains and teddy bears.

Woody's jaw dropped and his eyes grew wide. 'Wow, Buzz,' the cowboy said. 'That's really great! I didn't know you could—'

His sentence was cut off by a jolly 'Ho, ho, rrrrroar!' as RC rolled into the circle.

RC was decorated to look like a sleigh. And following behind him was Rex with a white cotton beard and a red sock hat.

'Sorry about the roar,' Rex said, even though no one had been scared. 'Sometimes I forget I'm Santa Claus, not a fierce bone-crunching carnivorous dinosaur!'

Rex went to the Christmas tree. He picked up presents to give to each and every toy. Bullseye was thrilled to have his bandana back. Mr. Spell got brand-new batteries.

'Your speaking was getting a little slow there,' Slinky Dog pointed out.

Buzz got a Star Command four-way outer space signal interceptor. His friends had put it together out of a small cardboard box, some sequins from an old doll's dress and lots of duct tape.

'Thanks, guys!' he said. 'It's just what I always wanted!'

One of the dolls gave Jessie a dress. Hamm's present was a quarter.

'Woohoo!' he shouted. 'That's as good as twenty-five pennies! Five nickels! Two dimes and a nickel! I'm feeling flush!'

And then Bo Peep pulled Woody over and gave him a big kiss. He turned as red as the Christmas lights. 'Aw shucks, Bo,' he said.

Woody looked at his friends. Buzz was right. Christmas without Andy wasn't better or worse. It was different. Spending time with people, and toys, you loved was what Christmas was really all about.

'Hey, Buzz, Woody, everyone!' Slinky Dog yelled from the edge of the bed. 'Check this out!' He pulled the window curtain aside. Outside, snow drifted down.

'It's a white Christmas!' he shouted. 'Merry Christmas, everyone!'

Woody smiled. 'Merry Christmas,' he replied.

FUN FOR
CHRISTMAS DAY

It's Christmas Day! Here are some ideas for fun games and activities you and your family can play.

PLAY CHARADES

Have everyone write down five to ten charades on a piece of paper. They could be names of books, films, songs or musicals. Put them all in a bowl and take turns acting them out. Remember – no talking allowed!

GUESS THE CELEBRITY

Write a celebrity's name on a post-it note and stick it to the forehead of another player. They have 20 questions to guess which celebrity they are!

HUM THE CHRISTMAS TUNE

Take turns humming a Christmas song or carol while everyone else guesses!

Alphabet Game

Choose a letter of the alphabet and a category, for example, the letter A and food. Everyone takes a turn saying an item that fits both criteria, for example, apple or avocado. The first person who can't think of an item loses!

Festive Jokes

Ask everyone to tell a funny Christmas joke – here are a couple of examples!

What happened to the elf who ate Christmas decorations?
They got tinsel-itis!

What goes, 'Oh, oh, oh!'?
Father Christmas walking backwards!

What did one Christmas tree say to another?
Lighten up!

Guess the Drawing

Have everyone write down five to ten objects, animals or people on a piece of paper. Put them all in a bowl and shuffle them up. Split into teams – each team will take a turn drawing their chosen item while their teammates guess. Set a timer for one minute for each turn.

BONUS ACTIVITY

MAKE A PAPER CHAIN

Paper chains are a great way to cheer up an empty room in the run up to Christmas!

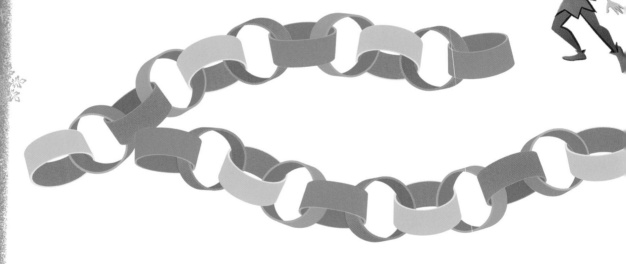

YOU WILL NEED

• coloured paper or
scraps of wrapping paper

• glue
• scissors

1. Cut strips of paper roughly 2 cm wide by 20 cm long. The number of strips you cut will determine how long your paper chain will be – around 30 is a good number but you can make your chain as long or short as you like!

2. Make a circle with one strip of paper and stick the ends together with glue.

3. Take another strip of paper and pass it through the circle. Glue the ends of the strip together so you have two connected circles.

4. Now take a third strip, put it through the second circle and glue the ends together again. This is how you make your paper chain!

5. Continue the process until you have used up all of your paper strips – you can stop early if you'd like a shorter chain, or cut more strips to make it longer!

6. Once you're happy with the length of your chain you can hang it up!

TOP TIP! You could use your paper chains to decorate your Christmas tree!

Use this page to count down to Christmas and keep track of all the fun, festive activities. Have you done them all?

1 DECEMBER

MAKE AN ADVENT CALENDAR

10

2 DECEMBER

DESIGN A CHRISTMAS CARD

16

3 DECEMBER

LEARN TO DRAW DUMBO

21

4 DECEMBER

BAKE CHRISTMAS BISCUITS

26

5 DECEMBER

MAKE AN OLAF DECORATION

32

6 DECEMBER

MAKE A CHRISTMAS TREE DECORATION

38

7 DECEMBER

WRITE A LETTER TO FATHER CHRISTMAS

44

8 DECEMBER

MAKE A SNOW GLOBE

50

9 DECEMBER

CHRISTMAS TRADITIONS

55

10 DECEMBER

MAKE A BAUBLE

60

11 DECEMBER

DESIGN YOUR OWN WRAPPING PAPER

66

PICTURE CREDITS

The publisher would like to thank the following
for permission to reproduce their images:
(t = top, b = bottom, l = left, r = right, c = centre)

10-11 © Juliasuena/Shutterstock.com; 44(c) © Jason Winter/Shutterstock.com;
50(c) © Anastasy_helter/Shutterstock.com; 51(br) © AnastasiiaM/Shutterstock.com;
55(tr) © TeymurazN/Shutterstock.com; 55(tl) © Marish/Shutterstock.com;
55(cr) © Abscent/Shutterstock.com; 55(cl) © GoodStudio/Shutterstock.com;
55(br) © TeymurazN/Shutterstock.com; 66(c) © Dzsenifer/Shutterstock.com;
88(c) © A Aleksii/Shutterstock.com; 94(c) © Irina Vaneeva/Shutterstock.com;
95(br) © Irina Vaneeva/Shutterstock.com; 99(tr, c, br) © antart/Shutterstock.com;
102(tl, bl, br) © nanmulti/Shutterstock.com; 103(tr, cl) © nanmulti/Shutterstock.com;
103(cr) © PinkPueblo/Shutterstock.com; 129(t, br) © flaxlynx/Shutterstock.com;
140(c) © Roi and Roi/Shutterstock.com